D0185154

ERIC LIDDELL

~

PURE GOLD

ERIC LIDDELL
~
PURE GOLD

A NEW BIOGRAPHY OF THE OLYMPIC CHAMPION WHO INSPIRED CHARIOTS OF FIRE

DAVID McCASLAND

AUTHOR OF THE AWARD-WINNING BIOGRAPHY OF OSWALD CHAMBERS

LION

Copyright © 2001 David McCasland
This edition copyright © 2012 Lion Hudson

The author asserts the moral right
to be identified as the author of this work

A Lion Book
an imprint of
Lion Hudson plc
Wilkinson House, Jordan Hill Road,
Oxford OX2 8DR, England
www.lionhudson.com
ISBN 978 0 7459 5571 1

Distributed by:
UK: Marston Book Services, PO Box 269, Abingdon, Oxon, OX14 4YN
USA: Trafalgar Square Publishing, 814 N. Franklin Street, Chicago, IL 60610
USA Christian Market: Kregel Publications, PO Box 2607, Grand Rapids,
Michigan 49501

First edition 2001
This edition 2012
10 9 8 7 6 5 4 3 2 1 0

Acknowledgments
Unless otherwise stated, all photographs appearing in this book are taken
from the Liddell family photo collection and appear courtesy of Mrs. Joan
Sommerville Nicol.

All rights reserved

A catalogue record for this book is available
from the British Library

Typeset in 10/13 ITC Galliard
Printed in Great Britain by Clays Ltd, St Ives plc

Editor's Note: In accordance with the Chicago Manual of Style, abbreviations
such as LMS and TACC appear in the text without periods between the letters.
In material quoted from articles and letters, place names and abbreviations
appear as they were originally written.

For Patricia, Heather, and Maureen

Contents

A Word About China

In this book I have chosen to employ the spelling of Chinese place names most commonly used by Westerners during Eric Liddell's lifetime. One exception is the use of Peking throughout the text, even though it became known as Peiping in 1928. A list of Chinese place names and their modern Pin Yin equivalents follows. It should be noted that the spelling of place names in China varied widely and was always changing; thus, the spelling in quoted correspondence may vary slightly from the glossary below. For example Tingchow-fu might be spelled Ting Chow, Ting-Chow, or Tingchow.

To many people in modern China the word "coolie" is offensive. During the historical period of this book, however, the word, as it was commonly used by foreigners, meant simply a Chinese worker who did hard labor for little pay.

Former Name	Pronounced	Modern Spelling
Ch'ao Yang	chow YAHNG	Chaoyang
Chefoo	chee FOO	Yantai
Chinwangtao	chin wang DOW	Qinhuangdao
Chungking	chung KING	Chongqing
Dairen	DIE ren	Dalian
Harbin	har BEAN	Harbin
Heng Shui	hung SHWEE	Hengshui
Honan	huh NAHN	Henan
Hsin Chi	sin CHEE	Shulu
Mukden	MOOK den	Shenyang
Nanking	Nan KING	Nanjing
Peitaiho	bay duh HUH	Beidaihe

Former Name	Pronounced	Modern Spelling
Peking	pee KING	Beijing
Shanhaikwan	shan hai GWAN	Shanhaiguan
Shanghai	shang HI	Shanghai
Shantung	shan DUNG	Shandong
Siaochang	SHAO zhahng	Zaoqiang
Taku	TAH Koo	Tangu
Techow	DER joe	Dezhou
Tientsin	tee in SIN	Tianjin
Tingchow-fu	ting chow FOO	unknown
Tsangchow	SAHNG joe	Cangzhou
Tsinan	jee NAHN	Jinan
Tsingtao	CHING dow	Quingdao
Weihsien	way SHIN	Weifang

Prologue:
Please Don't Go!

May 1941

Florence Liddell winced as the cabin floor shuddered slightly beneath her feet. Far below the water line, the *Nita Maru*'s engines rumbled to life, signaling that departure was nearing. Soon all guests would be required to leave the ship, and the gangway linking ocean liner to land would be removed. In years past, the prospect of a trans-Pacific journey always filled Flo with anticipation and excitement, but not today.

She glanced across the cabin at four-year-old Heather playing on the floor, then shifted her eyes to Patricia, sitting on Eric's knee. The little girl's hazel eyes looked straight into the eyes of her father as he spoke in what seemed to be unusually serious tones.

"Tricia," he said, "you're almost six years old and you're a big girl now. I want you to look after your mother, and I want you to look after Heather and help with this new baby that's coming. And I want you to promise me you'll do this until I return."

Tricia's golden curls bobbed as she nodded ascent to his every word.

"I promise," she said. "I promise."

To Flo, it seemed strange to be traveling on a Japanese ship, since that country's aggression in China was the main reason she and the children were leaving. But Eric had insisted it would be the safest way. Hitler was overrunning Europe, and no one could predict what would happen in Asia. Flo and the girls would be safer in Canada. She could have the baby there, and he would join them at the earliest opportunity. For now, he felt an obligation to the

London Missionary Society and to his colleagues to stay in China during these days of crisis and uncertainty. It would be a long two years apart, but it was best this way. Two years — it couldn't be more than that.

They had talked so much about this day that now, with nothing left to say, they spoke through their eyes and touch. How Flo loved him, this man she knew better than anyone on earth. Why did it seem they were always saying good-bye? Since the day they announced their engagement, they had been apart more than together.

And then it came. A ringing of bells, a loudspeaker announcement, and a blast from the ship's deep-throated whistle. They embraced and kissed, then Eric was gone. For a few minutes, Flo and the two girls sat in the cabin. Then they rushed upstairs to the ship's railing.

Tricia was the first to spot her father striding away on the pier, unmistakable in his sport shirt, white shorts, and knee-length socks. "There he is!" she shouted. Eric was nearly bald, but the spring in his step hinted at the athletic power that had carried him to a gold medal in the Olympics more than a decade and a half before. Suddenly, he turned and looked back at the ship. The girls waved frantically and Florence began to shout:

"Eric, don't go! Please don't go! I want to stay here with you! Please! Please don't go!"

She tried to run toward the gangway, but her feet refused to move. She shouted again, "Don't go!" Patricia wrapped her arms around her mother's waist and tried to comfort her, "It's all right, Mother. It's all right." Flo continued to cry out through her sobs. Then Eric faded from view and she felt herself cradled by loving arms. Slowly she awakened.

Sitting on the edge of Flo's bed, Patricia stroked her mother's white hair and held her against the terror that had invaded the night.

"It's all right, Mother. It's all right," Patricia said. "You were having a bad dream. Everything's all right now."

"It was so real," Florence said. "He was right there and I didn't want him to go. But when it happened I never shouted or begged him to stay."

"It was a long time ago," Patricia said.

"Yes," Florence said, regaining her sense of time and place. "A long time ago."

"Now we're at my house in Canada," Patricia said. "It's 1984."

Florence took a deep breath. So much had happened since that day in 1941 when their ship sailed from Japan. Maureen's birth in Toronto followed by the shock of the Japanese attack on Pearl Harbor. The years of waiting and praying after Eric and thousands of others were imprisoned in North China. Then the numbing news of his death.

For half a dozen years after Eric died, it was just the four of them: Florence, Patricia, Heather, and Maureen. Then Flo married Murray Hall, a Canadian farmer, and they brought another daughter, Jeannie, into the world. Following Murray's death from pulmonary complications came the incredible surprise of *Chariots of Fire,* the moving story of Eric's Olympic victory and his deep Christian conviction. The Academy Award-winning film had rekindled all Flo's memories.

She loved the movie. Despite all its dramatic liberties, the film captured Eric's winsome and humble spirit. Flo liked the Eric Liddell portrayed on screen, but she loved the real man far more. The mischievous Eric with the twinkling blue eyes and dry sense of humor. The shy Eric who agonized over speaking in public. The determined Eric who defied convention to court and wed her, a young woman nearly ten years his junior. The devoted Eric who loved God with all his heart.

Flo wasn't surprised that the world had come to admire the quiet Scotsman whose refusal to run on Sunday stood as a landmark of personal conviction. But there was so much more to the man she knew and loved. His lighthearted sense of fun, his deep compassion, his unselfish giving. How could anyone tell it all?

After her dream, Flo poured out a flood of memories as she and Patricia talked into the early hours of the morning. Perhaps she sensed that her own race was nearing its end. She had kept running all these years as part of her promise to Eric, to the girls, and above all to God. It had never been a race against the clock, but a contest against dark days of loneliness, heartbreak, and despair. She had met every obstacle head on with great faith and enthusiasm, determined to live and complete her most important task.

When Florence died on June 14, 1984, her obituary in the *Toronto Star* read: "*Chariots of Fire* widow dead at 72." It seemed appropriate that she and Eric should be linked again in death, as they had been in life.

Through an inspiring film, the world knows something of the Eric Liddell who ran for gold at the Paris Olympics in 1924. This is the larger story of the man who went the distance in life, and of the woman who ran with him in his greatest race.

PART I

THE MAKING OF A CHAMPION

1902–1924

Be still, my soul: the Lord is on thy side!
Bear patiently the cross of grief or pain;
Leave to thy God to order and provide—
In every change He faithful will remain.
Be still, my soul: thy best thy heavenly friend
Through thorny ways leads to a joyful end.

ONE

A North China Childhood

1902–1907

With a bump against the dock at Techow, the long, narrow houseboat reached the end of its two-hundred mile journey. For more than a week the Rev. James D. Liddell and his family had been winding their way south from the city of Tientsin along the Grand Canal. Now they faced a grueling overland journey to their mission station at Siaochang. James glanced at the November sky, relieved that it didn't look like snow.

From the deck, Chinese men wearing the traditional pigtail stepped ashore carrying immense parcels wrapped in rough burlap and tied with rope. Along the quay, coolies swarmed around shouting, shoving, and cursing, fighting for the heaviest items, hoping to carry something in exchange for a few coppers. Nearby, street vendors selling food and drink sat next to women sharpening scissors and men giving haircuts. To a Western observer it seemed like utter chaos and confusion. For the seasoned missionary it was just a normal scene in China.

James shouted in Chinese, giving instructions for the luggage and bargaining for the price all in one breath. From the tumult on the dock, two rickshaws carried the Liddell family and their belongings along the crowded streets to a crude Chinese inn where they would spend the night. Two-year-old Rob jabbered away in Chinese while Eric, ten months, slept soundly in his mother's arms. Through weary eyes, thirty-one-year-old Mary Liddell scanned the now-familiar sights of a Chinese town. Compared to the city of Tientsin, the town of Techow felt like the end of the world.

Although Techow was an important trading center, it was hardly a destination for anyone but the common people who lived in the town and on the surrounding plain. It certainly was not listed in the Thomas Cook guide of fascinating places to visit in North China.

Before Mary awoke the next morning, James had carefully loaded their belongings in two wooden-wheeled carts. He believed in packing properly the first time instead of repacking many times along the way. Since the carts had no springs and the roads they would be traveling were little more than ruts, a tightly tied load was imperative. The forty-mile trip to Siaochang would take most of two days if everything went well. If they broke an axle or encountered bandits, it would be a different story. In the first light of morning, James made a final inspection of the carts, then stepped back to photograph the carters as they hitched the mules. Before leaving, he carefully hid his camera deep in a bundle of clothing in Mary's cart. A bandit would have to dig deep to find that precious treasure.

After a quick breakfast and a hot cup of tea, James loaded Mary and the boys into one cart and walked beside them as the mules pulled the carts toward the ferry at the Grand Canal. Slowly the barge moved them through the muddy waters of the 1,200-mile-long waterway that was a lifeline of trade from Hangkow in the south to its northern terminus at Peking. Safely on the other side, the carts trundled down a dusty path, jostling and jolting the Liddells westward toward Siaochang.

A veteran missionary once said that the most comfortable way to travel in a Chinese cart was to pad it well with many thicknesses of quilts, put plenty of pillows at the back and sides, arrange several rugs for covering, and then — walk! It would be a long, rough ride for Mary, but the boys didn't mind a bit. Robbie considered it all a great adventure, and Eric made his feelings known only when it was time to eat. From time to time, Mary lifted the blanket covering Eric's face and gazed at his snippets of blond hair and the dimple in his chin. She loved her boys and couldn't imagine life without them.

Despite the fine dust billowing from the rolling wheels of the carts, it was a glorious winter day on the North China Plain. James was thankful for the warming sun, knowing that the paralyzing cold would soon be upon them. The dull brown landscape was dotted with plowed fields that had already yielded their autumn harvest of wheat, millet, and a coarse grain called *gaoliang*, used mostly for animal feed. Each year the land offered its promise of food for another year, but in China that pledge was often annulled by drought, flood, insects, or the pillaging armies of warlords.

The North China Plain lay flat and treeless over an area of eight thousand square miles, south of Peking and north of the Yellow River. Densely populated and heavily cultivated, the land supplied nearly everything needed by the people, from cotton for their clothing to mud bricks for their homes. In the section of the plain comprising what the London Missionary Society called its rural or "country fields" of Tsangchow and Siaochang, there were more than ten thousand villages with a total population of over ten million.

James scanned the flat landscape looking in vain for a tree or hill. How the cart drivers found their way was still a mystery to him. There were no roads, no landmarks, and each village they passed looked exactly like the one before. As the morning wore on, his mind ranged back over all that had happened to bring him to this day.

When he first volunteered for service with the LMS, the Rev. James D. Liddell had said: "I would gladly undertake the duties pertaining to a real pioneer situation." The society had obliged by posting him to Ch'ao Yang in Mongolia, two hundred fifty miles northeast of Peking. He had left his fiancée, Mary Reddin, in Scotland, knowing that he must prove himself on the field for a year and pass a Chinese language examination before she would be allowed to join him. James arrived in China on November 10, 1898, and a month later wrote the LMS Foreign Secretary in London, saying that he had already begun studying the language and was planning to take his exam the next May. He continued: "I expect that when you receive a wire saying I have passed, Miss Reddin will be sent to me."

During the first year he referred himself as "a poor show" in terms of effectiveness, but quite the opposite was true. Within six months he was visiting outlying villages to preach and meet with Chinese

Christians. Whatever James Liddell lacked in genius, he made up for in tenacity. Ever hungry to learn more of the country and its people, he traveled to the northernmost LMS station at Pei Tzu Fu, even after being warned that the road was infested with robbers.

His missionary colleague at Ch'ao Yang, Dr. Thomas Cochrane, had grown pessimistic about the LMS effort in Mongolia and felt the station should be abandoned and left to the Irish Presbyterians. "We should concentrate our efforts on people willing to listen," Cochrane argued, "on those who are anxious to hear the gospel." Although James was far from ready to accept that evaluation, in July, he and Cochrane were forced to leave Ch'ao Yang for several months when bandits threatened to take over the city.

This was an age of near anarchy in China when armed bands of marauders vied with warlords for control of towns and villages. Outlaws routinely kidnapped Chinese men believed to have wealth, then sent the family a severed eyelid or ear along with a note demanding money. If the ransom was not quickly paid, additional notes and body parts continued to arrive as the victim suffered a hideous torture. When the bandits lost patience, they often coated the victim with oil and set him afire in a public place as a warning to others. Women were often taken, and, according to one missionary, "the refinements of cruelty practiced upon the poor women dare not be mentioned."

Mary Reddin likely knew none of this when she sailed for China on September 11, 1899. She did know that James had passed his language exam, that she loved him and after six years of engagement, she was eager to become his wife. Whatever was ahead, they would face it together. Six weeks later she stepped off the ship in Shanghai and into James' arms. Her head was still swimming with the new sights and sounds when they were married at the Shanghai Cathedral on October 23. They left the next day to return to James' station at Ch'ao Yang in Mongolia.

In May 1900, letters arrived from Tientsin warning of serious trouble there and threats from a militant group known as The Society of Righteous and Harmonious Fists. Members of the group, called Boxers by Westerners, were determined to eliminate all foreign influence in China. In Ch'ao Yang, growing numbers of Boxers began to drill openly, reciting phrases they believed made them invulnerable to swords, knives and bullets.

After several months of very encouraging work, James sensed a marked change in the mood of the people toward the missionaries and their local converts. As James walked with several Chinese Christians to chapel one Sunday in early June, a group of Boxers began to shove and threaten the Chinese believers. Within days the situation became critical, forcing James and Dr. Cochrane to pack a few things and seek sympathetic Chinese friends to help them leave Ch'ao Yang. Cochrane's wife and children traveled in a cart while Mary, seven months pregnant, was carried in a sedan chair by six local Christians who risked death to help them. The Cochranes and Liddells made their way to a coastal city where they found passage on a boat to Shanghai.

Even as they departed, the threats turned to violence as the Boxers began a reign of terror across North China. They murdered some two hundred foreign missionaries, teachers and businessmen, but took greater vengeance on Chinese Christians and their families. Thousands fell to the sword. The Boxers also burned houses, schools and churches—anything that symbolized foreign domination and power. For two months they laid siege to the cities of Tientsin and Peking until an international military force from eight nations ended the uprising. Tragically, the foreign armies' rampaging sack of Peking planted the seeds of future rebellion.

In the relative safety of the London Missionary Compound in Shanghai, Mary gave birth to Robert Victor Liddell on August 27, 1900. The joy of his safe arrival was tempered by the peril of Chinese friends left behind. James wrote: "I commend the scattered flock to the Great Shepherd of the sheep, praying and believing that He will care and provide for them in this their time of need." Although the Boxers were put down and the Chinese government was forced to pay for damaged property, many people believed it was just a matter of time before the next anti-foreign movement swept China.

In November, the Liddells moved from Shanghai to Tientsin, a bustling port city and center of commerce eighty miles south of

Peking. There they awaited further assignment from the LMS. But during this period of transition, James was not idle.

Early in 1901, as many of the Chinese Christians began creeping back to their villages, James was given the task of helping them receive government compensation for their houses and churches destroyed by the Boxers. In what would become a life-long pattern in China, James left Mary safe in Tientsin while he traveled to Mongolia. Unsettled conditions in the wake of the Boxer Uprising made communication impossible, and for weeks Mary had no idea whether her husband was drinking tea with friends or in the hands of bandits. After prolonged delays in Chin Chou, James returned to Tientsin and on a second attempt finally reached Ch'ao Yang in July. For two months he assisted the remnant of Chinese believers there before returning home to Mary and baby Rob.

The Liddell's second son was born in Tientsin on January 16, 1902. James and Mary named him Henry Eric, and that is how it appeared in the LMS magazine, *The Chronicle,* in London. A few weeks later, as James walked to the British Municipal Building in Tientsin to register the birth, Dr. Ernest Peill, a missionary colleague asked, "Well, Liddell, what did you name the wee chap?" When James told him "Henry Eric," Peill said, "H.E.L. With those initials he'll have a hard time at school." James immediately returned home to confer with Mary, and the name was changed to Eric Henry.

Six weeks after Eric's birth, James again left Tientsin, this time in a blinding snowstorm, for a final return to Ch'ao Yang. After a three-day journey by train to Chin Chou, he met two men from the Irish Presbyterian Mission. From there, with a Chinese escort of twelve mounted men, they made their way into territory where lawlessness and anarchy still reigned. In spite of a journey that James called "both difficult and dangerous," he successfully oversaw the transfer of the LMS property to the Presbyterians.

Now, as he journeyed with his family to Siaochang late in 1902, it seemed impossible that all this had happened in the four years since James arrived in China. "More like four lifetimes," he thought to himself. Covering his face with a cloth to block out the choking dust, he perched on the shaft between cart and mules for a respite from walking. A cry from hungry Eric caused James to glance at the sun as it settled toward the horizon.

"Not much farther to the inn," he told Mary. She was a brave lady, this Mary Reddin, he thought to himself. The physical examination required of all prospective missionary wives had listed her as 5 feet, 3 inches and 8 stone (112 pounds). Regarding her general condition and powers of endurance, the doctor stated simply: "She is healthy and well developed but not robust." And if ever there was a country where strength and vigor were required, it was China.

The next afternoon as their carts rolled through the gates of the LMS compound at Siaochang, James pointed toward a completed three-story house standing between two other partially built structures of identical shape and size. "That's your new home," he said with a smile. Mary hardly had time to take it in before they were surrounded by a welcoming committee of missionaries and smiling Chinese. James set Rob on the ground, handed Eric to a lady standing nearby and helped Mary down from the cart. When her feet hit the ground, she watched in disbelief as the dust fell in clumps from her clothes.

In the rural area where James would be working, eighty churches had been destroyed and hundreds of Chinese Christians killed during the Boxer Uprising. In addition, the entire LMS compound at Siaochang had been destroyed. Missionary homes, medical dispensary, schools and a five hundred seat church were reduced to small piles of rubble. For the past few months James, along with Dr. Sewell McFarlane, had helped supervise the rebuilding as they started from scratch.

On December 6, 1902, J. D. Liddell wrote to George Cousins at LMS headquarters in London: "We, i.e., Mrs. Liddell and family are now all at Hsiao Chang. The house we are living in is finished until the Spring, when various little matters will require attention.

"One other house is nearing completion and the third will be ready about the end of March 1903.

"The superintending of the work was not easy, as constant watch had to be kept lest the many 'raw' workmen made mistakes.

"Dr. McFarlane and I think the houses are a credit to the Society, and ought to stand the wear and tear of many years."

At Siaochang the Liddells occupied one of three large Western-style family homes within the mud-walled compound. A fourth smaller house accommodated the single ladies. Mary's Chinese servants shopped for food, cooked, washed clothes and cleaned house while Chi Nai Nai, the "amah," looked after the children. As a trained nurse, Mary hoped she could assist medically at the mission or become involved in the educational work with the women. For a time she did, but her frail constitution and the demands of a growing family left Mary tired or feeling ill much of the time.

In October 1903, she gave birth to Janet Lillian, always called Jenny. Three days after the birth, Mary developed peritonitis. The missionary ladies at Siaochang attended her day and night while Dr. Ernest Peill applied all his knowledge, but she did not respond. One evening as she lay near death, Dr. Peill said to James: "There's nothing more I can do." The two men slipped from their chairs onto their knees and poured out their hearts in prayer for Mary. The next day she rallied and began a slow recovery.

In one of his annual reports, James wrote to the Foreign Secretary of the LMS: "Will you excuse me saying just a little — for your own ears — concerning my wife? She has struggled with this language amidst all that tends to hinder and discourage. She has tried to do what lay to her hand. But household duties and homeland sorrows* have taken a lot out of her. In her own quiet way she does far more than many would give her credit for. And if willingness to do much counts for anything, then she has done nobly."

As the children grew, Chi Nai Nai followed Rob, Eric, and Jenny around the compound at Siaochang. For a time, their wanderings were confined to the ground floor verandah on three sides of the house. Then it was down the steps with tentative forays toward the large stone church, the medical dispensary and the school for Chinese boys and girls. At first it was easy for Chi Nai Nai to keep up with them, but as their mobility increased, so did her frustration.

---

* Mary's mother died in 1903

On her tiny bound feet, she could not possibly run and catch them. Rob six, Eric four, and Jenny two ran off in three directions with Chi Nai Nai shouting after them: "Lobbie! Yellie! Jei-nee!" Dutifully, they would return because they loved her, just as she loved them.

During family prayers each evening, Eric was famous for going into fits of giggling, for which he would have to be sent from the room. But he was also a shy, sensitive child who often requested that they sing "The Ninety and Nine." When they reached the part about the little lamb, lost and alone on the mountainside, he always cried. He grew up learning that they belonged to God, but also to the LMS. Once as little Eric hammered nails into the verandah, Mary told him he mustn't do it because the house belonged to the mission. In frustration he laid down his hammer and asked, "Are we the mission's too?"

James spent much of his time visiting the surrounding villages, preaching in public on market days and meeting with local congregations of Chinese Christians to encourage them and their pastors. He thrived on the work, in spite of the exhausting travel on the North China Plain. In the spring, he battled the choking dust storms that swept down from the Gobi Desert. The long rains of autumn turned the rutted cart paths into a sea of trembling mud, two feet deep. Winter brought blowing snow and mind-numbing cold of minus ten degrees Fahrenheit. But weather rarely stopped James, and he was never sick.

The only thing that could defeat him was the heat. Summer on the North China Plain brought endless days of strength-sapping temperatures over 100 degrees Fahrenheit. The houses that kept the missionaries warm in the winter became ovens under the cloudless skies and the blazing sun. At night, with no fans to move the air, parents and children slept fitfully in ever-widening pools of perspiration. Prickly heat plagued the little ones while adults struggled to maintain some level of productivity. Their only relief was the annual pilgrimage to Peitaiho.

From Siaochang, it was a grueling four-day journey to the seaside cottages on the Gulf of Pei Chihli, 200 miles east of Peking. But once there, the women and children often stayed all summer, with the husbands joining them for the month of August. Some critics considered the annual holiday a luxury, but the missionaries saw it as a necessary time of recovery and recuperation. Accommodation at P.T.H., as it was affectionately known, ranged from the modest bungalows owned by various mission organizations to the opulent summer houses of business executives—the "taipans" of the Kailan Mining Administration, Butterfield and Swire, British-American Tobacco, and other international companies. Westerners roamed freely and safely along the beaches and through the village, attending tennis parties, concerts and sing-alongs. Evening gatherings ranged from cocktail parties for the business crowd to missionary Bible conferences with such noted speakers as Dr. F. B. Meyer of London. It was always a sad autumn day when the cottages were boarded up and the last missionaries returned to their places of service.

As James Liddell continued to visit the villages around Siaochang, he developed a growing conviction that the future of Christianity in China did not lie with him. In his report for 1904, he noted that he spent so much time traveling by very slow and exhausting means, he usually wasn't worth much at the end of the day. The best work, he believed, would be done by the local pastors who lived in the villages. Eventually, he would leave, but they would stay. His goal must be to train and encourage them. In circular letters to friends, and in his official reports to the London Missionary Society, James was careful to mention his Chinese colleagues by name and commend them for their faithful service to Christ.

"I cannot close this short review" he wrote in 1903, "without saying a few words of praise regarding three of our leading men, namely Chang Sung Mao, Pao Feng Ko and Ts'ui Chang Tu'ei. These men have been a source of strength and help throughout the year. We have other preachers doing noble work, but these three stand head and shoulders above the others."

During these years, Rob and Eric regarded everything that happened at Siaochang as an adventure. When torrential summer rains turned the LMS compound into an island, they splashed happily in the pools of water. An autumn plague of grub-like insects that destroyed eighty percent of the local crops became a contest to see who could pick the largest number off the garden plants and put them in a tin. While others were repulsed by the marauding vermin, the little boys stood near the compound gate and listened to what sounded like horses munching outside as the horde devoured almost all of the grain standing in the fields. A January blizzard that blocked all roads for two weeks became an occasion to bundle up in their padded coats and trousers for a romp through the snow.

They did not feel the isolation of their remote station, although it could be very trying for the adults. After the boys said a polite good-bye to Dr. and Mrs. Ernest Peill, who were departing for a new assignment at Peking, they could not understand why their mother wept for so long over the loss of these friends. Like most missionary children, they inhabited a safe, tranquil world, free of the burdens born by their parents, and removed from the sorrows of the Chinese people outside the compound walls.

In March 1907, Rob and Eric watched with wondering excitement as the servants packed the trunks with clothing and a few household goods. James and Mary kept talking of going "home" for a visit. Since Siaochang was the only home Rob and Eric had ever known, they could not picture what lay ahead. Mary was thrilled by the prospect of returning to Scotland for the first time in nearly eight years.

But no matter how hard she tried, she could not remove one dark cloud from the bright horizon of their furlough. When the homeland time was over and they returned to China, she knew that she must leave her little boys behind.

TWO

Another World

The green hills of Scotland were so unlike the North China Plain that five-year-old Eric couldn't stop looking and pointing. From Glasgow, a short train journey on the Forth and Clyde Railway brought the Liddell family to Drymen station at Croftamie. When they stepped off the train there in May 1907, a contingent of relatives and friends swept James, Mary, and the children into their arms. James' three sisters, Jane, Lizzie, and Maggie, were there, along with their seventy-three-year-old father. They piled people and belongings into a horse-drawn wagon for the one-mile ride to the village of Drymen, where James had lived from age ten to nineteen.

Fifty yards up the hill from the village square stood a two-story house called Ashbank where the Liddells had arranged to rent rooms from the Kirk family. From the upper window, Eric and Rob could gaze south across the magnificent Strathendrick Valley or watch the cattle drivers assemble their stock for the Saturday morning sale in the square. But neither Eric nor Rob was content to gaze for long. For once they were free to explore while three-year-old Jenny kept their mother company at home.

In this village of some three hundred, it was unlikely that the Liddell brothers could go anywhere without someone knowing who they were and what they were doing. On the south side of Stirling Road, near the square, Auntie Maggie lived with Grandfather Liddell above their small grocery shop where there was always fresh gingerbread for hungry boys. Auntie Lizzie MacFarlane and her husband, Uncle Robert, lived next door.

For the first time in their lives, the boys did not live in a compound surrounded by walls. Nor were they in the care of an ever-present Chinese amah. Rob and Eric explored their new world with gusto as they roamed the village in the company of local boys. Eric's vocabulary quickly grew to include a collection of profane words. When he casually used a few of them at the supper table, Mary reacted in horror. Once he understood that swearing was unacceptable, five-year-old Eric offered a simple solution: "Just tell me what all the bad words are, and I won't use any of them." Mary resigned herself to dealing with the problem as it arose, one word at a time.

For three months, Rob and Eric enjoyed a summer of glorious freedom. During family picnics on the banks of Endrick Water, they waded and splashed below the stately five-arched stone bridge. Their imaginations soared during day trips to nearby Buchanan Castle and visits to tranquil Balmaha Bay on Loch Lomond. James Liddell's ever-present camera recorded the family fun, often catching Mary with a broad smile.

On August 13 the boys began a new adventure when they entered Drymen Public School. The headmaster, John Hall, sporting a bushy handlebar mustache and slicked down hair, oversaw the work of Miss Wilson and another teacher in a two-room schoolhouse where the students were grouped by age. At recess, Rob would often be seen carrying a wooden rifle while Eric pursued the art of rolling a wooden hoop with a stick. But the Liddell boys never appeared in the school log book, which was reserved for noting those students who were exceptionally good or very, very bad.

On September weekends, the children scoured the roadsides and gullies around Drymen to pick brambles. With fingers and mouths turned crimson, Rob and Eric would arrive at Ashbank with a sack full of the local blackberries for the brass jelly pan on the back of the stove. October turned the leaves of the Rowan trees a flaming red and brought the first hint of frost as coal fires sent their plumes of gray smoke drifting lazily into the evening sky. Even the winter snow seemed to arrive as a welcome blanket of soft white to cover the sleeping hills.

The months ebbed away in the activities of everyday life. The family attended a local church and also participated in the evening Band of Hope meetings, singing the lively Moody and Sankey hymns. The Liddells were welcome guests in many homes, where their accounts of life in far-off China seemed exotic and exciting compared to village life in Scotland. James was often away for a week at a time speaking to churches on behalf of the London Missionary Society. At times, he seemed eager to return to the work in Siaochang, but Mary savored every breath of homeland air.

Rob and Eric had nearly outgrown their matching tweed suits by Easter when the pungent white blossoms burst out on the Hawthorne trees. With the coming of spring, Mary Liddell crossed an emotional line beyond which a dread of the future overshadowed the joy of the present. After school recessed in June, the Liddells would have a scant three months together before their furlough ended and James and Mary placed their boys in the School for the Sons of Missionaries. From the porch of Ashbank, Mary scanned the hills around Drymen and pondered the future. No one in the LMS would think it strange for her to take her boys to boarding school, kiss them on the forehead, tell them to be good, then walk away for seven years. But she could not fathom the possibility. As she watched the children walk up the hill from school, a new resolve began to take shape in the deepest part of her. When James left for China in September, she would not go with him.

It may have been an earlier visit to the School for the Sons of Missionaries that helped convince Mary she must follow this course. The SSM, as it was often called, occupied a plot of ground in Blackheath, a village along the railway line nine miles east of central London. The school was housed in a somber, four-story brick building that the current headmaster described as "inconvenient, cold and dark, and much too small for the number of boys it accommodates." The boys themselves called it "the old barn."

Inside, long gloomy stone corridors paralleled the big schoolroom, which ran the entire length of the building. Eighty boarders, all sons of foreign missionaries, lived upstairs in two large dormitories and several smaller ones. Light entered through high, vaulted windows with leaded panes, but it struggled to reach the interior rooms. Small diamond-shaped swing windows provided only a hint of fresh air.

The school was flanked on one side by the station of the South-Eastern Railway line. From early morning until late at night, coal-burning trains rumbled through, spewing plumes of soot-laden black smoke. The asphalt-covered playground, known as "the Bear Pit," lay ten feet below the level of a private road in front of the school. At the end of that road stood the Blackheath Congregational Church.

On September 14, 1908, James Liddell entered the names of his two sons in the SSM registration book. Although sorrowful at leaving them, in his heart James believed it was best for everyone. The next day he sailed alone for China. Mary and Jenny would remain in England for a year to see how the boys settled into school.

That night Mary gazed at a postcard photo of the Home and School for the Sons of Missionaries. While it might be adequate as a school, she could never accept it as a home. She and Jenny moved into furnished rooms in a nearby house, planning to stay there at least through the long Christmas holiday. On occasional Sunday afternoons and half-holidays, her boys would not be farmed out to local families or guardians. They would come home to her.

In the meantime, her sons had to face boarding school life on their own. Like all the boys, Rob and Eric were known to masters and fellow students by their surnames only. Throughout their years at the school, Rob would be Liddell i (one) and Eric, Liddell ii, (two) with the lower case Roman numerals indicating their order of birth.

During their first days at SSM, Rob and Eric endured the usual ragging and mild bullying from the older boys. Perhaps the most punishing rite of initiation was running a gauntlet between two lines of lads who snapped them with knotted handkerchiefs. They were also introduced to the "fag" system, in which each younger boy was required to do errands and menial jobs for an older boy. Through it all, Eric stayed close to Rob and often leaned on his older brother for strength and support.

Each morning the boys donned the school uniform of dark trousers and jacket with a broad white Eton collar. After half an hour of "prep" time, they assembled for breakfast — usually cold porridge, bread, and a pat of butter. On alternate mornings a dab of marmalade replaced the porridge.

A regimen of academic classes, including science, history, foreign language, scripture, mathematics, history, English, and geography, carried them up to noon. The midday meal usually included some form of meat. Whenever mutton appeared for lunch, the boys dubbed it "dead missionary" because the somewhat improved meal invariably followed the visit of a parent home from the foreign field. The most common dessert, called "putty and varnish," was a suet pudding topped with molasses. The abhorred amalgam of leftovers at the end of the week was known as "resurrection pie."

Afternoons were devoted to classes and outdoor sports, followed by tea and a study period each evening. At 9:00 P.M., the boys received a slice of bread covered with the dripping of fat from the day's roasted meat. Eric considered this an indigestible mass, and on more than one occasion he found a way to deposit his unswallowed mouthful into the wastepaper basket.

Because there was no daily hot water, the boys stood over a small basin and half-heartedly dabbed at the dirt from sports and play. Once a week they descended to the basement boot room where they took their turn in a tank filled with warm water. In groups of ten to twelve, the boys took a giant step along the road to cleanliness. No doubt the periodic visits to the nearby Ladywell Baths for swimming instruction served a dual purpose.

SSM's headmaster, W. B. Hayward, believed in discipline primarily as motivation on the inside, but also as correction on the backside. Boys who flagrantly violated the rules would be invited to "bend over and receive three of the best" from his cane. Hayward established the prefect system in which senior boys were given responsibility for much of the daily regimen. They could issue "order marks" or demerits which could cost a boy his weekly free time. And the prefects were free to wield a thick cord known as a "tally whack."

As Rob and Eric navigated these sometimes threatening new waters, at least for that first year they had a safe haven nearby. For a month at Christmas and Easter, Mary welcomed her boys "home" where she and Jenny were staying. On June 26, the school closed early after two boys were sent to the local hospital, one with diphtheria and the other with scarlet fever. Mary quickly swept Rob and Eric off to Berwick-upon-Tweed for a summer with her family.

But she could not stay with them forever. On September 14, 1909, Mary paid her last visit to Blackheath to say good-bye to her sons. They talked and hugged and promised to write every week. As much as they all tried to avoid crying, the tears came as they embraced for a final time. Then the boys were excused to go out and play.

After a brief meeting with the headmaster to discuss the details of guardianship and holidays, Mary left through the massive front door. Hesitantly, she walked to the edge of the building and glanced down into the playground. Rob and Eric were engrossed in a game of touch rugger with several other boys and did not see her. Mary wanted to call out, but knew it would be wrong to prolong the farewell. She turned and walked away, wracked with sobs, knowing that she would not see her sons until James' next furlough—six years away. The next day she and Jenny sailed for China.

⁂

One observer described the religious life of the SSM as "active without being forced." Attendance at Sunday morning church service was required, and most boys went to the Congregational church next door. When an outbreak of measles or influenza placed everyone under quarantine, the masters and senior boys conducted the Sunday services themselves in the school.

The prefects and other seniors who often meted out discipline were revered by the junior boys. When Eric and his classmates played their game of "table rugger" on the trestle tables in the dining room, they named their counters after the school rugby heroes of the day: Rawlinson, Claxton, and Carnagie; Fahmy, Harmon, and

Hills. Their age and athletic prowess made them demi-gods in the eyes of the younger boys. But far beyond sports, the example of the older boys helped set the moral and spiritual tone of the school so that, honesty, integrity, and character permeated every aspect of school life.

Everyone could recite the school motto: Gloria Filiorum Patres — "The fathers are the glory of the sons" (from Proverbs 17:6: "The glory of children are their fathers.") — but its meaning was caught rather than taught. SSM did not try to push its students into missionary service, but certainly held it up as an honorable and noble vocation. Present and former missionaries often addressed the boys, and the entire student body went en masse to the annual Missionary Demonstration at Westminster Chapel in London. Sacrifice and separation were accepted, by parents and children alike, as part of the missionary calling. None liked it, but few questioned its necessity.

With all its austerity and discipline, the School for the Sons of Missionaries had a saving grace — the people inside its walls. The dismal building at Blackheath was filled with boys whose main goal in life was having fun. They came from every corner of the earth, often speaking Hindi, Arabic, or Chinese better than English. Given a moment of free time, they could instantly launch a round of marbles in the dining hall, or resume an ongoing game of touch rugger on the playground. The latter reigned as the favorite pastime at SSM. Touch rugger involved getting a tennis ball to the opposite wall of the playground. Points, known as "tries," were scored by touching the ball to the wall. The game demanded quick passing and lightning reflexes, which later stood the smaller SSM boys in good stead on the rugby pitch when they encountered the larger players from rival schools.

The boys also tended a menagerie of pet birds and lizards on the little side playground known as the Aviary, always managing, in the process, to carve their initials into the red-brick arches. With a passion for adventure and exploration, they soon learned every nook, cranny, and hiding place in the building. In a darkened dormitory room, after an evening pillow fight, they told horrifying snake stories from India, and South Sea tales of being tossed over the breakers of a coral reef in a native canoe.

During spring excursions to the nearby town of Hayes, they roamed the common and quickly formed battle lines for a cone fight, with ammunition provided by the local trees. They gathered lizards to take back to school and encased tadpoles in the lime water bottles from lunch. Before reaching Blackheath, most of the future frogs died in the lethal mixture of pond water and lime cordial.

Any teacher who lacked the ability to create interest and maintain order could be mercilessly teased and punished by these young sons of missionaries. One intimidated young instructor, fresh from university, hit a mental block in the middle of reciting the Lord's Prayer and received not a word of help from his students, who enjoyed watching him squirm. More than one junior master was sent packing within months of his arrival because he could not control his classroom.

Mr. George Griffiths, however, was not one of these. Any new boy who decided to test "G. G.", as he was affectionately known, quickly discovered the diminutive Welshman to be more than his match. Although he stood less than five feet tall, G. G. could use his fiery temperament to good advantage when the occasion required it.

Latin could have been a daily ordeal with a dull master, but G. G. made it almost fun. With a masterful blend of quick wit and good humor, Griffiths created classroom order more through interest than authority. One student recalled the time in class when G. G. was asked to explain the contemporary meaning of the Latin word *vestige*. The amiable master replied that one day the boys might be caught by the police while swimming naked in the river and accused of being without a "vestige of clothing." With a twinkle in his eye, Griffiths went on to say that at the subsequent police-court proceedings they might be able to argue that the charge brought against them was unfounded because they had been wearing a pair of sock suspenders at the time of the alleged offense. The boys laughed, and Griffiths directed their attention once again to Caesar's commentaries on the Gallic Wars.

G. G. never forgot the name or face of a student. Many alumni who approached him at the annual Old Boys' Day after an absence of a dozen years were stunned to be greeted by name. Above all he was kind, fair, and dedicated to his task. Every day during his twenty-nine-year tenure at the school, Griffiths walked the two and a half miles from his home to the school and back.

Mr. Sydney Moore was another favorite of the boys. Moore came to the school as a breath of fresh air in 1903. A widely traveled man who spoke six continental languages, Moore's initial academic assignment was daunting: to instruct every boy in the school in spoken and written French; instruct three-quarters of them in spoken and written German; and teach some scripture, English, and European history. The enthusiastic young master managed to do all that and more. He swept into the French classroom in his flowing academic robe with an enthusiastic, "Bon jour!" In class he spoke only French and insisted that his students do likewise. Under his influence, boys from SSM began to carry off top prizes in language competitions involving larger and more prestigious British schools. In addition, he conducted a well-attended voluntary Bible class for the boys.

Men like Griffiths and Moore were typical of the faculty attracted to SSM by Headmaster Hayward, whose energy and forward thinking shaped the life of the school and did much to overcome its inadequate physical resources. For years Hayward longed to move SSM to a new location, not for himself, but for the boys. In 1912 his dream became reality when the school moved to the premises of the former Royal Naval School in nearby Mottingham and became known as Eltham College.

For the first time, the boys had a playing field of their own — a place for cricket and rugby. A place to play and room to run. Just the ticket for ten-year-old Eric Liddell.

THREE

Eltham College

1912–1919

On Sunday, February 3, 1912, Eric awoke to a world wrapped in white. He could only hope that the snow would last beyond church services and the mandatory letter-writing period following the noon meal. If so, he and the other boys might have a chance to improvise sleds and play outside.

Eric gazed out the window and thought how different it was to see trees and fields instead of the busy streets of Blackheath. And their dormitory was warm, unlike the drafty "old barn." The boys eagerly gathered near the radiators to savor the luxury of their new surroundings. Since returning to school on January 30, each day had brought fresh discoveries of the glories of their new location at Eltham College.

That afternoon, Eric had more than enough news to fill the required weekly letter to his parents. He told about the gymnasium, lawn tennis courts, swimming pool, and playing field. The school had its own chapel and a separate sanatorium for boys with contagious illnesses. He and Rob had enjoyed their Christmas holiday and were feeling fine, even though influenza had struck half the boys in school just before the term ended. As usual, he ended by hoping everything was all right in China.

But, as usual, everything was not all right in China. During the previous three months, outnumbered troops of the old Manchu dynasty had battled the Chinese revolutionaries who gave no quarter to their vanquished foes. In the city of Sianfu an estimated 10,000 Manchus — men, women, and children — had been slaughtered, and their area of the city burned to the ground. Anti-foreign mobs, unconnected with the revolutionaries, had destroyed some mission buildings in that city and killed eight foreigners. All across China, villagers fled to avoid the clash of rival armies, and many foreigners feared for their lives. In Peking, five-year-old Pu Yi had been deposed, to become forever known as "the last Emperor." Christmas Day had found Sun Yat Sen stepping ashore in Shanghai to hail the overthrow of the Manchu Dynasty and briefly become president of the new republic before it quickly disintegrated into warring factions.

But all that was likely unknown or at least uninteresting to the tousle-haired ten-year-old writing to his parents. Eric hurriedly signed and sealed his letter, gave it to a monitoring prefect, then dashed outside with the rest of the boys. At the moment, he was far more concerned with sledding than with politics in China. As long as the weekly letter arrived from his mother, he felt his family was all right in Siaochang, even though the news was always at least six weeks old.

At the beginning of the new term, a recent Cambridge University graduate joined the Eltham College staff as a classics master. Augustus Pountney Cullen loathed his given names and preferred that his colleagues call him A.P., Gus, or simply Cullen. At the age of twenty-two, Cullen sported a bushy mustache and a handsome Douglas Fairbanks look. As a scholar and sportsman, he entered fully into the life of the school, giving talks on the heroes of the Greek classics and coaching the boys in swimming. His initial impressions of young Eric Liddell were: (1) the boy was not likely to set the world on fire academically; and (2) when it came to classroom and dormitory pranks, Eric was not as innocent as he looked.

The move to Eltham College also brought the advent of non-boarding students known as "day boys." Many were the sons of local residents with no connection to a missionary society. The tuition from the "day bugs," as the boarders called them, helped undergird the always-precarious financial status of the school.

The school year marched along to the cadence of eagerly anticipated events: Mr. Tucker's yearly visit with his fascinating collection of mechanical toys; the July outing to Vinson's strawberry fields at Belvedere, where the boys could pick and eat all they wanted; and the summer holidays, which Liddell i and Liddell ii usually spent with relatives in Drymen or Berwick-upon-Tweed.

As 1912 drew to a close, Rob and Eric were surprised to learn that they had a new brother, Ernest, born December 12 in Peking. Even nine-year-old Jenny had not guessed why she and her mother had gone to stay with friends in Peking after the summer at Peitaiho, instead of returning to Siaochang. After Mary's brush with death following Jenny's birth, being near a proper mission hospital in a major city seemed to be a wise choice. But Mary was not able to sustain good health in China for long.

At Siaochang, in late October 1913, Mary began suffering periodic attacks of agonizing pain in her stomach. James sent a courier to Tsangchow to summon their longtime friend, Dr. Sidney Peill, who arrived the next day. After his examination, Dr. Peill said that he suspected gallstones but suggested getting a second opinion. A doctor came from Peking, confirmed the diagnosis, and said Mary should return immediately to Britain for an operation. On December 18, 1913, James, Mary, Jenny, and one-year-old Ernest sailed from Tsingtao on the Princess Alice.

Rob and Eric were amazed to hear that their family would arrive in London at the end of January 1914, a year earlier than their father's scheduled furlough. But their excitement at being reunited was tempered by one look at their mother's ashen face, much more drawn and lined since they last saw her more than four years previously. After a one-day visit, the boys returned to school while the rest of the family left for Edinburgh, where successful surgery, combined with being home near her family, quickly restored Mary to health.

The Eltham College annual sports day in April took place on a soggy field during intermittent rain showers. Under the towering plane tree in front of the school, the military band of the Lewisham

Industrial School kept spirits enlivened throughout the day. Eric won the long jump, high jump, and 100 yard dash in the under-thirteen age category. Rob, competing against older boys in the higher age bracket, placed first in the long jump and third in the 220 yards race.

The Liddell family spent the six-week summer holiday at a house in Spittal, a seaside resort near Berwick-upon-Tweed. Every morning, James, Rob, and Eric swam together in the bracing North Sea. Ten-year-old Jenny, eager to show her older brothers how well she could swim, put one foot in the frigid waters and retreated to a sun-drenched chair on the front porch of their seafront cottage. She preferred the warmth of the Bohai Sea at Peitaiho.

Then, early in August, James returned home one afternoon with a newspaper whose entire front page bore only three words in massive type: BRITAIN AT WAR! Mary took a deep breath, reassuring herself that the conflict with Germany would end long before her boys would be required to go and fight. Eric was twelve and Rob a few weeks short of fourteen when war fever swept the nation and young men began enlisting by the thousands. "Not my boys," Mary prayed each morning. "Please, let it end soon."

In September, when Rob and Eric returned to Eltham College, Jenny was enrolled in the School for the Daughters of Missionaries, known as Walthamstow Hall, in Sevenoaks, Kent. Despite the beautiful surroundings and the encouragement of sympathetic older girls, she missed her family terribly. Christmas holidays brought a brief respite, but when she returned to Sevenoaks at the end of January, her letters bled with pain at the prospect of being left in England when her mother, father, and Ernest returned to China in the spring. One of her friends at school said simply, "Jenny Liddell will die if she is left behind."

Once again, Mary faced the sickening prospect of leaving a child in an English boarding school while she returned to China, half a world away. If it were the only way, she would do it. But was it absolutely necessary? The LMS had reassigned James from rural Siaochang to the city of Peking, where there were many good schools. Even if Jenny attended the China Inland Mission boarding school at Chefoo, she would be home for three months of the year. To settle the matter for herself, Mary traveled by train four hundred miles from Glasgow to Sevenoaks and met privately with Miss Sophie Hare, the headmistress at Walthamstow Hall.

Seated in Miss Hare's study with its parquet floor and polished wood paneling, Mary asked, "Would you consider me foolish if I wanted to take Jenny back to China?" During their frank discussion, the white-haired and somewhat imposing headmistress showed great sympathy for Mary, describing her own feelings of sadness as she watched missionary parents return after a seven-year absence and fail to recognize their own daughters. Many girls, upon completing school, had come to Miss Hare saying that they did not really know their parents, and that she meant more to them than their own mothers. Mary thanked her for her honesty and said, "If it's all right then, Jenny will leave school in a few weeks and return to China with us."

It was a sad parting on March 13, 1915, as James, Mary, Jenny, and Ernest said good-bye to Rob and Eric. In two weeks the boys would be released from school for the month-long Easter holidays, but the sailing date was fixed and could not be delayed. Rob gave Jenny a ring and tiny kitchen stove for her dollhouse, and she responded with a tearful hug. Eric tickled two-year-old Ernest, who squirmed away to see Jenny's new treasures.

Mary took Rob by the shoulders and marveled that he was taller than she. Seven years until their next furlough. He would be a grown man before she held him again. And Eric would likely be in university. She left the final words to James, whose strong handshake, prayer, and good-bye would have to keep the boys until they all met again.

Between the ages of six and a half and thirteen, Eric had lived in a family home with both parents for only a hundred days. One of his contemporaries wrote of their Eltham College experience as the sons of missionaries: "We reckoned in pennies and often had none of them for long periods. Many of us remained at school through the holidays; by modern standards we seldom went out. And so we came to know each other intimately, like brothers, and we formed each other. The school was our family, and did for us not only a school's job, but much of what a family circle does for those who have one."

Academically, Eric's interests centered on mathematics and science. Under Master D. H. Burleigh, chemistry became a grand adventure of discovery. In the laboratory Eric learned to draw sulfuric acid by mouth into a pipette while concentrating on the careful procedure rather than the potential danger. Burleigh loved his subject and, through his enthusiasm, lit a fire of interest in young Eric Liddell. Outside the classroom, Burleigh garnered Eric's further admiration by winning the 1915 Masters/Old Boys 220 yards race in 26 seconds flat.

As Eric and Rob grew into their teens, their personality differences were clearly evident. Rob was vocal and outgoing; Eric was quiet and shy. Rob joined the Literary and Debating Society, while Eric shunned any kind of speaking before a group. Even at Master Sydney Moore's weekly Bible classes, which Eric faithfully attended, he never offered a comment during the discussions. Rob participated in a number of dramatic presentations, while Eric's only stage appearance is said to have been as the Dormouse in a school production of *Alice in Wonderland*. According to one account, he brought the house down simply by acting in his normally shy and quiet way. Eric's peers dubbed him "The Mouse," a nickname that persisted throughout his years at Eltham.

While Rob seemed completely at ease in situations of student leadership and public address, Eric did everything possible to avoid them. When pressed for a decision on a matter of urgency or importance, Eric often responded, "Ask my brother. Rob will take care of it." And perhaps because Rob was older and a little more serious in nature, he usually did take care of it.

But they were loyal brothers and close friends. If there were any conflicts between them, they are not recorded. On the athletic field, they teamed together in cricket and rugby despite their difference in age. Because World War I siphoned the older boys from schools across England, Rob, Eric, and their classmates rose to varsity competition much sooner than they would have under normal circumstances. At sixteen, Rob captained the Rugby First XV with fourteen-year-old Eric playing beside him on the wing. Their lackluster season of three wins, seven losses, and one draw was considered respectable, but certainly did not command the front page of the December 1916 *Eltham College Magazine*. That was reserved for the college's Roll of Honour, noting that "five more of our brave soldiers have fallen, making a total of twelve who have been killed on Active Service."

During the first few months of the war, it had been a grand adventure for the boys to watch battalions of recruits passing by on route marches, and to catch occasional glimpses of airplanes. Even the inconvenience of food rationing had been accepted as "doing our part" for the war effort. But the conflict, which some thought would be won by Britain in a matter of months, had become a murderous stalemate in the muddy trenches of the Western Front. The Battle of the Somme in the summer of 1916 claimed the lives of more than a million men on both sides of the war. And there was no end in sight, no apparent answer to Mary Liddell's prayer, "Please let it end soon."

When a Cadet Corps was formed at Eltham College early in 1916, both Rob and Eric joined. Rob thrived on the discipline and challenge, rising to the rank of Cadet Sergeant. Photographs of Rob in uniform show him relaxed, smiling, and looking every bit the leader. Eric seemed to tolerate his own participation in the corps as a necessary responsibility, but inside he was as stiff and uncomfortable with the whole idea of war as he was in his ill-fitting cadet uniform. Eric was not a pacifist, but deep in his heart he embraced peace as his ideal and preferred to confine his combat to the sports field.

Pacifism was recognized as a personal conviction, but it was not a popular stand in England. Most people regarded the truly brave men as those who fought and died "For God, King, and Country." Men of military age who were not in uniform often received looks of disdain from women at home who at times stopped them on the street and accused them of cowardice.

But England and its European neighbors were not the only countries wracked by military conflict. J. D. Liddell's missionary report for 1917 said: "This winter finds China suffering from Flood, Famine, Plague, and War. As I write, North and South oppose each other, and one sees little hope of a proper settlement. The Country seems to be drifting into a hopeless state of confusion, and it is difficult to see how order will be produced from the present chaos."

Just before Rob completed his studies at Eltham College in April 1918, he and Eric alternated in capturing first and second places in six of the nine senior division athletic events at the Annual Sports Day. The record read like an All Liddell contest:

CROSS COUNTRY RUN: (1) R. V. Liddell (2) E. H. Liddell.
LONG JUMP: (1) E .H. Liddell (2) R. V. Liddell.
HIGH JUMP: (1) R .V. Liddell (2) E. H. Liddell
HUNDRED YARDS OPEN: (1) E. H. Liddell (2) R. V. Liddell.
HURDLE RACE: (1) R. V. Liddell (2) E. H. Liddell
QUARTER MILE: (1) E. H. Liddell (2) R. V. Liddell

Eric tied the school record of 10 4/5 seconds for the 100 yards, but at the end of the day, Rob had won the Senior Championship, edging out his younger brother by only four points.

After the Easter holidays, Rob entered the University of Edinburgh to study medicine, leaving Eric at Eltham. It was the first time they had been separated since Eric's birth. In October 1918, Rob served a short stint on active duty with the Artists' Rifles (2/28th London Regiment), but was not sent overseas. A few weeks later no one was more relieved than Mary Liddell in China to hear that the Armistice had been signed and finally peace had come.

At the eleventh hour on the eleventh day of the eleventh month, Eric joined the Eltham College faculty and students in a special chapel service commemorating the end of the war. They thanked God for peace and victory, remembering those who had given their lives in the conflict. As the Roll of Honour was read aloud, it seemed to chronicle the past decade of Eric's life. His rugby heroes from Blackheath days were dead: Rawlinson, Claxton, and Carnagie; Fahmy, Harmon, and Hills. His teammates at Eltham, Badger and Piper, would not take the field again. The war had taught them all that life was fragile, and that at any moment a man could be swept up by events far beyond his control.

If any phrase summed up the philosophy that permeated Eric's years at Eltham College, it was "play the game." Unlike its modern counterpart, meaning to pretend, to "play up and play the game" embodied the ideals of integrity, justice, fairness, and tolerance. In principle, those ideals formed the moral and ethical backbone of the far-flung British Empire. Included in this challenge to live by the highest code of personal behavior was a sense of duty to help infuse these ideals among people and societies where they seemed all but unknown.

In an address to the entire school, Headmaster George Robertson had compared their responsibilities as Christians to "play the game" to the situation of the children of Israel who received the Promised Land as a gracious gift and trust from Almighty God. "Like them," Robertson had said, "we are called upon to correct our faults and to do our part in the Covenant recognizing the immense responsibility involved in our heritage." God's gifts of faith, health, and knowledge were undeserved and must never breed arrogance on the part of those who received them. They were to be used unselfishly to help bring a better life to others.

Three times a year, in April, July, and December, the *Eltham College Magazine* appeared with news of that term. Only once during Eric's twelve years at the school did his name appear for academic merit. Apart from that and a commendation for achievement in carpentry, all other mentions of his name were in connection with sports. During his last eighteen months at Eltham, he continued to excel in athletic competition and received the Blackheath Cup as the best all-round sportsman. As captain of rugby during the 1918 season, the *Eltham College Magazine* said of him: "He has captained the team with marked success throughout the season, and has been the mainstay of the three line. His kicking is excellent, and his speed and remarkable swerve have decided the issue of several matches. He is the best tackler, and the team is inclined to rely too much on him. He is inclined to be too lenient with the slacker of the team."

Although immensely popular among his peers and highly regarded by them, one honor at Eltham eluded Eric — the Bayard Prize. Determined solely by a vote of the boys themselves, the award was given annually to the one among them who had exerted the best influence during the year. Rob received the Bayard Prize in 1918, but in 1919, when Eric might have been favored to win, it was awarded to another senior boy. Eric's quiet, shy, self-effacing personality did not give him the aura of a leader. While holding himself to the highest standards of morality and effort, he never insisted that others strive as he did, and found it impossible to reprimand the rugby team slacker. That was Eric's way.

Eric left Eltham College in the spring of 1920, hoping to pursue a degree in Pure Science. But there was just one problem. The University of Edinburgh wouldn't accept him.

✵ FOUR ✵

Running and Rugby

Traveling north from London in March 1920, Eric Liddell pondered his identity and his future.

If Master Sydney Moore, the gifted foreign language teacher, had not left Eltham College in 1915, Eric might have completed his studies with full credit in French. As it was, he could not become a student at the University of Edinburgh until he had raised his level of language proficiency and obtained an entrance certificate.

At the age of eighteen, it seemed very strange to be an Old Boy of Eltham College with his boarding school years behind him. He would not miss being known as Liddell ii, although until Rob left Eltham, the title had always given him the privilege of deferring critical decisions to Liddell i. He would miss the camaraderie and friendship of the other boys, along with the genuine concern and academic expertise of the masters. At least most of them. If he ever became a teacher, he certainly had examples of all sorts to emulate and avoid.

In another week, his mother, sister, and younger brother would arrive in Edinburgh. Mary Liddell had, once again, left China a year before James' scheduled furlough in order to make a home for Rob and Eric. It might be her last opportunity before the boys married and established homes of their own. Eric looked forward to living with Rob and being together again as a family, but he also had much to accomplish in the next few months. He would need to find a French tutor and also work to earn some money for school.

Four hours into the journey north, the train rumbled across the Royal Border Bridge at Berwick-upon-Tweed. Eric recalled the summer holidays he and Rob had spent nearby with his mother's relatives. Many times the two of them had played beside the River Tweed, skipping stones across the water and watching the trains thread their way over the tall stone arches of this same bridge.

The Tweed rises in the Borders Region of Scotland, and for most of its last twenty miles forms an undulating line of demarcation between the Scots and the English. Near Paxton, the border turns north and east, running overland, while the river widens until it flows into the North Sea at Berwick.

Although the town had last changed hands from Scottish to English hundreds of years before, its nationality was still a matter of discussion. When travelers asked, "Is Berwick in England?" the locals always answered, "For the time being."

Eric knew that as soon as he opened his mouth in Edinburgh, people would wonder about his origins because he had no trace of a Scottish accent. If they asked, "Are you a Scot?" perhaps that same answer — "For the time being" — would be the best one for a young man of Scottish parentage, but born in China and educated in England.

In early April, Rob and Eric were eagerly waiting on the platform at Edinburgh's Waverley Station when Mary, Jenny, and Ernest arrived home from China. A horse-drawn cab carried the newly reunited family to a furnished flat in Gillespie Crescent, not far from the university. After a separation of five years, it took a bit of time to get reacquainted. Rob, nearing twenty, had completed two years of his medical studies and acquired a girlfriend in the process. Mary and Jenny professed to be happy for him, but were quite disappointed that they would have to share him with Miss Ria Aitken. Eric, whom Mary had last seen at thirteen, still had to be coaxed to tell of his athletic achievements and honors at Eltham College.

Mary quickly realized that the little boys who had needed her in the past were now independent young men. Everyone struggled a bit as new roles and responsibilities were defined by trial and error. Seven-year-old Ernest proved to be the free-spirited, fun-loving catalyst that quickly drew everyone together, and within a few weeks, they were all enjoying each other immensely.

Eric found a French tutor, and acquired a job on a farm outside Edinburgh. By six every morning, he was bicycling to the countryside where long days of hard work marked his summer holiday. Before autumn arrived, the family moved to a larger flat on Merchiston Place, near "Holy Corner," so named because churches stood on each of the four points of the intersection. One of them, Morningside Congregational Church, became the Liddell's home congregation. Mary, Eric, and Jenny all joined the church where Rob had become a member two years before. Eric participated actively in the Young People's Union, where he became known as a young man of high principle and a committed but quiet follower of Christ.

That autumn, Eric began his studies at Heriot-Watt College. Under an existing agreement with the university, his courses in mathematics and science would count toward graduation. His 94% in first year Inorganic Chemistry earned him a tie for first place in that class. After obtaining the Scottish Universities Entrance Board Certificate, he signed the matriculation book and officially entered the University of Edinburgh on February 23, 1921.

A few weeks later, a fellow student caught up to Eric as he walked to class.

"I understand you did some running at Eltham College."

"A little," Eric replied.

"Why don't you turn out for the University Athletic Sports day at the end of May?"

"I'm awfully busy," Eric said. The words seemed strange to his own ears, even though his academic load was daunting. Too busy to run? To do the thing he loved?

"I could give you a hand," the fellow offered.

"Thanks, but I don't really need any help with physics and chemistry," Eric said.

"Not with the science. With your running. I could help you train."

Eric wavered. "If I could find the time... ."

"Why don't you meet me at the athletic field tomorrow at three?" the would-be trainer asked.

"I guess I could spare an hour to limber up a bit," Eric said, and they shook hands on it.

Neither Eric nor his new friend knew much about technique or training, but the green grass and open air roused Eric's spirit and made him realize how much he had missed running. Every afternoon for a week they worked on starts and wind sprints before timing Eric in a few 100-yard dashes. But almost as soon as they had begun, the month-long Easter holiday intruded on their training schedule.

When Eric blithely announced that he was taking a week-long bicycle trip with four friends, his new trainer objected. "That's absolutely the worst thing you can do," he protested. "You'll come back stiff as a board and your muscles will be like uncooked spaghetti."

Eric appreciated his concern but was not about to miss the ride of a lifetime through the Highlands from Edinburgh to Fort William. Once there, he and his friends planned to be on the summit of Ben Nevis, Britain's highest peak, in time to see the sun rise. Clad in tweed suits, complete with white shirts, vests, and neckties, they pedaled their way for 130 miles through some of the most spectacular scenery in Scotland. To the northwest, snowcapped peaks lined the horizon as they coasted through green valleys and struggled over hills dotted with grazing sheep.

In the early darkness of the appointed morning, they slipped out of the hostel in Fort William and began their trek up Ben Nevis. After hiking five miles on a rocky path, they reached the 4400-foot summit, only to find it wrapped in swirling mist. The sun rose, but they saw none of its splendor that morning on the barren, fog-shrouded top of "the Ben."

Six days after setting out, they arrived back in Edinburgh, tired but exhilarated by the journey. And when Eric returned to the track, he learned painfully that his novice trainer had been right. He could barely walk, much less sprint, and his muscles had absolutely no spring. With only a month left before the Varsity Sports, he set to work, trying to regain the speed that had carried him to an Eltham school record of 10.2 seconds in the 100 yards.

Rob and Eric welcomed their father to Edinburgh on May 3, 1921. Since they last saw him, his hair and mustache had turned white, but his energy had not diminished. At the age of fifty, James Liddell was always ready for a vigorous walk or a swim. His good humor and laughter brightened the family circle and made it complete. For the first few weeks he was free to be at home with the family before the demands of deputation work for the London Missionary Society would carry him away to address Congregational churches across Britain. And he was eager to watch his second-born son run.

On the last Saturday in May, Eric made his way along Colinton Road to the Edinburgh University Sports Ground at Craiglockhart, just over a mile from the Liddell flat. Craiglockhart boasted one of the few tracks in Scotland where runners could cover a straight 220 yards. Wooden bleachers stood in front of a two-story pavilion that contained a clubhouse above and the athletes' dressing room below. Eric walked through a door marked "Players Only" and savored the warmth inside. He hung his overcoat on a hook, then selected an empty wooden equipment locker and sat on the lid while he removed his shoes.

G. Innes Stewart was favored to repeat as sprint champion in the 100 and the 220-yard events that day. Stewart, severely wounded and twice decorated during World War I, was a popular favorite who maintained a strict training regimen prior to the Varsity Sports. When he took the field that afternoon, he took little notice of the unknown freshman in the longish black shorts and white vest, standing on his right. But during the first 100-yard heat, Stewart kept glancing from the corner of his eye at the new runner, who refused to let up as they hurtled down the track. He beat Liddell by less than a stride. In the 100-yard final, Eric reversed the order, edging Stewart by inches and finishing first in 10.4 seconds.

Later that day, in the final of the 220, Stewart broke the tape ahead of Eric by the slightest margin, winning in 23.4 seconds. Some spectators remarked that young Liddell had a curious running style, swinging his arms high, lifting his knees nearly to his chest, and, at the finish, throwing his head so far back that his eyes, if they had been open, would have seen only the sky.

"Quite an ungainly action, that lad," said one man through teeth clamped on his pipe stem.

"Aye," answered the fellow next to him. "But he beat Stewart once and almost again. Odd style or not, he's fast."

With this performance at Craiglockhart, Eric was immediately chosen to run for the Edinburgh team against athletes representing Glasgow, Aberdeen, and St. Andrews Universities. With only three weeks to train for the Intervarsity Sports, Eric was taken to Edinburgh's Powderhall Stadium. He knelt on the cinder track, the first he had ever seen, and sifted the strange material between his fingers. Nearby, the professional runners danced around as if they were stepping on hot coals, dug holes for their toes, and endlessly practiced their starts. Did they expect him to make a fool of himself like that? Apparently so.

Self-consciously he began to do the exercises he had been shown. He worked his shoulders, shrugging and twisting to loosen the muscles, feeling that everyone must be watching him. He danced on his toes, bent and stretched, then executed a series of 10-yard dashes, wondering how all this could possibly help since he was doing everything but run.

Powderhall Stadium hosted competition between professional runners, as well as dog racing where money changed hands with every heat. In addition, it offered a place for amateur runners to train. On one side of the oval track, Eric and the short distance men went through their paces. Across the infield, the whippets barked and pranced, waiting their chance to chase the "rabbit" and bring a windfall of shillings to the man who picked the fastest dog.

One afternoon at Powderhall, a stout, diminutive man wearing a tam-o'-shanter cap approached Eric and extended his hand.

"Tom McKerchar," he said.

Eric introduced himself and gripped the man's hand.

"You're too tight," McKerchar stated abruptly. He pressed his fingers into Eric's back just below the shoulders. "Your muscles are hard here and in your legs. If they aren't softened, they'll snap."

Eric had seen this man working with some of the other runners, but knew nothing about him except that he spoke with knowledge and authority.

McKerchar gestured toward a group of runners. "Join those lads out there for a turn around the track."

Eric complied and handily won the impromptu race, stopping immediately after crossing the finish line. Approaching McKerchar, he asked confidently, "How was that?"

McKerchar folded his arms across his chest and looked at the ground for a moment before fixing his eyes on Eric. "If you want a breakdown," he said, "you're going about it in the best possible manner. Never stop after you break the tape. Jog on, walk a little, give your muscles time to finish the race."

Recalling this first encounter with McKerchar, Eric said later: "Thus, being thoroughly humiliated, feeling that my reputation had been dragged through the mud, that my self-respect was still wallowing in the mire, and that if I didn't get into the clutches of a trainer soon, every muscle in my body would give way and I should remain a physical wreck till the end of my days — I was then in a fit mental condition to start an athletic career."

Tommy McKerchar earned his living in the printing trade, but he found his life as an athletic trainer. He was forty-four years old when he first shook Eric Liddell's hand at Powderhall. Standing 5' 5" and bulging above his belt, he looked more like a bulldog than a greyhound. He could not outrun the slowest man at Powderhall, but he understood muscles and tension and tone. With a cigar clenched in his jaw, Tommy could watch a man run and know instinctively how to help him improve. Although he may have received some pay from the professional runners he trained, he took Eric Liddell under his wing for the sheer joy of it. Under the strict amateur code of the day, Eric could not hire a trainer, but Tommy could volunteer and work for nothing.

As McKerchar offered corrections to Eric on the track, he rarely had to say anything more than once. In fact, athlete and trainer said little to each other as their bond of trust and respect grew. After every workout, Eric would strip and lie on the table in the training room, where Tommy would massage his muscles carefully, sometimes painfully, pushing, kneading, loosening, realigning, so that the fibrous sinews could drive the pistons of the legs without hindrance. From the very beginning, Eric placed himself figuratively and literally into Tommy McKerchar's hands.

On June 18, Eric Liddell and G. Innes Stewart took first and second respectively in the 100 and 220-yard races at St. Andrews. A week later, Eric again won both sprints at the Scottish Amateur Athletic Association Championships in Glasgow. For the rest of the summer, he trained at Powderhall under McKerchar's eye two to three times a week. Before the running season ended in mid-August, Eric had competed in eleven meets in Scotland and Ireland, raising eyebrows wherever he ran.

On August 11, 1921, an article in the *Glasgow Herald* confidently stated, "E. H. Liddell, Edinburgh University A.C., is going to be a British champion ere long, and he might even blossom into an Olympic hero. His success has been phenomenal; in fact it is one of the romances of the amateur path. Unknown four months ago, he today stands at the forefront of British sprinters, and possibly by this time next season he may be not only a Scottish but an English champion. Liddell, as much because of his supreme grit as because of his pace, is a great figure in modern athletics, and is destined to be still greater in the near future."

While Eric created a stir in the press with his athletic triumphs, the immediate impact on the Liddell household was a growing lack of space. Cups, trophies, cutlery sets, ribbons, and medals seemed to be everywhere. Amateur athletes won no money or lucrative endorsements, but valuable prizes abounded at every contest. Mary began to worry about thieves breaking in, and Jenny expressed her own concern about who was going to polish all the silver. "Surely not I!" she protested.

Rob celebrated his twenty-first birthday by asking Ria to marry him, and she joyfully accepted. With the presentation of a ring, they became officially engaged, although the wedding would have to wait until Rob completed his medical studies. He also announced that he had decided to pursue a career as a medical missionary and hoped to work in China. James was pleased with Rob's decision, and Mary was ecstatic at the prospect that her son and possibly her grandchildren would be close to them in China. Perhaps it was her reward for enduring the long years away from him.

During the 1921 autumn term Rob and Eric played rugby for Edinburgh University. Both were three-quarter backs, playing on the wing where their speed and agility could be utilized to the best advantage. Their renewed partnership, dormant since Eltham College days, did not go unnoticed by the press. One article stated: "E. H. Liddell has been carrying off chief honours in the Edinburgh University Rugby Back division, but it should not be overlooked that his brother, R. V. Liddell, is also making a name for himself in the same team. 'R. V.', the elder of the brothers, intends to devote himself to mission work in Manchuria. The football association of the Liddells is likely to prove of great value to their University team, and it will be no surprise if next year they are found playing together in the big games." Only Rob knew that this season was his last, having decided he must give up sport for the sake of his medical studies.

Eric stood 5' 9" and weighed 155 pounds, hardly a picture of the brute strength associated with rugby. But what he lacked in brawn, he made up in quickness and sheer determination. And he loved the game, perhaps even more than running. Many connoisseurs of rugby football had little use for sprinters on the team. Cinder track men were accused of being prima donnas, flinching from making tackles and wanting only the glory that came with taking the ball on a fast pass, sweeping past the last defender and scoring a try. But those charges were never leveled against Eric. One sportswriter described him as "a tireless and dogged defender, and when he smother tackled you, you stayed smothered."

Of Eric on the field, *The Student* magazine said "[he] has that rare combination, pace and the gift of rugby brains and hands; makes openings, snaps opportunities, gives the 'dummy' to perfection, does the work of three (if necessary) in defence, and carries unselfishness almost to a fault."

To the working men in the factories and coal pits, university rugger was mildly interesting, while games between city or regional clubs were much more important. But international matches were a matter of patriotism and fierce national pride. On December 8, 1921, the first "trial" match for Scottish international team selection drew 8,000 spectators to Galashiels, thirty-five miles southeast of Edinburgh. Eric scored five tries during the match, and kept pace with the mercurial and often unorthodox play of A. L. Gracie on the wing.

Although their years at Eltham College overlapped, Eric and Gracie had never played together on a First XV because of their age difference. Gracie, six years older, was the son of Rev. T. Gracie, a missionary with the British and Foreign Bible Society in Ceylon. At Eltham, Gracie walked away with every academic, athletic, and leadership award in the school before entering Oxford University in 1915. As a young lieutenant in the British Army, he had served with distinction during World War I and received the Military Cross.

On the day before Christmas, Liddell and Gracie took the field together in a second "trial" match at Edinburgh's Inverleith Stadium. Once again, their tremendous speed and lighting reflexes carried the Scottish team to a one-sided victory. Gracie's unpredictable moves and passes never caught Eric by surprise. Their teamwork seemed almost telepathic, often leaving dazed defenders sprawled on the ground. Adrian Stoop, legendary rugby fly-half and later president of England's Harlequin Club, said of Gracie's unorthodox methods: "He did everything wrong, but did it so quickly that nobody could catch up with him."

There was no greater honor for a rugby player than to be selected as a member of his country's national team. And that was exactly where Eric Liddell found himself at the beginning of

1922. The Scottish International Team would play four matches, against France, Wales, Ireland, and England. If they won all four, they claimed the Grand Slam. Defeating their three UK opponents would give them bragging rights for the Triple Crown. And the winner of Scotland vs. England claimed the Calcutta Cup, a coveted silver trophy made from melted-down rupees given by members of an English rugby club in India during the time of the British Raj.

Whereas cricket was a gentleman's game of bowling, batting, and fielding played in white trousers during fair weather, rugby was more often a contest of mud and blood. On January 2, 1922, a record crowd of 37,000 packed Colombes Stadium in Paris, hoping to see the French teach the Scots a lesson. On a field already soaked by heavy rain, the two teams churned the pitch into a quagmire as they slogged through a second-half downpour to a 3-3 draw. The match against Wales at Inverleith in early February ended at 9-9. Eric's play was solid but unspectacular, with none of the breakaway scoring that had led to his selection in the December trials. Three weeks later, Scotland managed a 3-point victory over Ireland at Inverleith, and *The Scotsman* newspaper offered this evaluation: "The real disappointment of the game was the non-success of E. H. Liddell, not perhaps so much because of any real failing, as by the fact that his pace was not the tremendous asset that it was expected to be. Yet it was to Liddell's credit that he was able to snatch at the chance of winning the game. That he is a great player in the making there is no doubt, but there were times when he showed a rawness in his work and a lack of resource when cornered."

Once again Eric was reminded that in the world of high profile sport it was difficult to live up to people's expectations and always perform as wonderfully as the fans wanted. He didn't spend much time agonizing over criticism in the press, but no one was more disappointed than he when an injury during a pick-up rugby game kept him out of the international match against England at London's Twickenham Stadium. He had to be content with earning three caps, one for each international match played, and with having given his best each time.

Even while playing university and international rugby, Eric managed to tie for first place in Second Year Inorganic Chemistry and Physical Chemistry. He also served as secretary of the Young People's Union at Morningside Congregational Church, and taught a Sunday school class for poor children in the needy Cowgate area of Edinburgh.

For much of the winter, James Liddell traveled the UK in deputation work on behalf of the London Missionary Society. But this time his entree with many audiences was not his twenty-five years in China, but the fact that he was the father of Eric Liddell. Mary was used to James being gone, but now she also had to be content with much less time with her older sons. With the demands of university studies and sports, she felt fortunate to see them at meals.

Eric gave no clear indication about his future plans, but since Rob had expressed a strong interest in going to China as a missionary doctor, his father was not beyond some behind-the-scenes nudging in what he felt was the right direction. On January 14, 1922, James wrote to Nelson Bitton, Foreign Secretary of the LMS, encouraging him to approach Rob directly about possible service with the society. "There is no question as to his earnest devotion to our Lord Jesus Christ, and the winning of men to Him," James wrote. "All other things in time and by experience adjust themselves to one's life devotion. We are helping him all we can on such matters as wide tolerance with folk who may differ, seeing the best in every one, mission policy, looking at principles, etc, and we are quite sure he will in due time be a decent, hard-working missionary."

Rob had little use for any religious enterprise that was not centered on personal conversion to Jesus Christ, and he freely said so. His outspokenness caused some concern in LMS circles, although mission officials hoped he would mellow in time. An early evaluation of Rob in the LMS files reads: "Now ready to offer himself for medical work in North China to the L.M.S. Very earnest attractive fellow. At present considerably on the stiff side in theology, and attached to the narrower evangelical opinions of Edinburgh. A great capacity for development is obvious in Robert Liddell, and he possesses very strong character."

Unlike Rob, Eric rarely expressed a strong opinion on anything. When others engaged in a heated discussion, Eric would remain on the sidelines, a half-smile on his face, considering the issue, but saying nothing. His convictions, like a deep river with a strong current, carried him along forcefully but silently, never intruding into the lives of others.

Eric's 1922 running season began on May 27 at the Edinburgh University Sports with a record setting 10.2 in the 100-yard dash, and first place finishes in the 220 and 440-yard races. He served as captain of the university team for the Intervarsity meet at Aberdeen and the Scottish Championships at Powderhall. As the summer progressed, once again the Liddell home bulged with the spoils of his victories in other amateur races. Mary and Jenny each received a gold watch with their names inscribed on the back. Cabinets temporarily housed glassware and tea knives, destined for relatives and friends. On the mantle, a collection of clocks ticked away the hours toward the Liddell family's autumn return to China.

For two weeks in September, a cabin at Coldstream rang with the laughter and conversation of the six Liddells, savoring a final holiday together. James snapped photos of Ernest, now nearly ten years old, standing in the middle of the bridge over the Tweed, with one leg in Scotland and the other in England. Jenny, almost nineteen and growing prettier by the day, pondered the odd fact that during their entire furlough, while Eric was becoming the best-known athlete in Scotland, she had never watched him play rugby or run a race. Some women attended such sporting events, but there had always been other things that required her attention. Rob's fiancée, Ria, joined them for a few days, lending her musical talents to the family sing-alongs. In the evenings they played games and by day explored the grounds of a magnificent estate known as the Hirsel, seat of the Lords of Home since the early 17th century. Eric enjoyed the quiet and the brief respite from his taxing schedule. Soon, he would resume his studies and be back on the rugby pitch with the University First XV.

For a final time before leaving, Mary sat between Rob and Eric and brushed her hand across their thinning hair, so rapidly retreating from their foreheads. "Too many hot showers," she asserted. One look at her husband's balding pate would have proven a genetic link, but Mary would have none of it. "Don't wash your hair so often," she told them again as they ducked away from her strong fingers, trying to massage non-existent hair follicles into new life.

In mid-October, James, Mary, Jenny, and Ernest embarked on the six-week voyage to China and a new post in the city of Tientsin. Rob and Eric moved into rooms at 56 George Square, in a hostel sponsored by the Edinburgh Medical Missionary Society. There was hardly time for any of them to mourn the parting.

By the time the Liddells reached China in early December, Eric was a sure selection for his second season of international rugby. Sportswriters predicted an even better season than the last for Scotland with Liddell and Gracie on the wing and a host of returning players. In January, a solid victory over France set the stage for a February showdown against Wales at Cardiff Arms Park, where Scotland had not won in thirty-three years.

Some Scots likened playing Wales in Cardiff to playing the devil in Hades, such was the power of the team's national ground. The spell cast by a home field with a Welsh crowd could hex a more powerful opponent into foolish blunders that would cost them a victory. And then there was always the weather.

Days of continuous rain before the match left so much water standing on the pitch that members of the Cardiff city fire brigade appeared with a pumper truck to try to drain the field. Gracie, Scotland's captain, said that with soft ground and a slippery ball the game would be decided by brawny forwards fighting up the middle rather than by fleet backs trying to get outside. In the end, it was Gracie who would prove himself wrong.

Long before the kickoff on Saturday, February 3, Cardiff Arms Park bulged with an overflow crowd of 40,000. After the gates were closed, another 2,000 boisterous Welshmen, many of whom had spent the morning in nearby pubs, were turned away. Only the tact and forceful diplomacy of the police on duty prevented a storming of the gates or a mass scaling of the fences. Just before the match began the crowd inside hushed, then stood to sing the Welsh national anthem. The blend of powerful, harmonious male voices with the distinctive tang of the Welsh language evoked a level of emotion far beyond the size of the tiny, but fervent nation. For many people, hearing a stadium full of Welshmen sing "Mac hen wlad fy, nhadau yn annwyl i mi" (O land of my fathers, O land of my love) would have been worth the price of admission. But the miners and farmers and factory workers had come for a football match, and both teams were determined they should have one.

Throughout the first half, wide open scoring chances eluded both sides. The Welsh cheered in amazement when Johnson, not noted for his speed, overtook Liddell from behind and tackled him a yard short of the goal line. At the end of the first half, Wales led 3-0 on a penalty goal. Early in the second half, the ball came to Eric on the outside, and with the way clear ahead of him, he brought the crowd to its feet as he threw back his head and dashed across the goal line as if he were breaking the tape in a 220-yard dash. But Wales quickly countered to regain the lead. With less than two minutes remaining and Wales ahead 8-6, Gracie took the ball on a long cross-field pass. Dodging and weaving his way through the center of the Welsh team, he broke tackles and eluded the last defender to score the winning try.

As soon as the game ended, hundreds of Welsh fans leaped the barriers and headed straight for Gracie, the man who had snatched an international victory from them. Before the Scottish back realized what was happening, they lifted him shoulder high and carried him off the field toward the pavilion. The Scottish team watched in amazement as the Welsh honored the game's hero for his inspired play. In Gwalia they had a word for it — "hawl" — grit, determination, guts, and they honored it in anyone, even if he had just beaten them.

Eric's comment to the press was: "A jolly good game, and one of the finest international matches I have ever played in." The fact that all the glory had gone to Gracie was just fine with him.

After Scotland defeated Ireland 13-3 in a drizzling rain, the team was poised to win the Grand Slam and the Triple Crown with a victory over England on the Scots home ground at Inverleith. On March 17, before a crowd of 32,000 in perfect weather, the Scots lost by two points. The newspapers commended Eric for his tenacious play and team contribution, even though he had not scored during the match. After shaking hands with the English victors, Eric left the field knowing that this had likely been his last international rugby match.

The Olympic Games were just over a year away and there was a great deal of talk about his being selected for the 100 and 200-meter races. Much would depend on his success on the track during the coming season. If he was chosen, he would be expected to forego rugby competition to avoid injury before the next summer's games.

But it was all conjecture at this point. Nothing definite. What Eric was certain about as he pondered his future was that he wanted to serve Christ with whatever gifts he had been given. But he had no idea how his athletic ability could be put to use for the kingdom of God. In his own eyes, he seemed to possess so few of the skills he thought necessary for Christian ministry. Not only was he not an orator, he dreaded the thought of speaking in public. Forty thousand shouting fans in a stadium didn't bother him at all, but forty people sitting quietly in a church hall terrified him.

One night, he decided to tell the Lord that he wanted to serve Him and leave it at that. Whatever the Master asked, he would do. In his room at 56 George Square, Eric knelt and spoke a simple prayer. As he turned out the light and slipped into bed, he had no idea that he would soon be the subject of a discussion that would alter the course of his life.

FIVE

Turning Point

April 1923

Why don't we have a meeting for men only and invite Eric Liddell to come and speak?"

The suggestion was so straightforward and so preposterous that it caught everyone by surprise. Like a pebble tossed in a quiet pond, it took a few seconds for the ripples to reach the shore of possibility in the small circle of young men who heard it.

"Would he come?"

"Has he ever spoken about his faith in a public meeting?"

"Does he have any faith to speak about?"

The queries tumbled from a dozen university students huddled around a coal stove in a church basement. As members of the Glasgow Students' Evangelistic Union (GSEU), they were nearing the end of a two-week Christian campaign in Armadale, a coal mining town twenty miles west of Edinburgh. At the moment, their efforts to reach the young men of the town seemed as futile as trying to heat their freezing church basement quarters with a small fire. With only three days left in the campaign, they were casting about for a way to gain a hearing among the miners and foundry workers, who much preferred a pint at the pub to a place in a pew.

"What do we know about Eric?"

"Son of a missionary; member of a church."

"Runs like the wind!"

"Seems sympathetic toward the Christian faith."

"His brother Rob campaigned with us last year."

"Who'll go and put the question to Eric?"

All eyes instinctively turned toward David Patrick Thomson, a divinity student who had co-founded the GSEU one year earlier. D. P., as he was always known, stood to his full height and said, "If Scotland's best known athlete comes to Armadale, it could be a great day for the gospel of Christ. Let's ask the Lord to send him." With heads bowed around the glowing coals, they voiced a prayer in perfect harmony with the one already spoken by Eric a few days before.

Around noon the next day, D. P. Thomson unfolded his broad, 6' 2" frame from the cab of the petrol lorry in which he had hitched a ride to Edinburgh. Already that morning he had stopped in a nearby town to make a bid on a man's personal library, and he was planning to scour the shelves of nearby James Thin Booksellers for bargains. D. P. never began a day with only one thing to do. But his most important business lay at hand.

When he knocked at 56 George Square, Rob Liddell opened the door. After the two exchanged a few pleasantries, D. P. got to the point. Did Rob think Eric would consider coming to Armadale the next evening to speak about his faith in Christ? Rob, in a reversal of sorts, said, "You'll have to ask my brother," and climbed the stairs to summon him. A few minutes later, D. P. shook hands for the first time with the fastest man in Scotland.

No one who knew D. P. Thomson could imagine that he simply asked Eric Liddell to come to Armadale and let it go at that. The invitation would have included a vivid description of the opportunity to lift Christ up before a group of men who wouldn't walk across the street to hear a preacher, but who would come from all over town to hear a rugby internationalist. D. P.'s infectious enthusiasm not only made it seem imperative that Eric come and speak, but made it sound completely possible for a young man who dreaded the public platform. Under Thomson's spell, scores of people had already volunteered for tasks that had always seemed out of their reach, simply because it seemed absurd to say no to a man who was so convinced they could do it.

Eric paused for a moment, pondering the invitation, then glanced up and with a broad smile said, "All right, I'll do it." D. P.

thundered his delight and invited Rob to come and speak as well. After giving them a few particulars about the meeting, Thomson was off down the street in his loping stride, buoyed by the success of his mission.

The next morning while Eric tried hard not to second-guess his decision, a letter arrived from his sister, Jenny. Sent weeks before from China, it ended with a verse of Scripture: "Fear not for I am with thee; be not dismayed for I am thy God; I will strengthen thee, yea I will help thee; yea, I will uphold thee with the right hand of my righteousness" (Isaiah 41:10). The verse Jenny sent him, at just that moment, came as a confirmation that he was on the right track and that God would give him the strength he needed.

Armadale carried the reputation of a rough town, the kind of place where a stranger wouldn't walk the streets on Saturday night unless he was looking for a fight. In nearby Bathgate, the more cultured population considered their soot-faced neighbors a bad-mannered lot, likely as not to eat their own young. To a visitor, the men of Armadale could seem cold and aloof, scarcely responding to the outsider's "Hello" on the street. But it was a matter of perception. A slight nod or a flick of the eyes was greeting enough between miners, who often did no more than that to say good morning to their mates as they boarded the elevator for the descent into the pits. Among themselves, they were a loyal clan who cared for their own, sharing what they had to make it through lean or troubled times. But their emotions and thoughts of eternity lay buried as deep in their souls as the seams of coal they wrested from a reluctant earth.

The "men only" meeting commenced at nine o'clock that Friday night in the Armadale Town Hall. Nearly eighty men walked halfway up a steep hill from the town center and took their places, not really knowing what to expect. Rob Liddell spoke first, but, in D. P.'s opinion, lacked cohesiveness and did not seem at his best. Eric followed, expressing quietly and simply what Jesus Christ meant to him. D. P. closed the meeting and later noted that Eric had done remarkably well for a first appearance and had said some telling things. Everyone thought the meeting had been worthwhile.

Although few realized it, the men present that night had seen and heard the most popular athlete in Scotland take his first public stand for Christ. Whatever they thought of his content and delivery, they could not doubt his sincerity. And the effect of the evening had been far more profound on the speaker than on those who heard him. No one but Eric knew what a giant step of faith he had taken that night.

A week later, Eric joined members of the GSEU at Rutherglen, near Glasgow, where he and D. P. addressed an evening meeting of 600 young people. As in all of the student campaigns, there was no request for public response at the end of the meeting. Instead, D. P. invited those with spiritual concerns to meet in another building to learn more about what it meant to accept Christ and commit their lives to Him. Student leaders were available to talk and pray individually with any who wanted personal counseling.

By the middle of April, Eric had decided to officially join the GSEU, and had committed himself to campaign with them whenever possible. It was far more than a decision to become a celebrity speaker. Most of the student campaigns were held during university holidays. At the invitation of local churches, GSEU members spent up to two weeks in a town, sleeping on straw mats in a church basement and doing their own cooking. Posting handbills and delivering invitations door to door, along with speaking to small groups in schools, churches, and open air meetings were duties shared among the campaigners. With only thirty-four members, there were no prima donnas in the GSEU.

On May 26, 1923, Eric won the 100, 220, and 440-yard events at the annual Edinburgh University Sports. A dozen meets awaited him before the running season ended in mid-August, but his new race of faith and personal witness for Christ had brought him fresh exhilaration and purpose. On May 28 he wrote to Thomson saying that he was a changed man since the day D. P. had asked him to speak at Armadale, and that a new joy had come into his life.

When Eric later chronicled his own journey of faith, he expressed this turning point in these words:

"I was brought up in a Christian home where the stories of the Bible were often told and became familiar to me. In school, the stories of the Bible and the teachings of Christ were placed before me. The beauty of the Christian life began to appeal to me. The time came when the appeal of Christ became more personal and I began to realize that it was going to affect my life. In this experience of Christ there was a sense of sin but that was not nearly so great as the sense of being called to do a piece of work for which I was absolutely unqualified.

"My whole life had been one of keeping out of public duties but the leading of Christ seemed now to be in the opposite direction, and I shrank from going forward. At this time I finally decided to put it all on Christ — after all if He called me to do it, then He would have to supply the necessary power. In going forward the power was given me. Since then the consciousness of being an active member of the Kingdom of Heaven has been very real. New experiences of the Grace of God, sense of sin, wonders of the Bible have come from time to time. All these fresh experiences have given me fresh visions of our Lord."

The Armadale speaking engagement had seemed such a simple invitation, but saying "yes" had changed his life.

SIX

The Road to Paris

1923–1924

The 1923 Amateur Athletic Association Championships in London commanded close scrutiny from the British Olympic Committee. From their vantagepoint at Stamford Bridge stadium, committee members compared the names of Britain's most promising athletes with their performance on the field, hoping to draft a preliminary list of possible team members for the 1924 Paris games.

On Friday, July 6, Harold Abrahams, the Cambridge University sprinter, faced Eric Liddell for the first time. Abrahams had competed in the 1920 Olympics at Antwerp but was eliminated in the quarterfinals of the 100 meters. Determined to win a gold medal in Paris, he had defied a widely held tenet of amateurism and hired Sam Mussabini, a professional coach. At Stamford Bridge, many observers believed Abrahams and Liddell would duel for the British championship in the 100 and 220, but the anticipated showdown did not materialize. In a second round heat of the 220, Eric beat Abrahams by five yards, and Harold's slow time kept him from the finals. In the 100-yard dash, Abrahams was eliminated in the second round and did not face Liddell either in the heats or in the final.

Late Saturday evening, July 7, word reached D. P. Thomson that Eric had won the 220 final and also broken the British record for the 100 yards in the time of 9.7 seconds. "A year from now, he could be an Olympic champion at those same distances," Thomson murmured to himself. "Fastest man on earth." That night he began to ponder the possibility of going on a world evangelistic tour with Eric in the winter of 1924–25, when their university studies were complete. "We could reach the young people of the Empire well," he mused. D. P. simply did not believe in small dreams.

A week later, the famous English pottery-making city of Stoke-on-Trent, affectionately known as Smoke-on-Stench, hosted the 1923 Triangular International. There, Eric was scheduled to face Harold Abrahams in the 100-yard dash. Although no particular rivalry existed between the two, everyone hoped to see them go head to head for the first time at 100 yards. However, before the meet began, Abrahams reported that he had a septic throat and withdrew from the competition. Eric took the 100 yards in 10.4 seconds and, as expected, moved through the 220 heats toward the final, which he had never won in this annual meet between Scotland, Ireland, and England. Many felt this was his year.

In the minutes leading up to the final of the 220, Eric was hardly the picture of intensity and concentration. Actually, he seemed more concerned with the other runners' success than with his own. Walking from one opponent to another, Eric offered the use of his small trowel to dig starting holes in the cinder track. With that completed, the Flying Scotsman wandered down the line, smiling, shaking hands with each runner and wishing him all the best. Some spectators quipped that Liddell was merely saying good-bye to his opponents, because after the gun it was the last they would see of him. On this day, as on many others, that's exactly what happened as he raced to victory in the 220. Between the starter's pistol and the tape was the only time Eric did not intentionally put others ahead of himself.

His actions before the 220 at the Triangular International were typical of his behavior at every meet. Liddell's teammates and opponents alike respected his kindness on the infield as much as his determination on the track. A rival from Aberdeen University recalled sitting on the cold turf in shorts and singlet one blustery day, awaiting the start of his race. Eric noticed him and, without a word, draped his own university blue blazer over his opponent's shoulders and walked on. During a sports day at Craiglockhart, a black runner to whom no one else had bothered to speak wandered alone among scores of other contestants. Eric approached, linked arms with him, and they talked together until the young man's event was called. Gentleness, sportsmanship, and genuine concern for others did not make headlines, but won for Eric the admiration of his peers.

After winning the 100 and 220 at Stoke, Eric had a chance to sweep the sprints with a victory in the 440 final. But he had taken scarcely three strides in the race when the dream appeared shattered. J. J. Gillis, an English runner, trying to move inside on the unlaned cinders, knocked Eric off the track, causing him to stumble onto the infield. Thinking himself disqualified, Liddell stood for a moment until a Scots judge shouted for him to go on. He set off after the others, a good twenty yards behind the pack.

Tommy McKerchar watched in disbelief as Eric's spikes shredded the rain-soaked track. His legs pumped furiously, gradually cutting the gap between himself and the leaders. McKerchar had trained hundreds of athletes to go deep and summon all they had in a race, but he had never seen any man run like Eric was running now. Tommy threw his cigar on the ground and joined the crescendo of cheers that rolled like thunder from the stands.

Around the final turn, Eric was running fourth, now only ten yards behind Gillis. With forty yards remaining, Liddell strained past another runner, then threw his head back and ran with wild abandon. The crowd went into a frenzy as he broke the tape two yards ahead of Gillis, then collapsed into the arms of his Scottish teammates. They carried him, gasping and heaving, to the pavilion, where he summoned enough strength to refuse a swallow of brandy, requesting instead only a drop of strong tea.

For an hour, Eric lay on the table as McKerchar massaged life back into his quivering muscles.

"You turned 51.2," Tommy said. "Scotland won by half a point."

Eric managed a smile. His time after being knocked off the track was only one second more than his record-setting win a month before in the Scottish Intervarsity meet.

Those who witnessed the race could not describe it without shaking their heads in wonder. There was no way a runner could make up that distance over 440 yards. But Liddell had done it, they had seen it, and they would never forget it. If Eric had never run another race, he would have been enshrined in Scottish hearts for his courage alone.

But the victory left him physically spent. Two weeks later at the Glenpark Harriers Meet in Greenock, Eric ran only one race, the 100-yard handicap, and did not place. Was this the same young man who had set a British record in the event only three weeks before in London? Many who had come to see the Flying Scotsman were concerned at his lack of finishing power.

After the Saturday races, Eric stayed on in Greenock to address an open air meeting the following evening. Reporting on the event, the *Glasgow Herald* said: "The meeting was one of a series held on Sunday evenings throughout the summer months at which talks are given on Christianity. Mr. John Kerr, the well-known cricketer was chairman, and there was a large attendance.

"In his address, Mr. Liddell said there could be no neutrality where Christianity was concerned. Each one came to the crossroads at some period of his life, and must make his decision for or against the Master."

It had been only four months since Eric had faced his own crossroads and publicly declared his allegiance to Christ at Armadale. By his own admission, that decision had transformed his life. But the next turning point was closer than he imagined.

During the four remaining meets of the summer, Eric did not win a race. At the British Games Meeting held at London's Stamford Bridge stadium in August, he placed fourth in the 100 yards, and he did not run in the 220. In other Scottish meets, his performance was lackluster at best. Yet his overall achievement on the track marked him as a likely choice for the British Olympic team. He had agreed to forego winter rugby competition to avoid injury, and the road to Paris seemed clear. But several months earlier a decision had been made that would present a major hurdle for Eric Liddell.

The minutes of the British Olympic Association Council meeting on March 27, 1923, recorded that "the Programme for the Games of 1924 had now been received and after translation would be circulated to governing Bodies and Associations." The note appeared almost as a postscript to the more important issues of housing for the British athletes in Paris and the council's strong opposition to Germany being allowed to participate in the 1924 games.

Most prospective team members received the schedule of events sometime in late 1923. And as soon as Eric read that the 100-meter heats were to be held on a Sunday, he knew what he must do. He would tell the committee that he could not run in that event. It was not an arrogant refusal; not a stubborn "I will not," but rather a heartfelt "I can not."

Eric believed the Christian Sabbath belonged to God and was to be kept as a day of worship and rest. Many devout Scots of the day held the same non-negotiable conviction about Sunday, but none of them was favored to win the 100 meters in the coming Olympics. Eric had no desire to make a show of his decision, but the resulting publicity was out of his control. Many people applauded him as a man of conviction, willing to sacrifice an almost certain gold medal in the 100 meters to remain true to his principles. But there were vocal critics who felt that when it came to Olympic competition, personal religion should take a back seat to patriotism and national honor. There is no evidence that Eric himself agonized at all over the decision. In his mind, it was simply the right thing to do.

But running was not the only thing on Eric's mind. With only a few months until his university graduation, he pondered his calling in life. He had considered going to China as a teacher, but was not ready to make a long-term commitment to a mission agency. Theological education was a possibility, as was a year of teacher training.

Unlike his brother, Rob seemed certain of his way. In December 1923, he completed his medical studies and set his course for China as a missionary doctor. He and Ria joyfully announced a May wedding date. Preliminary indications from the LMS were that if the candidate committee approved Rob, he and Ria would be assigned to Tingchow-fu, a remote inland station in South China.

In the meantime, Rob would gain practical experience as resident doctor at the Cowgate Dispensary, run by the Edinburgh Medical Missionary Society.

A few days before Christmas Rob and Eric spent an evening with Dr. and Mrs. Ahmed Fahmy, who had retired after thirty-three years as LMS missionaries in South China. Dr. Fahmy, born in Alexandria, Egypt, to Muslim parents, had given his life to Christ when he was eighteen — at the cost of his family's denouncement and severance of all ties with him. Following his medical education in Edinburgh, Dr. Fahmy had established a pioneering medical mission work in Changchow. His elder son, Eric, an outstanding athlete and 1908 graduate of SSM at Blackheath, had been killed while leading a charge against German trenches in World War I. The Liddell brothers remembered Eric Fahmy as a skilled member of the Old Boys' Football club at Eltham during the winter of 1913–14.

Rob and Eric listened intently as the Fahmys realistically described missionary life in China, a country perpetually in crisis of one kind or another. Every bit of work, for body or soul, was accomplished against the backdrop of floods, famine, marauding bandits, political corruption, and war. In Chinese, the word "crisis" combines the characters from two other words: danger and opportunity. That was the essence of taking the gospel to the land where both Rob and Eric had been born.

On this evening, the Liddell brothers took it all in, not with the ears of children listening out of duty, but with the hunger of young men eager to embark on the adventure of their life's work. There was no question of the need in China, and Rob was sure of his call. The evening fueled his desire to be sent to a pioneer station. Eric's leaning toward China was strong, but he had not yet settled on God's way for him.

When news of Rob's possible appointment to South China reached Mary Liddell in Tientsin, she sat down and wept. The LMS might as well send him to South America. Tingchow-fu was a thousand miles, as the crow flies, from Tientsin, and no one in China, not even a crow, could travel in a straight line for long. After mulling the situation for several weeks, Mary wrote an impassioned letter to Nelson Bitton, the foreign secretary, pouring out her heart in the hope that the LMS might reconsider their decision and send Rob and Ria to North China.

She wrote in part: "We have practically been separated from him since he was eight years old, except when we saw him during furloughs. Not that we do not believe in guidance from God nor that the pain of separation has to be faced and borne often for Christ's sake (if it is necessary). It may be that my mother's heart is crying out for my son, but on the other hand if God shows me that His will and desire is to have my boy working for Him in Ting Chow, then I bow to His will and say 'His will be done,' for I know a man will only do his best work if he is in the place God wants him to be in."

Mary no doubt meant what she said about bowing to the will of God, but while the decision was still up in the air, she organized a bit of additional pressure to sway the appointment toward North China.

After Rob received an appeal from the LMS district committee in North China, asking him to consider coming to a hospital there, he told Mr. Bitton he felt no call to North China. His own heart was drawn to Tingchow-fu. Bitton, in the uncomfortable position between a heartbroken parent and a determined young missionary candidate, saw both sides of the issue. He wrote to Mary Liddell saying that initially they had thought of sending Rob to a hospital in Hong Kong for a year's training before he proceeded to his station in Fukien province. "Since, however, receiving your letter on Saturday I have been giving a lot of thought to it because I must own the letter touched me somewhat deeply."

In the context of a divine call and supernatural empowering for the task, missionary service retained a strong human dimension that could never be ignored. Like many others, James and Mary Liddell had paid a high price to serve God and the people of China. For most of a decade and a half, it had cost Mary the agonizing separation from her older two sons, and no one felt her yearnings more acutely than her own colleagues. While they had to consider the pressing needs of an entire field of service, they could not ignore

a mother's heart. As a compromise, the LMS decided to send Rob
and Ria to Shanghai for their first months of service, thus allowing
them to visit the Liddells during the summer before proceeding to
South China.

When Eric began the new school term in January 1924, two things
were clear: (1) God loved him; and (2) D. P. Thomson had a
wonderful plan for his life. The irrepressible leader of the GSEU asked
Eric to join him for a year's campaigning across Britain, beginning
in September. As usual, Thomson did not merely ask, but painted a
picture of unparalleled opportunity for evangelism among youth — a
unique moment that would never come again. Eric agreed to consider
the proposal and weigh it against the pull of China.

In the meantime, the issue of his Olympic participation had
to be resolved. After informing the Olympic authorities of his
decision, he was quite willing to explore alternatives with them.
The first possibility in the committee's mind was for Eric to alter his
perspective. While it was true that the preliminary heats for the 100
meters were on July 6, the first Sunday of the games, they did not
occur until the afternoon. There would be plenty of time for Eric
to attend morning worship services, then race late in the day. But
he did not see it that way. When a determined committee member
reminded him that the Continental Sabbath ended at noon, Eric
replied, "Mine lasts all day."

Sir J. E. K. Studd, a noted member of the British Olympic
Association Council, appreciated Eric's Christian conviction. As
an outstanding English cricketer of forty years before, Studd had
organized D. L. Moody's evangelistic meetings at Cambridge
University in 1882. Three years later, J. E. K.'s younger brother,
C. T. Studd, an equally famous athlete, sailed for missionary
service in China as one of the celebrated Cambridge Seven. J. E.
K. Studd and some of his fellow Council members supported Eric
Liddell's stand on the Sabbath, but there were others who called
for him to reconsider.

Along with sacrificing his place in the 100 meters, Eric gave up two other races in which Britain held high hopes of winning the gold. The qualifying heats for the 4 x 100 and 4 x 400 meter relays occurred on weekdays, but the finals were scheduled for Sunday, July 13. Again, some tried to persuade Eric that he could worship in the morning, then run to the glory of God in the afternoon, all without compromising his convictions. But Eric remained unmoved.

The Council appealed to the International Olympic Committee, requesting that "athletes who object to running or taking part in any game on Sunday, be given a chance to have their race or event arranged on another day." On January 22, 1924, word came that the appeal had been denied by the IOC, saying they could not ask any other committee, including the host country, to make those changes.

Since neither Eric's mind nor the schedule of events could be changed, he agreed to train for the 200 and the 400-meter races. He was not considered an Olympic contender at either distance, although some gave him an outside chance in the shorter race. McKerchar himself was not a religious man and had no personal reservations about Sunday sports, but once Eric's decision had been made, Tommy accepted it and set out to prepare his protégé for the races he had agreed to run. If Eric could win on heart alone, then the 400 belonged to him. But Tommy, more than anyone, knew it would take much, much more to win at the longer distance. Down at Cambridge, Sam Mussabini convinced Harold Abrahams that he could find him an extra two yards in the 100. McKerchar would have to find an extra three hundred yards for the Flying Scotsman.

Because Eric rarely talked about his athletic career, many of his twelve fellow residents in the Edinburgh Medical Missionary Society Hostel were unaware of his faithful training. To the casual observer, he seemed to place little importance on preparing for the Olympics. But two or three afternoons a week Eric met Tom McKerchar at Craiglockhart or Powderhall, learning the pace and strategy of the 400 meters. A man who ran the first half of a 400 at full speed would have no finishing power and would likely lose in the last twenty yards. But a sprinter who held too much in reserve at the beginning could not hope to make up the difference down the home stretch.

The fine balance between pace and stamina was only a single tick of the stopwatch. But in a race that would likely be decided in tenths of a second, one tick was enough to win … or lose.

At the hostel, Eric asked for no training diet, being content to eat what was served to everyone. Mrs. Taylor, who prepared the meals and knew Eric well, was always surprised that his only request beyond the ordinary fare was for a cup of coffee after dinner on special days. On race days, he avoided "pastry, plum pudding, and all foods that," in his own words, "would obviously be too heavy as passengers for the afternoon." However, on one occasion he broke his own rule and ate plum pudding at the noon meal. Later that afternoon he ran the second fastest quarter he had ever run in Scotland.

Eric regularly gathered his more sedentary housemates for a run around the George Square gardens and beyond. After outfitting them in his collection of international rugby jerseys, Eric led them as far as they were willing to go. Near the end of one long run, a passing motor bus honked a challenge that Eric readily accepted, easily outrunning it up a long hill.

Instead of campaigning with the GSEU over the 1924 Easter holiday break, Eric found himself on the way to the United States in the company of a two-mile relay team from Cambridge University. He had been invited to compete with them in the Penn Relays at the University of Pennsylvania, an annual event drawing 4,000 athletes from over 500 colleges and universities. This opportunity would provide Eric an early start for the running season and give him a taste of the American competition.

The journey began badly, with Eric leaving behind one of his suitcases, then suffering from prolonged seasickness. Three days before the meet began he stepped gingerly onto the track at Franklin Field for his first workout, only to be met by a raft of reporters and photographers. "Liddell was afraid to step very fast," wrote a correspondent for the *Philadelphia Inquirer*, "but he did give the big crowd on hand a real treat when he followed Starr down the straightaway at racing speed.

The tall, thin Scotsman seems to have lots of speed, even though he runs with form not used much in America."

Twenty-four hours before the relays began, a newspaper ad trumpeted the first day's main attractions: "CAMBRIDGE UNIVERSITY, ENGLAND, COMPETES TOMORROW IN SPRING MEDLEY RELAY CHAMPIONSHIP. ERIC LIDDELL, OF EDINBURGH UNIVERSITY, MEETS AMERICAN COLLEGE CHAMPIONS IN INTERNATIONAL 220 YARDS TOMORROW."

In the eyes of many spectators, however, the Flying Scotsman failed to live up to his advance billing. Eric finished second in the 220 final, a scant yard behind Louis Clarke of Johns Hopkins University. The next day he placed fourth in a near-photo finish in the 100 yards final. With only thirty inches separating the first four runners, most people in the stadium had no idea who had won until the official announcement came. The Yanks were only too glad to trumpet their victories over Liddell in the sprints and also over the Cambridge team in the sprint medley and two-mile relays.

Far from being discouraged, Eric felt he had learned a great deal and that he had turned in an adequate performance. As always, he was as gracious in defeat as he was in victory. Besides, he had enjoyed a grand time seeing the sights of Philadelphia, having lunch at the famous Wanamakers department store, and savoring the hospitality of the Philadelphia Cricket Club.

On the return voyage aboard the SS *Republic*, Eric appeared at the masquerade ball as an American Indian, wrapped in a bedsheet and sporting a cobweb duster in his headband. The mixed company aboard the ship included a number of attractive young women, with whom Eric enjoyed a game of cards and a dance or two. There was no shortage of adoring young ladies wanting to meet a prominent athlete, but Liddell remained as elusive on the dance floor as he was on the track. A few girls caught Eric's eye, but none stole his heart.

Eric enjoyed people of all sorts in a variety of social situations, and although he did not smoke or drink, he never looked down on those who did. He lived his life on the basis of his own bedrock convictions, without condemning those who did not share them.

He thoroughly enjoyed his trip to America even though it ended with the unfortunate disappearance of the two suitcases containing all of his souvenirs.

Back in Edinburgh, the pace of Eric's life accelerated dramatically. During the next ninety days, he completed his final term of university studies, sat for his final examinations, and stood up for Rob as best man at his May 17 wedding. Eric also decided to set his course for China, hoping to teach science at the Anglo-Chinese College in Tientsin. He would join D. P. Thomson for evangelistic campaigns in the autumn and spend the following year preparing for his missionary service.

When Eric began the summer running season on May 19, seven meets lay between him and the Paris Olympics, although, at the moment, neither he nor anyone else was officially a member of the British team. Near the end of May, the Council of the British Olympic Association sent a required list of provisional team members to the French authorities, clearly stating that they were not bound by this list and that they deferred final selection until after the Amateur Athletic Association Championships in London. No matter what an athlete had achieved in the past, a poor performance, an injury, or a convincing defeat at Stamford Bridge could be the end of his Olympic hopes.

On Friday evening, June 20, Eric faced the daunting task of running two 220s and two 440s in the space of only three and a half hours. He won all four races and qualified for the finals. The next day, Eric finally secured his place on the Olympic team with a second place finish in the 220 behind H. P. Kinsman of South Africa. Less than an hour later, Eric took first in the 440. His time of 49.6 seconds showed improvement, but hardly marked him as a top Olympic contender at that distance.

When the final roster for Paris appeared, Harold Abrahams was slated for the 100 meters, the 200 meters, and the long jump. Eric Liddell would run the 200 and 400 meters. With both men entered in the furlong, many Britons hoped they might yet witness a duel between Abrahams and Liddell for a gold medal in Paris.

SEVEN

Olympic Champion

1924

On June 16, 1924, the USS *America* steamed out of Hoboken, New Jersey, leaving no doubt about its cargo and destination. Port and starboard on the hull, in letters ten feet tall, the words AMERICAN OLYMPIC TEAMS brought a chorus of cheers from the crowds gathered along the pier. As the liner slipped down the Hudson River into New York harbor and past the Statue of Liberty, it seemed every person on board was at the rail, savoring a last glimpse of the country whose honor they would seek in Paris.

Four days earlier, Horatio Fitch had arrived in Boston for the final Olympic trials in the 400 meters. He and his fellow hopefuls had brought everything needed for a trans-Atlantic journey without knowing whether they would sail for Paris as members of the American team or return home carrying a heavy load of suitcases. Now, aboard the *America*, Fitch received his Olympic uniforms and wondered aloud why the official competition shirt had half-sleeves instead of being a lighter and cooler singlet. "In Paris, a man is not permitted to show his bare shoulders at a track meet" he was told. Based on other information circulating aboard ship, it seemed that different rules governed the "uniform" of the dancers at the Moulin Rouge.

During the ten-day Atlantic crossing, 250 athletes divided their time between recreation and training. A six-foot-wide strip of green cork flooring circled the upper promenade deck, providing a track where the sprinters and distance men could do a bit of work while dodging the morning walkers and the afternoon waiters serving tea. Weightlifters, boxers, and wrestlers grunted through a daily regimen of sit-ups and medicine ball drills; swimmers practiced their strokes while restrained by a stationary harness in a fifteen-foot-square canvas tank filled with seawater. The swimmers, including a boisterous nineteen-year-old Johnny Weismuller, frequently marched around the deck singing, led by the Kahanamoku brothers and three other Hawaiians, all playing their ukuleles. The unofficial anthem of the voyage became "It Ain't Gonna Rain No More."

But beneath all the nervous energy lay the unflagging desire to win. Every day on the cork track, Fitch concentrated on the instructions of Coach A. Alonzo Stagg and wondered if he could beat the world's fastest quarter milers, including the Flying Scotsman.

When the Americans disembarked at Cherbourg, France, on June 25, Eric Liddell was donning his spikes for an afternoon race at the annual Edinburgh Pharmacy Athletic Club Sports. His presence there helped draw several thousand spectators and boosted the gate receipts in support of the local athletic club. In an exhibition handicap race at 150 yards, Eric took second and gave the crowd another chance to debate his chances in France. Three days later he ran his final race before the Olympics, finishing fourth at 300 yards in another handicap race. His countrymen sent him off with a skirl of the pipes and hearty wishes for success in the games.

The wounds of World War I had not completely healed as the athletes from forty-five nations converged on Paris. Just a decade earlier, the wanton destruction of life and land had begun with pistol shots fired in Sarajevo by a revolutionary supporting the Serbs' right to the disputed provinces of Bosnia and Herzegovina. The assassination of Archduke Francis Ferdinand of Austria-Hungary had seemed like an isolated incident until the cords of secret alliances and political intrigue dragged the nations of Europe and beyond into a nightmare of trench warfare and poison gas. During the next four years, some ten million soldiers and five million non-combatants died before it was all quiet on the Western front. A scant hundred miles from Paris, endless rows of white crosses lined the fields of Flanders. The map of Europe had been redrawn by the victors, and across a six-hundred-mile swath, from France to

Belgium, farmers and peasants had toiled to remove the tangled barbed wire, replant splintered trees, and fill in the death holes of no-man's land.

Baron Pierre de Coubertin, architect of the modern Olympic games, had hoped that Germany would send a team to Paris, but the other nations refused to invite their former enemy. They had not forgotten and would not yet forgive. Former members of the Central Powers, including Austria, Hungary, Bulgaria, and Turkey, were allowed to send teams to Paris, but not Germany. Not for another four years. But most of the old animosities could at least be set aside for a time in the spirit of peaceful athletic competition.

The mood in Paris itself was anything but somber. People flocked to see the beautiful singer and dancer, Mistinguett, and listen to the songs of Maurice Chevalier in the Folies Bergere. The more adventurous thronged La Revue Negre to hear the latest black American jazz bands. Pablo Picasso splashed his non-traditional inner self on canvas, while Igor Stravinsky electrified the world of symphony and ballet. Ernest Hemingway and F. Scott Fitzgerald were living the high life and writing of its emptiness. And Gertrude Stein, dame of the city's avant-garde literary scene, declared that "Paris was where the 20th century was." The river of liberty and license rising in the United States during the Roaring Twenties had already breached its moral banks in the city by the Seine.

On Saturday morning, July 5, the athletes attended a religious service at the Cathedral of Notre Dame. That afternoon at the opening ceremonies, 2,000 Olympic competitors marched through the Marathon Gate into Colombes Stadium to pledge themselves to uphold the Olympic ideal of sportsmanship and fair play.

Eric Liddell hardly recognized the site of his international rugby debut two years before. The stands, now enlarged to accommodate 70,000 spectators, glistened under a fresh coat of blue and gold paint, but showed many empty seats. The British team, dressed in blue blazers, white flannel trousers or cream pleated skirts, and straw hats circled the track behind the contingents from the United States, Finland, and France. Two airplanes circled so low overhead that men hand-cranking movie cameras could be clearly seen. Then, in eager anticipation of what lay ahead, the athletes stood together on the field as the Olympic flag was raised and a battery of 75mm guns fired in salute. During a series of speeches and the taking of the Olympic oath, the realization crept in that they would soon know which of them would achieve the Olympic ideal of "*Citius, Altius, Fortius*" (Faster, Higher, Stronger).

On Sunday morning, the entire British team gathered at the Tomb of the Unknown Soldier, where the Prince of Wales laid a wreath in honor of their countrymen who had fallen in battle. For the rest of the day, Eric followed his usual Sunday observance while Harold Abrahams began his quest for gold in the 100 meters. As Harold advanced through the afternoon heats and the semifinal, he was the epitome of focus and determination.

The next afternoon, Eric sat in the stands near the starting line as the six finalists lined up for the most important race of their lives. Down on the track, Abrahams carefully positioned his toes in the starting holes as Sam Mussabini's words echoed in his mind: "Only think of two things — the report of the pistol and the tape." Ten and three-fifths seconds later, Abrahams crossed the finish line a step ahead of the American sprinter Jackson Scholz and became the first Englishman ever to win the Olympic 100 meters. After all the training and trying, and the terrible anguish of uncertainty, Abrahams had done it. He had done it indeed.

Eric joined the thunderous ovation that was silenced only by the hoisting of the Union Jack and the playing of "God Save the King." At the end of the day, Liddell was thrilled for Abrahams and perhaps somewhat relieved that his own refusal to run on Sunday had not cost the Empire a gold medal after all. But Eric's time of being a spectator at the games had come to an end. Tomorrow would begin four straight days of competition, first in the 200, then the 400 meters. In both races, his prospects for a gold medal were considered slim. One pessimistic British reporter had written: "It is unfortunate that E. H. Liddell's religious scruples will not permit of him running on Sunday, which rules him out of the short sprint, for I am not at all confident regarding his prospects in the 400 metres."

The next morning after a light workout, Eric lay on the table as Tommy McKerchar massaged the tension out of his muscles. McKerchar was one of the official trainers assigned to the British track and field team, but his primary charge for the next four days was Liddell.

Outside the training room, visible heat waves rose from the roof over the half-empty grandstand. High ticket prices and soaring temperatures had combined to keep thousands of would-be spectators away from the games. But merchants selling bottled water at premium prices could barely keep pace with the demand among those who came.

"Perfect running weather," Tommy muttered. Eric agreed, but knew that the same heat that kept him limber also sapped his strength after repeated races. He would have to qualify in two preliminary races on Tuesday and a semifinal on Wednesday afternoon to reach the 200-meter finals in the evening.

In the first-round heats for the 200 meters, British hopes soared when Harold Abrahams defeated Charley Paddock, the world amateur record holder. There could be no sweeter victory than to beat the Americans in the 100 *and* the 200. After Abrahams and Liddell advanced to the second round of the 200, their teammate Douglas Lowe electrified the crowd with a homestretch sprint to win the final of the 800 meters. Britain now held the gold in two races where they had not been favored, and they were looking to Abrahams to continue the winning streak. An Edinburgh newspaper asked the question in everyone's mind: "Will Abrahams complete the double?"

At 6:00 P.M. on Wednesday, July 9, Abrahams and Liddell lined up against a formidable quartet of Americans in the 200-meter final. George Hill, Bayes Norton, Charley Paddock, and Jackson Scholz were all capable of Olympic record time, even on the reddish cinder track that had been softened by a morning rain. With the late afternoon sun shining brightly, thousands of British hands clutched tiny flags, hoping to wave them in victory if Abrahams could only triumph again.

After a clean start, the pack ran evenly for the first eighty meters, but at the turn Abrahams was two steps behind. He seemed flat as he lagged farther behind with each stride. Eric's arms churned like windmills, and his legs pounded the track, straining to overtake the leaders. At the tape, it was Scholz (21.6), Paddock (21.7), and Liddell (21.9), with only three-tenths of a second separating first and third place. Abrahams finished last, but even so was less than a second behind the winner.

The next day many British newspapers focused on Abrahams's disappointing loss rather than Liddell's significant achievement. The *Edinburgh Evening News* headlined its Olympic news article: "BLANK DAY FOR BRITAIN — OUR FAILURE IN THE 200 METRES." *The Scotsman* was more specific: "ABRAHAMS FAILS IN 200 METRES." Only the *Glasgow Herald* proclaimed what seemed to be overlooked by everyone else: "LIDDELL HOME THIRD IN 200 METRES." It seemed a strange lack of Scottish enthusiasm for a favorite son who had won a bronze medal.

For many athletes, the most taxing part of Olympic competition was not the event itself, but the anticipation and the waiting. On Thursday, the first round of the 400 meters was scheduled for 3:00 in the afternoon, with Eric slated to run in the fourteenth of seventeen heats. After nearly an hour of waiting, Eric cruised to an easy victory, while Fitch of the U.S. had only to jog down the track against one opponent for both of them to advance. In the second round, as the favorites continued to win and the field narrowed to twelve runners, Joseph Imbach of Switzerland stunned the crowd by setting a new world record of 48.0 seconds. But disappointment stalked the British team as Toms fell after hitting an upright stake supporting the string lane-marker. In addition to chalk lines on the track itself, white strings supported by thin, shin-high stakes separated the lanes. Most of the athletes had never competed in such an arrangement and lived in fear of disqualification. And more than one spectator wondered how Eric Liddell could avoid catching a spike on the strings while running with his head back and his eyes closed.

As exciting as the 400-meter heats had been, the afternoon belonged to Paavo Nurmi of Finland. Known as "Peerless Paavo," he ran like a machine and seemed to crush all opposition effortlessly. Nurmi rarely smiled, rarely talked, and made it clear that he ran for himself, not Finland. He was virtually unstoppable. He won the 1500 meters, setting a new Olympic record, and at the tape he hardly looked winded. Less than an hour later, he lined up for the final of the 5000 meters. Not an athlete or trainer had left the infield, as everyone sought a trackside vantage point to watch Nurmi attempt the impossible.

Months before, in an effort to stop Finnish domination of the events, the French officials had scheduled the finals of the 1500 and 5000 meters half an hour apart. A furious protest by the Finns lengthened the interval to fifty-five minutes, which should have been enough to thwart anyone's attempt to run both races. Anyone but Nurmi.

For the first nine circuits of the 500-meter track, Paavo carried a stopwatch in his right hand, regularly noting his time. At the beginning of the final lap, he tossed the watch aside, his signal to the rest of the field that he considered the race won. With teammate Vilho Ritola on his heels, Nurmi maintained his long, rolling stride, increasing speed only when he sensed Ritola closing the gap. Paavo won by two seconds, setting a second Olympic record within an hour. Athletes and spectators alike were left shaking their heads at the Finn's remarkable endurance — and wondering what it would take to make him smile.

Nurmi was admired for his athletic prowess, but he was not popular with other athletes or the press. Eric, on the other hand, made friends wherever he went. His congenial spirit and habit of shaking hands with competitors before each race endeared him to athletes and spectators alike. Far from trying to impress others, Liddell went joyfully about his business, completely unaffected by the occasion.

That night at a Paris hotel, a group of coaches gathered around a table to discuss who would win the 400 meters the following day. The Americans favored Fitch but couldn't discount Imbach, the Swiss who had set a new world record in that day's competition. The banter went back and forth until Jack Moakley, the revered track coach at Cornell University, spoke up. "That Liddell's a hell of an awful runner," Moakley said, "but he's got something. I think he's got what it takes."

The next morning as Eric left his quarters at the Hotel Moderne, one of the British team masseurs pressed a folded note into his hand. Eric thanked him and added, "I'll read it when I get to the stadium." Later, during a quiet moment in the dressing room at Colombes, Eric unfolded the paper and read: "It says in the Old Book, 'Him that honours me, I will honour.' Wishing you the best of success always." Eric had never doubted his decision not to run on Sunday, but the barbed comments about his disloyalty and selfishness in putting his personal religious beliefs above the national interest had always hurt. It came as a great encouragement to know that someone shared his conviction, and to be reminded that the honor God gave, whatever form it might take, was all that really mattered.

In the first 400-meter semifinal heat, Horatio Fitch established a new world record of 47 $4/5$ seconds. His teammates showered him with congratulations and assurances that no one could beat him in the final. Liddell won the second heat in 48 $1/5$ seconds, well off Fitch's mark. The field had been narrowed to six men, who now had two hours to rest and think about the most important quarter mile of their lives. In the dressing room, McKerchar massaged Eric in characteristic silence, both of them knowing there was nothing more to say.

When the runners drew their lanes for the final, Canada's Johnson received the coveted inside position. Eric's teammate Guy Butler was in lane two, still formidable even with a strained thigh muscle. Because of this, he could not crouch as the other runners and had to begin from a standing start, a distinct disadvantage. Imbach, the Swiss flyer, held lane three, and the American, Coard

Taylor, running on an injured ankle, was assigned to four. Horatio Fitch in lane five would run next to Liddell, whose draw of the outside lane had been greeted with disappointment by the British team. Because of the staggered starting positions, the other runners were all initially behind the man in the outside lane, leaving him no way to gauge his pace against the rest of the field.

In Edinburgh, two of Eric's housemates at the EMMS hostel had wired a set of metal mattress springs to serve as an aerial for their crystal radio set. Since they couldn't afford to go to Paris, an attempt to hear the race by wireless was the next best thing. George Graham-Cumming signaled Greville Young to be quiet as the announcer's voice crackled through his earphones. The race was about to begin.

At 6:30 P.M. the summer sun still shone as Harold Abrahams shunned his Olympic competitor's free seat above the starting area and paid ten shillings for a place near the finish line. Across the track, Eric made his customary round of shaking hands as the runners prepared their starting holes. Standing nearby on the infield, Captain Philip Christison, leader of the Queen's Own Cameron Highlanders, decided to strike up the band and give Eric "a blow of the pipes" to send him on his way. While the official starter in his white linen duster made his final check from man to man on the track, the pipers skirled out eight bars of "Scotland the Brave" before anyone could stop them.

A voice from the loudspeaker called for quiet as the starter raised his pistol, bringing a hush across the stadium. Then came the commands: "A vos marques! Prêts!" The sound of the gun and a clean start brought a roar from the crowd that increased as the runners hurtled down the track. Abrahams' brow furrowed with concern as he watched Eric sprint as if he were running 100 meters instead of 400. "He can't possibly keep this up" he murmured. Nearing the halfway point, Eric led by three yards and was clearly running at full speed. Those in the stands timing with their own watches shook their heads in disbelief as Liddell clocked 22.2 seconds at 200 meters. There was no way he could continue that pace for the entire race.

With 100 yards remaining, the crowd gasped as Imbach snagged a spike on the lane marker and fell to the track, unable to get up. But Eric seemed oblivious to everything except his own race.

Back in Edinburgh, Graham-Cumming leaped to his feet, clasping his earphones and shouting the announcer's words after him: "They've cleared the last curve. Liddell is still leading! He's increasing his lead! Increasing and increasing! Oh, what a race!"

Down the final stretch, Fitch strained to narrow the gap, sure that Eric must slow down and "tie up" at any second. Instead, he saw Liddell throw his head back and put on a burst of speed that carried him to victory by five meters. Fitch, Butler, and Johnson crossed the line as Coard Taylor's ankle gave way, sending him sprawling onto the track. The determined American crawled the last ten yards to finish fifth.

The crowd went wild. A man in the stadium produced a huge Union Jack and began waving it triumphantly. Eric walked about on the track catching his breath, shaking hands with Fitch and smiling broadly as photographers swarmed around him. The crowd quieted as a voice announced the results of the race, then erupted again at the news that Eric Liddell had set a new world record of 47 $^3/_5$ seconds.

And back in Edinburgh, two young men danced around a room, unable to stop shouting, "He won! He won!"

Rob cabled the news of Eric's victory to Peitaiho, where the Liddells were besieged with well wishers from among the missionaries and business community on holiday. Mary shook her head in wonder, thinking back to the childhood illness at Siaochang, which had left Eric so weak that a well-meaning friend had said mournfully, "That boy will never run again."

The following morning, the same newspapers that had hedged about Liddell's chances in the 400 now proclaimed his great victory. "A WONDERFUL TRIUMPH!" "ELECTRIFYING RACE!" British journalists, who had complained of having to endure repeated playings of "the mournful strains" of "The Star Spangled Banner," now heaped praise on Eric for rescuing the British Empire both athletically and musically at Colombes.

For Eric, there was a great feeling of joy but no sense of receiving God's blessing for refusing to run on Sunday. He had won — that's all. Decisions based on principle needed no circumstantial vindication. The Almighty was gracious, but not obligated to give first place in any of this world's contests to the person who did His will.

Sunday, July 13, marked the final day of the track and field events. Again, Eric's Sabbath convictions kept him out of Olympic competition, this time in the finals of the 4 x 100 and the 4 x 400-meter relay races, in which Britain won silver and bronze, respectively. Instead of running, Eric preached at the Scottish Presbyterian Church in Paris. In reporting the event, a British newspaper published a photo of Eric shaking hands with the pastor and headlined it "British Olympic Champion in the Pulpit." Even after his stellar performance, the newspaper caption said: "If we had been able to use Liddell we should probably have won a relay race, but his religious views do not allow him to run on Sundays." The remark seemed to be a mixture of reluctant respect tinged with lingering regret.

Throughout the previous week, the British and Americans had both enjoyed the company of royalty. The Prince of Wales and Prince Henry cheered on the British team, while Hollywood stars Douglas Fairbanks and his wife, Mary Pickford, known as "the king and queen of movieland," hobnobbed with the Yanks. Among the competitors themselves were a number of future luminaries, whose stars were just beginning to rise: Johnny Weismuller of the American swim team captured three gold medals; French tennis player, Rene Lacoste, nicknamed Le Crocodile for his tenacious play, earned a bronze in the doubles; and 6' 4" Yale University rower, Benjamin Spock, who aspired to be a doctor, took home a gold in the eight-oared sculls. These men would go on to worldwide fame in film, fashion, and medicine that would eclipse their Olympic triumphs.

On Sunday night, Eric attended a farewell reception at the Continental Hotel given by the British Olympic Association for athletes from countries outside of the expansive British Empire. During the occasion, a Scottish lass who had heard Eric preach that morning determined that she would dance with him during the evening, but she could never penetrate the crowd of athletes surrounding Eric. Liddell spent the evening shaking hands and commending his fellow Olympic competitors. It never occurred to him that he was the only member of the British team to have won two medals in individual races. Part of what endeared him to others was his ability to enjoy his success while being completely detached from any sense that he was responsible for it.

Horatio Fitch, in his Olympic diary, penned this tribute to Eric: "Tho a sprinter by practice, he ran the pick of the world's quarter milers off their feet. Tho a small man, he makes his legs move fast enuf to beat his rangy competitors. His form is all wrong by our standards, for he runs almost leaning back, and his chin is almost pointing to heaven, yet he won his race on pluck and stamina. And most difficult of all, he had to set his own pace all the way, where one instant's faltering judgment would have meant defeat."

During the previous three years, Eric had reluctantly accepted the publicity and notoriety of being a well-known Scottish athlete. He had no idea, however, of the reception awaiting him as an Olympic hero.

The Victor's Crown

Summer 1924

No one was more elated by Eric's Olympic victory than D. P. Thomson. With plans already in place for a series of evangelistic campaigns together, Thomson knew that Eric's gold medal would become the drawing card for hundreds of young men who cared little about Christianity but would flock to hear an Olympic champion. D. P. took immediate steps to link his friend's running spikes with "the feet of those who preach the gospel of peace."

On Monday, July 14, as Eric and the rest of the British track and field team headed home across the English Channel, the *Glasgow Herald* hit the streets with an article by D. P. headlined: "E. H. LIDDELL: SCOTLAND'S OLYMPIC HERO." After highlighting Eric's family background and athletic achievements, the article concluded:

> "The announcement that Liddell is to preach in the Scottish Kirk at Paris (That event took place yesterday) serves as a reminder that our champion's main interest does not lie on the athletic field. To multitudes who know little of football or running, the name of E. H. Liddell is fast becoming known as a speaker to young men, whose presence in the pulpit or on the platform serves as a reminder that the finest athletic prowess often goes hand in hand with enthusiastic and effective spiritual work. Liddell's career on the running track may be drawing to a close, but his great work among young people in the interest of a vital and whole-hearted Christian discipleship is only just beginning, and the effects of that

work are likely to be as far-reaching as the fruits are great. China is the goal Liddell has in front of him and having completed his science course at Edinburgh University, he looks forward to a period of combined theological training and evangelistic campaigning before following his brother out to the mission field."

Two days after arriving back in Edinburgh, Eric donned a black graduation gown with green hood, denoting the Faculty of Science, and marched into the cavernous McEwan Hall for the university's graduation ceremony. Inside the magnificent circular domed building, the dignified proceedings, steeped in tradition, were often enlivened by the presence of an assembly of vocal undergraduates in the top gallery. They occupied chairs, aisles, and staircases, and during the conferring of degrees, their candid remarks often flowed from the gallery. They did, however, have a self-imposed limit on rowdiness, and on one occasion had removed one of their own by passing him overhead, person to person, from the top gallery, down the curving stairwell, and out the door, without ever touching the floor. But on July 17, 1924, the university's vice-chancellor, Sir Alfred Ewing, was way ahead of the undergrads.

Applause ranging from polite to hearty greeted a distinguished company of a dozen notables as they accepted the honorary degree of Doctor of Laws. Following that, through nearly half the alphabet of those receiving their Bachelor's degrees, everything proceeded normally. But when Eric Liddell stood along with those in his row, murmurs and applause began to ripple through the crowd. By the time he mounted the steps to the platform, cheers erupted and the entire assembly rose in a standing ovation that continued until Dr. Ewing's requests for quiet were honored.

In an unprecedented departure from convention, Sir Alfred spoke directly to Eric: "Mr. Liddell, you have shown that none can pass you except the examiners." Laughter swept the audience, followed by sustained applause and cheers. To the surprise and delight of everyone there, Sir Alfred continued: "In the ancient Olympic contests the victor was crowned with wild olive by the High Priest of Zeus, and a poem composed in his honour was presented to him. The Vice-Chancellor is no High Priest, but he speaks and acts for the University; and in the name of the University which is proud of you, and to which you have brought fresh honour, I present you with this epigram in Greek, composed by Professor Mair, and I also place upon your brow this chaplet of wild olive."

Eric, smiling, flushed with embarrassment, and crowned with the garland of honor over his receding hairline, walked back to his seat as the top gallery burst into "For He's a Jolly Good Fellow." After the ceremonies, he emerged from McEwan Hall and was met by a crowd of young men who seized him, sat him in something resembling a sedan chair on poles, and hoisted him onto their shoulders. Seeing that resistance was futile, Eric beamed with enjoyment as they carried him along the streets of Edinburgh toward the imposing St. Giles' Cathedral for the university commemoration service. As the procession moved along George IV Bridge, people on the street waved flags and handkerchiefs, while those watching from offices above joined in cheering Liddell. At one point, an automobile passed by, and the proper and aristocratic Lady Sleigh leaned out the window to wave at Eric.

At St. Giles', he was greeted with repeated cries of "Speech, speech!" Stepping down from the chair and surveying the crowd, he said quietly: "I really hardly know what to say on this occasion because there are many here who deserve this just as much as I do."

The crowd answered with cries of "No, no!"

Pausing briefly, Eric continued: "Over the entrance to the University of Pennsylvania, there is written this, 'In the dust of defeat as well as in the laurel of victory, there is glory to be found if one has done his best.' There are many here who have done their best, but have not succeeded in gaining the laurel of victory. To these, there is as much honour due as to those who have received the laurel of victory. Thank you all very much for this reception."

That would have been enough exaltation for an entire day, but it was only the beginning. At a University Union luncheon for the honorary graduates, Eric was toasted for his Olympic victory and was asked to speak to the distinguished gathering.

In his self-deprecating style, Eric told them that he was a short-distance runner owing to a defect in his constitution. He was extremely short-winded and, therefore, would not detain them long. He continued: "The papers have told you that my action is extremely bad, but that can probably be traced to my forefathers. It is well known in Scotland that the Borderers used to visit England now and then and escape back as quickly as possible. It was no doubt the practice of my forefathers to do this, and the speed with which they returned from England seems to have been handed down from generation to generation. One does not look for correct action when one is returning from raids, and probably this explains my own running action.

"Athletics is part of educating the whole person. A man is composed of three parts — mind, body, and soul, and only when we instruct each part in such a way that one is not overestimated, but each receives proper emphasis, will we get the finest and truest graduates from our University. As we realize that we not only have to store our minds with knowledge, but to educate our bodies for the strenuous life we must go through, and also remember that we are spirit as well, then we will send out graduates who are really worthy of taking their place in any part of life."

His ordeal of speaking ended, Eric sat down in relief, hardly aware of the loud applause.

But if he thought the day's festivities had ended, his hopes of peace and quiet were shattered once again when he emerged from the luncheon to find a company of his fellow university athletes pulling a brightly decorated carriage in which he and Sir Alfred Ewing were invited to ride. They took the scenic route along the famous Royal Mile to the Castle of Holyrood, then into the city center and down Princes Street, the main thoroughfare, with the local police gladly cooperating to clear the way. In front of a balcony where several female graduates were having tea, Liddell was compelled to make another speech. They finally arrived at the vice-chancellor's house where Ewing was expecting a company of prominent people for afternoon tea. Sir Alfred invited Eric and the carriage pullers to join them, but before entering the house, the vice-chancellor told the crowd outside that "never before in the course of a single day had he basked in so much reflected glory!"

The next evening, more than a hundred Edinburgh civic leaders and churchmen gathered in Mackie's Dining Saloon to honor Eric at a formal dinner. In speech after speech, he was praised, lauded, thanked, commended, and honored for his athletic achievement and for upholding the Christian Sabbath.

When Eric finally rose to acknowledge their tributes, he said that he found it difficult to speak after so many brilliant speeches had already been made. Holding a program in his hand, Eric mentioned that when he arrived for dinner, the first thing that caught his eye were the initials E. H. L. on the program. "My parents had first named me Henry Eric Liddell, but before it became officially registered, a friend suggested to my father that the initials H.E.L. might be rather awkward. This evening would certainly have been an occasion on which they would have been awkward."

Knowing they would expect some comment on the Olympic Games, Eric told about receiving a note from one of the British trainers on the day of the 400-meter final. "On it was written the words: 'He that honoureth me, I shall honour.' It was perhaps the finest thing I experienced in Paris, a great surprise and a great pleasure to know there were others who shared my sentiments about the Lord's day. Next winter, I hope to do a little work for the church, and if you desire to help me in that work, just give me your prayers. Thank you very much indeed for giving me such a great honor tonight."

At the close of the evening, a telegram was read before being sent to Eric's father: "Large gathering Edinburgh; chairman Lord Sands cordially congratulates his father and mother on Eric's wonderful feat and still more on his noble witness for Christian principles."

After the dinner, a taxi took Eric the short distance to Waverley Station, where he boarded an overnight train for London. Alone at last, he collapsed into his berth and fell asleep before the train jerked to a start. Tomorrow, he had a track meet to run against the Americans.

Every one of the fourteen events in the USA vs. the British Empire meet at Stamford Bridge was a team effort. Each race was a relay, and every field event involved a composite score from multiple competitors. The athletes had faced each other in Paris, but today things would be somewhat rearranged. Eric arrived refreshed and ready to run his two quarter-miles, one in the mile medley and the other as anchor in the 4 x 440-yard relay.

In the mile medley, Eric misjudged his pace in a fast start and lost his quarter to Charley Brookins. Poor baton passing by the British team resulted in two more races lost, and at the end of the day the USA had won the meet by eleven events to three. But in the midst of the overall disappointment, the 30,000 British fans would remember this as the day they witnessed "Liddell's epic quarter." As anchorman in the 4 x 440-yard relay, Eric received the baton seven yards behind Horatio Fitch. The swift American, who had finished less than a second behind Liddell in Paris, was determined to carry the final lap for the USA. At the last turn, with a hundred yards remaining, Eric began to close the gap. Then, with the crowd cheering themselves into a frenzy, he surged past Fitch on the straightaway to win by four yards. On an afternoon dominated by the Americans, the British fans consoled themselves with the knowledge that Liddell had, by his courage and determination, won a great race and saved them from almost complete humiliation.

The downside of the meet for Eric was that his participation kept him from attending Rob's ordination to missionary service in Edinburgh on the same day. But it gave him the pleasure of paying a surprise visit to Eltham College a few days later and speaking to the throng of cheering boys in the same quadrangle where he had walked as a student only four years before. Of course, Eric knew better than anyone how difficult it was to separate the boys' cheers for him from their joy at being given an entire day off from school for the occasion.

Two days later, Eric must have wondered if the Olympic celebrations would ever subside as he attended a luncheon given in his honor by the Edinburgh Town Council. During a congratulatory speech, Sir William Sleigh, the Lord Provost of Edinburgh, mentioned that in the days of the ancient Olympic games it was customary to honor the victor by erecting a statue and exempting him from all public taxes. But since they had no authority in the area of taxes, the city presented Eric with a permanent reminder of his Olympic triumph, a beautiful gold watch and chain bearing an inscription from the Corporation of Edinburgh.

For this occasion Eric had asked that D. P. Thomson and Tom McKerchar be among the invited guests. In responding to the honor and gift from the city, Eric again relied on self-effacing humor. "I feel rather privileged at having my talent found out for me," he told the crowd. "When I was at school, the Headmaster drew up a report in which he said, 'I do not think Liddell is as good as he appears to be, but somehow I cannot catch him.' This was how my talent for speed was first discovered."

Glancing at the table where McKerchar sat next to D. P., Eric continued. "In all the mentions of my Olympic victory, one thing has been forgotten and that is the great part my trainer, Mr. Tom McKerchar, has played in my success. For the last four years, he has coached me and shown me exactly how to run the various races. When I ran my first quarter mile at Edinburgh University, my trainer really ran it for me, before sending me out to try it on the track. I have much for which to thank Mr. McKerchar in all my success."

Eric sat down to a chorus of loud cheers and applause, for this banquet, as well as all the others, celebrated more than an athletic victory. Lord Sands reminded the assembled guests that it was not because Eric Liddell ran the fastest of all the runners in the world that they were there. "It is because," he said, "this young man put his whole career as a runner in the balance, and deemed it as small dust, compared to remaining true to his principles. There are greater issues in life than sport, and the greatest of these is loyalty to the great laws of the soul. Here is a young man who considered the commandment to rest and worship high above the fading laurel crown, and who conquered. It was St. Paul, the tentmaker of Tarsus, who watched the Olympic Games weary centuries ago and wrote,

'They who run in a race run all, but one receiveth the prize. So run that ye may obtain.'"

Eric had another month of running before the summer season ended and he entered the Scottish Congregational College. His appearance at the remaining meets was primarily as a celebrity whose participation helped raise funds for the host organization. After a Saturday of rain-dampened competition in Greenock, the town of his father's birth, Eric stayed on to address a Sunday evening meeting as he had done the previous year. This time, however, there were not hundreds of people, but a crowd of several thousand who came and stood in the rain to hear "the Olympic champion" speak on the text, "Remember now thy creator in the days of thy youth."

Barely eighteen months before, Eric Liddell had told the Lord he wanted to serve Him with the gifts he had been given, but could see no way to do that. After all, his strengths were speed, agility, and determination, not theological prowess or eloquence. But on the heels of Eric's prayer, D. P. Thomson had appeared asking him to come to Armadale and tell a group of coal miners what Christ meant to him. Eric's "All right, I'll come" had opened the door to a new experience of faith and service. Now, as an Olympic champion, he had been given a much greater gift of honor and responsibility.

With this came all the dangers of fame and popularity. Men admired him, young women adored him, ministers used him as an example of Christian conviction, and people on the street recognized him wherever he went. It would take a great deal of spiritual and emotional maturity for twenty-two-year-old Eric Liddell to cope with the kind of success that had turned men's hearts and tripped their feet since the beginning of time.

NINE

Christian Campaigner

1924–1925

In mid-August, Eric traveled to Galashiels for his final meet of the summer. Many believed it would be his last appearance on a Scottish track before he left for China in a few months, and thousands flocked to the Netherdale Football Ground to watch him run. He didn't disappoint them with his second place in the 100 yard handicap and a 54.0 victory in the 440 during a pouring rain.

While in Galashiels, Eric met Loudon Hamilton, a young man of rollicking humor and dynamic faith. Standing six feet three inches tall, with rugged good looks and a carefully clipped bushy mustache, Hamilton exuded an infectious enthusiasm for life. Yet only a few years before he had been mired in hopelessness and anger. He and Eric took a long walk beside the wide, meandering River Tweed, and talked openly about a dynamic spiritual movement through which Hamilton's life had been radically changed. Liddell listened intently as Loudon, five years and a world war older, described his own life-changing encounter with Christ.

As a nineteen-year-old artillery officer, Hamilton had witnessed the mind-numbing slaughter at the Battle of the Somme. During four months of carnage, British casualties exceeded 20,000 men a week. Describing his wartime experience, Loudon said: "The careers of most of the best fellows I knew ended in a burst of machine gun fire or a puff of shrapnel." A year later during the Battle of Passchendaele, Hamilton shook his fist at the stars one night and cursed God for allowing it all to happen. What faith he previously possessed died that night. With wounds and a decoration for valor, he returned after the war, cynical and disillusioned.

In 1921, while studying philosophy at Oxford, Hamilton was asked to entertain a visiting American educator, Frank Buchman. At a loss for what to do, he invited Buchman to the weekly meeting of "The Beef and Beer Club." Two dozen young men, many of them decorated veterans of World War I, crowded into Hamilton's rooms where they "smoked long pipes, drank long tankards of beer and talked long hours about how to put the world right — with no conclusions."

Buchman, a middle-aged Lutheran minister wearing a business suit, sat quietly in a corner of the room as the air filled with blue tobacco smoke. He said nothing until an hour before midnight, when someone finally asked what he thought about it all. The American surprised them by stating that he agreed with everything that had been said during the evening. "Of course the world has got to change," he said, "but that change might begin with people." And he told the story of two Cambridge students who had taken an entirely new approach to life. The room grew silent, a few pipes went out, and no one knew quite what to say.

Hamilton dismissed the meeting at midnight, hoping to be rid of Buchman, and was horrified to hear his atheistic roommate invite the American to breakfast. The next morning, Hamilton supplied a gargantuan meal to keep his visitor eating and not talking. But again, Buchman told brief stories of men whose lives had been transformed by the simple experiment of turning themselves over to Christ. "If you let God change you," Buchman said, "He'll use you to change the world."

A few weeks later at a "houseparty" where the main topic of conversation was a personal experience of Christ, Hamilton admitted his own need "for a change and a clean-up," and opened the door he had slammed in God's face.

Hamilton summed up his experience in the statement: "Sin is the disease; Christ is the cure; the result is a miracle." Sitting under an overhanging tree on the bank of the Tweed, he told Eric of the great adventure of discovering God's guidance by listening to Him each morning during a quiet time. The practical result was a life of complete honesty, integrity, and freedom. "I want to live so that God can say 'hello' to me anytime of the day or night," Hamilton said with deep feeling.

Eric was intrigued by the idea of being guided by God, and particularly challenged by the concept of seeking to live each day by the Four Absolutes: absolute honesty, absolute purity, absolute unselfishness, and absolute love.

"I used to prefer Einstein's theory of relativity," Hamilton said with a twinkle in his eye, "Relatively honest, comparatively pure, reasonably unselfish and occasionally loving. It was easier. But it's not God's way."

At the time, the spiritual movement Hamilton described to Eric had no name and no official membership. It would be another four years before a journalist in Pretoria, South Africa, referred to Hamilton and a group of visiting young evangelists as "the Oxford Group." Even then, the movement remained a way of life to be embraced rather than an organization to join.

Eric left Galashiels with a new determination to live absolutely for Christ, and a new fire kindled in his heart to see people changed by the gospel. That was exactly what D. P. Thomson had in mind as well, and in this way the two men were exactly alike. In almost every other way they could not have been more different. Perhaps that's why they made such an engaging and effective evangelistic team.

Eric was shy and reserved while D. P. was gregarious and outgoing. In a church or open air meeting, Eric spoke quietly and conversationally. D. P.'s booming stentorian voice would carry to the last seat in the house, or across a rugby field. While speaking, Thomson would range from one side of the platform to the other. In contrast, Liddell seemed riveted to the pulpit, rarely gesturing with his arms or hands, but often rising on tiptoe, perhaps the habit of a runner. Eric's enthusiasm was quiet and steady; D. P.'s vitality was boisterous and unrestrained.

Thomson, like so many men of his generation, had been shaped by World War I. Eric had been a twelve-year-old at Eltham College when D. P., along with his older brother, Pringle, and five cousins all joined up to fight the Great War. Thomson soon found himself in

Salonika as a young lieutenant in charge of a field bakery providing bread for 60,000 men. With a natural bent toward business, he quickly became a master at planning, organization, and logistics.

Two years later, in August 1916, D. P. lay in a Liverpool hospital, convalescing from heart and stomach problems, when he received word of his older brother's death in France. Before the war ended, his five cousins were also dead, and D. P. alone was left of the seven who had enlisted together. "If I were spared to come through," he said, "I could never go back to business. In a new and deeper way now, mine was a dedicated life."

Eric himself was no stranger to the reality that today's opportunity for Christ was all a person could count on. Two weeks after Eric returned from Paris, Rob had undergone a routine surgery. But something went wrong, requiring a second surgery. Instead of spending ten days in the hospital, Rob languished during two months of serious illness and bed rest while the ship on which he and Ria were scheduled to sail for China departed without them. In Tientsin that same autumn, Mary, Jenny, and Ernest all suffered from the ravages of the flu. Eric believed it was good to make plans, but he also knew that it was never wise to think that the future was in his control.

⚘

The team of Thomson and Liddell began their evangelistic campaign in September 1924 with a series of meetings in Dundas Street Church, Glasgow. Crowds ranging from 450 to 600 filled the church each night to hear Eric speak about what it meant to live as a Christian. D. P. followed with an appeal to decide for Christ, urging his hearers to consider carefully the implications of fully yielding themselves to God. There was no call to "come forward" during the meeting, but all wanting to know more or seeking personal counsel were invited to adjourn to another room.

The large number of young people remaining after each meeting prompted some critics to assert that D. P. and Eric were playing on the emotions of their audience. Eric's father, responding to a letter he had received about the Dundas Street meetings, wrote to the LMS foreign secretary: "It is certainly very gratifying that Eric has so fully entered into this spiritual experience, and is desirous of passing on what is his possession, that others might also enjoy the same. My wife and I are perfectly sure he has the illumination that will be as an anchor for life if he keeps in touch with Jesus Christ. We are very glad the team is not stressing theology as such, but getting the young life to face their personal relation to the Saviour. 'What will *you* do with this man who is called the Christ'? From what we know of Eric we are sure he will not seek to harrow any one's feelings, or seek to publicly uncover what any one wishes to be kept sacred. But I guess he'll want very honest dealing as between individuals and their Lord. We could never dream of connecting Eric with sensational methods. Our hope is that the churches will be helped, and many young people make the great decision."

In a subsequent letter, James Liddell tempered his positive feeling about Eric's activities with parental concern: "We hear that Eric is having strenuous times between work and meetings. We hope he will not undertake too much while still doing study. He is one who finds it difficult to refuse work."

One of Eric Liddell's greatest strengths was his willingness to accept every invitation he possibly could to speak a word for Christ, regardless of the size or "importance" of the audience. One of his greatest weaknesses was the opposite side of the coin: whenever he saw a pressing need or was asked to perform any act of Christian service, he found it almost impossible to say no.

In October Eric took up residence in the Scottish Congregational College in Edinburgh and began a year's course of theological study. From the outset, his studies suffered from the regular and often prolonged interruptions of the speaking commitments that already filled his calendar. On several occasions during the year he accompanied members of the Glasgow Students' Evangelistic Union for missions of a week or more in Kilmarnock, Irvine, Ardrossan, and other Scottish towns.

Thomson, a great believer in publicity, led teams door-to-door distributing notices of the meetings and in posting handbills throughout the towns. To stir up additional interest in the meetings, the students often challenged the local rugby team to a game. Even with Eric on their side, the young evangelists didn't always win, but they never failed to attract a crowd. Before these games, Eric sometimes ran exhibition races against the town's swiftest harriers, always giving a generous handicap to the challengers. Win or lose, he shook hands all around before and after the race, smiling and congratulating his opponents on a job well done.

In addition to his demanding schedule with the GSEU, Eric accepted a number of speaking engagements from schools and churches, including his own Morningside Congregational Church in Edinburgh. Since 1921, Eric had served faithfully as a Sunday school teacher and president of the Young People's Union at Morningside. While watching him develop athletically and spiritually, Rev. Moffatt Scott and members of the congregation had given him a nurturing church home in which to grow. Now they welcomed him to the pulpit for three consecutive evenings of outreach to youth.

But a week before the meetings began, Eric was sobered by the news that D. P. Thomson's younger brother, Robert, had died after a short illness in London. The Thomson brothers were remarkably close, having been led to Christ on the same night at the ages of eight and eleven. As young adults, they remained best friends, thinking vigorously together about philosophy and theology, and collaborating on a recently published series of handbooks on modern evangelism. Everyone who knew Robert Thomson considered him a genius. He was always working on some new invention, and at the age of twenty-five was serving as assistant lecturer in physical chemistry at Kings College, London. D. P. called him "the finest Christian I ever knew." And now he was gone.

Once again, the frailty of life and the shortness of time fueled D. P. Thomson's sense of urgency to preach the gospel. And this time Thomson's deep loss touched Eric Liddell as well. It could have been his own brother, Rob. It could have been Eric himself, or any one of his most promising friends. In a new way, the brevity of life became intensely real to both men as they spoke of Christ to young men and women who often gave little thought to eternity.

"The brothers I loved so dearly and admired so greatly had both been taken," D. P. said, "and I was left. In some small measure at least it must be my aim to fill their place." Thomson often said he would rather set ten men to work than do the work of ten men, but everyone who knew D. P said that somehow he managed to do both.

≋

In early December, Eric said good-bye to Rob and Ria as they sailed for China, assuring them that he would not be far behind. A January letter from Shanghai said they had begun half a year of medical and language training before assuming their post in South China—and, they were living in the house where Rob was born.

Six hundred miles north in the city of Tientsin, Eric's plans for coming to China were the subject of frequent discussion. The principal of the Tientsin Anglo-Chinese College, Dr. Lavington Hart, arranged for passage money to be given to Eric, hoping he would be there by spring. Hart desperately needed a science teacher, and the sooner Eric Liddell arrived, the happier he would be. J. D. Liddell expected his son in May, but the details remained unsettled.

January also brought Eric the news that Tommy McKerchar, a father again at the age of forty-seven, had named his newborn son Eric Liddell McKerchar. Eric agreed to be the boy's godfather and proudly attended his christening.

Before Eric settled on a departure date for China, he had to decide whether he would run that year or not. In one sense, it seemed impossible for him to train consistently with his academic and speaking load. Many people thought he should quit while he was at the pinnacle of his athletic achievement. But if Tommy would give him a hand with training, he might consider running in a few meets, concluding with the Scottish Championships at the end of June. McKerchar's broad smile was all Eric needed to set his departure for China in early July.

In addition to the GSEU and his own speaking commitments,

Eric had agreed to join D. P. Thomson in conducting a series of "Manhood Campaigns" for the YMCA, which still maintained the strong spiritual purpose for which it was founded. In cities throughout England Eric and D. P. held meetings in YMCA halls, spoke to students at the large public schools, and addressed diverse groups ranging from a crowd of airmen at a Royal Air Force depot to an assortment of working boys in London. From the Theatre Royal in Manchester to a pub in County Durham, they brought the message of Christ to audiences known for ignoring evangelists.

But no city offered the challenge of London. Frank Carter, General Secretary of the London Central YMCA, knew the pulse of the young men living at the Y. Some were university students, others intent on success in the banks and business houses, and a number were struggling to find their way in the great city. That's why he insisted that D. P. and Eric play by his rules when they came to London Central.

"No more than four days," Carter had told Thomson during their initial discussion about the mission. "You'll meet in the lounge where the men can sit on sofas and in easy chairs. They'll be free to smoke and ask questions, but there will be no invitation during the meeting. I'll open each session with a one-sentence prayer, then it's over to you."

D. P., who had never heard such arrangements for an evangelistic meeting, agreed out of respect for this man of great vitality known by everyone as "the Guv'nor." Frank Carter looked intently at Thomson through the small circular lenses of his wire-rimmed glasses and smiled.

"After each meeting," Carter continued, "the chapel will be available for those who wish to use it. You and Liddell will each be provided with a room where you can talk privately with anyone seeking counsel."

On a Saturday night in April, D. P. and Eric attended a smoking concert at London Central where a jazz band played in a casual atmosphere. During the evening, they made their way around to various tables for personal introductions to the men. The following Monday evening, at the first "Manhood Campaign" meeting, Eric and D. P. each took his turn standing behind a small table, telling the men what Christ meant to him. In a sign of respect and perhaps even reverence, every pipe and cigarette went out within five minutes after Eric began to speak. The second night, the two young evangelists counseled men until after midnight. And on the final evening, eighty men came to the chapel, first kneeling in silence to search their own hearts, then listening to Thomson's clear explanation of how they could commit themselves fully to Christ. Again, he and Eric dealt individually with men until nearly midnight.

In their final mission together, they teamed up for twelve days of Young Life Campaign meetings in Edinburgh. In the public schools there, Eric was welcomed as a hero. Each day he and D. P. took their message of faith and commitment to those who could not or would not attend the evening meetings in a church. Even so, the nightly services drew people from a cross-section of the city.

On the opening night of their campaign, an audience of 1200 listened to Eric explain why he and Thomson were there.

"We are here to place before you the call and challenge of Jesus Christ. Many of us are missing something in life because we are after the second best. We are placing before you during these few days the thing we have found to be best. We are putting before you one who is worthy of all our devotion — Christ. He is the Saviour for the young as well as the old, and He is the one who can bring out the best that is in us."

He concluded by making commitment to Christ a matter of personal choice.

"Are you living up to the standards of Jesus Christ? We are looking for men and women who are willing to answer the challenge Christ is sending out. If this audience was out and out for Christ, the whole of Edinburgh would be changed. If the whole of this audience was out for Christ, it would go far past Edinburgh and through all Scotland. The last time Edinburgh was swept, all Scotland was flooded. What are you going to do tonight?"

A local journalist wrote: "What is particularly marked in the manner and method of their appeal is the fact that both men rely not upon emotional fervour at the expense of reason, but on the direct challenge both to mind and heart of intelligent and robust young manhood. The challenge that they fling out to the youth of this generation is definite enough. It is a call to men to pledge their loyalty to Jesus Christ and to invest personality, gifts, life itself in the service of the Kingdom of God."

After the big kickoff rally, the crowds decreased each night to a low of 500 by the weekend. D. P. had been bold enough to book Usher Hall, with seats for 3000, for the closing meeting the next night. A sympathetic minister said he would cut short his Sunday evening service and lead his entire congregation to the meeting to help make up the shortfall. D. P., concerned over the prospect of concluding their meetings with a small group huddled together in a huge hall, gladly accepted his offer. The next evening, The Reverend Dr. James Black and his large congregation arrived just before eight o'clock to find Usher Hall filled to capacity and an overflow meeting being hastily organized at a nearby church.

The meeting brought to a close Eric's heavy speaking schedule of the previous nine months. It had been remarkable not so much because he had spoken scores of times to thousands of people, but because he had spoken publicly at all. Now, only two years beyond his first timid testimony at Armadale, he had put fear behind him and grown in his ability to communicate the message of Christ. No one would call him eloquent, but his humility and sincerity overcame any lack of platform skill. His listeners knew that he spoke from his heart and from his own experience. Like the Master he served, his words rang with authority.

Eric's illustrations came from the things he knew best — the chemistry laboratory, the rugby field, and the running track. In his quiet, direct manner, he compared giving one's life to Christ with choosing the captain of a team. "Have you ever sought a leader in everyday life?" he asked. "In Jesus Christ you will find a leader worthy of all your devotion and mine. I looked for one I could admire, and I found Christ."

❦

Three days after the Edinburgh campaign concluded, Eric was back on the track at Craiglockhart for the annual university sports day. In four short years, he had come from unknown freshman to nationally acclaimed Olympic champion. And despite the concern of those who feared that his strenuous speaking schedule had thrown his training into disarray, Eric captured first place in the 100, 220, and 440. Ten days later he repeated the triple victory at St. Andrews against runners from all four Scottish universities.

On each of the next three Saturdays, Eric ran in local meets to benefit the host athletic club. On the Sundays following each meet, he preached in a nearby church, always taking time after the services to talk with the young people and sign autographs. With less than a month remaining before his departure for China, he gladly accepted every invitation he could, whether it was preaching to a thousand or giving prizes to a dozen Sunday school scholars on a Sabbath afternoon.

At the Scottish Amateur Athletic Championships in Glasgow, Eric gave the 15,000 spectators more than they hoped for. The newspapers called it "Liddell's Triple Triumph" as he swept first place in the 100, 220, and 440 for the third time in a month. At the end of the day, he anchored the Edinburgh University team to victory in the one-mile relay, making up a ten-yard deficit on his leg of the race. For the third consecutive year, Eric Liddell received the coveted Crabbie Cup as the most meritorious competitor in the championship meet.

When asked if he was leaving the track forever, Eric replied that he was leaving for the next four years. But even the door of hope he left slightly ajar did little to lessen the sense of national loss. Harold Abrahams had suffered a career-ending leg injury during long jump competition and was also gone from the track. "No Liddell; No Abrahams" lamented the press.

An enthusiastic crowd packed Eric's farewell service in Glasgow. A thousand people who were turned away from Renfield Church filled nearby St. John's Wesleyan for an overflow meeting. Responding to the tributes and a great ovation, Eric stood to speak and looked toward D. P. Thomson.

"Two years ago," he told the audience, "I was faced with the biggest problem of my life. I had been asked to assist at an evangelistic campaign in Armadale, but at the time had never addressed a public gathering. I was very reluctant about accepting the invitation. The morning after being invited, I received a letter from my sister in China, and it contained this text: 'Fear not, for I am with thee; do not dismay, for I will guide thee.' Those words helped me make that decision, and since then, I have endeavored to do the work of my Master."

The valedictory gathering in Edinburgh also required an overflow meeting in a nearby church. Again, leading churchmen and civic leaders paid glowing tributes to Liddell the sportsman and the Christian. In his response, Eric said that he was going to a country where his work, on the surface at least, would be different. But through his opportunities as a teacher, he hoped he would be able to lead many a Chinese boy to Christ in the same way he himself had been led.

On Monday morning, June 29, Eric took a final look around his room at 29 Hope Terrace, the stately Edinburgh home that housed the Scottish Congregational College. It had been quite a year.

As he closed his suitcase, a horse-drawn cab, minus the horse, arrived outside to a chorus of cheers. His friends were not about to let him depart unnoticed. A four-wheel landau carriage with the top down awaited him in the driveway.

Principal T. Hywell Hughes gave his most famous student a final handshake, and the two exchanged a look of mutual admiration and appreciation. Eric resigned himself to the fanfare and, with a broad smile, entered the carriage. Decorated from spokes to posts with red, white, and blue streamers and pulled by a team of university athletes, the vehicle attracted hundreds of followers as it rolled through the city streets toward Waverley Station. Along the route, the crowd following tossed streamers and sang "For He's a Jolly Good Fellow" and "Will Ye No Come Back Again?"

When the cab came to rest on the wrong platform, Eric set off on foot to make his train, only to be carried back to the carriage, which was finally maneuvered to the correct location. And then came the inevitable cries of "Speech! Speech!"

Eric stood in the cab and expressed his heartfelt thanks for their hearty send-off and their good wishes. He said he was going abroad to try and do his part in the great task of unifying the countries of the world under Christ, and he hoped that everyone at home would do their bit as well. He wanted them all to share the motto: "Christ for the world, for the world needs Christ."

Once inside the railway car, Eric lowered the window and continued to shake hands with those who crowded around. He grasped the walking stick extended by a man who could not get close enough to touch his hand. And then he led the crowd in singing two verses of the hymn "Jesus Shall Reign Where'er the Sun." As the train pulled away, the well-wishers, waving handkerchiefs and hats, followed it to the end of the platform.

Eric sank into his seat, once again amazed at the outpouring on his behalf. As the train passed Dunbar, the North Sea sparkled to the east and the familiar landscape held his gaze. With new eyes of appreciation, he savored these last glimpses of Scotland.

He stopped at Berwick-upon-Tweed to spend the day with his mother's relatives. Then, with the far-north summer sky still glowing an hour before midnight, he boarded the overnight train to London and fell into a peaceful sleep.

He was off to run another race, one that would test him far beyond anything he had known. At the peak of his athletic career with the world at his feet, twenty-three-year-old Eric Liddell turned away from it all and set his face toward China.

PART II

THE GREATEST RACE

1925–1942

Be still, my soul: thy God doth undertake
To guide the future as He has the past.
Thy hope, thy confidence let nothing shake:
All now mysterious shall be bright at last.
Be still, my soul: the waves and winds still know
His voice who ruled them while He dwelt below.

TEN

The Anglo-Chinese College

1925–1926

The Trans-Siberian Railroad stretches for nearly 6,000 miles from Moscow to Vladivostok, crossing the Ural Mountains and skirting the southern tip of beautiful Lake Baikal. During its first dozen years of construction, some 70,000 workers moved nearly 80,000,000 cubic feet of earth, stripped the timber from 108,000 acres of forest, and constructed bridges across six major rivers.

Eric Liddell, like most others, traveled the Trans-Siberian for speed, not comfort. Instead of a leisurely ocean voyage with ports of call at Colombo, Singapore, and Hong Kong, there were hurried platform stops at Omsk, Irkutsk, and Ulan Ude. But instead of six weeks at sea, the entire journey from England to China could be made in one-third the time. The price was enduring cramped quarters and the uncertainties inherent in crossing national borders where the officials spoke no English and cared little whether foreign passengers reached their destinations or not. If there was turmoil in Manchuria, the train from Harbin south to Tientsin might not be running. In that case, Eric might wait there for days, or travel on to Vladivostok and book passage on a ship making the long swing around the southern coast of Korea. But on this journey, everything worked like a Swiss clock.

On July 18, Eric stepped off the train at the seaside resort town of Peitaiho, exactly fourteen days after leaving London's Victoria Station. His mother and father, along with Jenny and Ernest, were there to welcome him "home" to China. For the next six weeks, he had no official duties except to relax, enjoy his family, and get acquainted with his colleagues in the missionary community.

Eric wrote to a friend in Britain: "I had a splendid voyage out here... I do not think that the distance can be done in much less a time for I had only three long stays; about ten hours at Berlin; eight at Moscow and six at Harbin. All along the way I was most fortunate having as my companions Germans, Russians and Chinese in the various countries who could all speak English and the required language, so my trip was made quite simple. From Moscow to here I had some Russians whose ideas were not quite the same as mine, but despite this we managed to get along smoothly."

A week after Eric reached Peitaiho, Rob and Ria arrived from Shanghai. For the first time in three years, the Liddell family was complete again. Even though Rob and Ria were being posted far away to South China, everyone seemed content to focus on the moment and enjoy each day they were given together. But the realities of life in China could never be ignored for long.

Along with hugs and handshakes and good wishes, Eric had also been greeted with the news that his career as a missionary teacher might be over before it ever began. A few weeks earlier, on May 30, colonial police in Shanghai had fired into a surging crowd of protesting Chinese workers and students, killing several of them. Outrage among Chinese students over "the Shanghai incident" quickly spread throughout North China, resulting in early closure of a number of schools, including the Tientsin Anglo-Chinese College where Eric was scheduled to begin teaching science. Wild rumors circulated that the principal, Dr. Samuel Lavington Hart, brandishing a pistol in each hand, had expelled all the students and driven them out, refusing to allow them to take their final exams. The combination of a rising Chinese nationalism, Communist agitation, and smoldering anger over decades of Western domination had produced a volatile mixture that threatened to explode without warning.

In his letter, Eric continued: "I have been here now for three weeks and find that many of the people here find it difficult to give a good account of the political position. One thing we do know and that is, there is a prejudice against the British and a few days ago there were placards pasted up all over this little seaside resort.

"We do not know yet what to do about the reopening of the T.A.C.C. but hope to meet together tomorrow to discuss the plans. Not only are the students anti-British but they are also anti-Christian, although they deny this last statement."

Eric had come to China with a four-year commitment to teach science, help with sports, and see if he was cut out for missionary service. At the end of the trial period, he would be free to return to Britain with no further obligation. His father hoped, as did many others, that Eric would sense this as his calling from God and apply to join the London Missionary Society and become a career missionary under its auspices. In the meantime, his salary would be paid directly by the college, to which he was ultimately responsible.

For nearly twenty-five years, the Tientsin Anglo-Chinese College had been the vision and heartbeat of its founder and current principal, Dr. Lavington Hart. Educated at the Sorbonne in Paris, St. John's College, Cambridge, and London University, Hart had established himself as a brilliant physicist and lecturer in Britain. But in 1892 he left his promising career and, along with his brother Walford, sailed for China with the LMS. Within two years of their arrival, both Walford and his new bride were dead of dysentery. Lavington and his wife, Elsie, moved from Wuchang to Tientsin, where Hart founded the college, with the objective of taking the gospel to the sons of Chinese businessmen and government officials through Christian education. While a great deal of missionary effort went into helping the poor, the Chinese gentry remained largely untouched by traditional missionary methods. Dr. Hart's passion was to influence the country's future leaders by educating them and letting them see Christianity lived out through their teachers.

But every year brought continuing uncertainties, and Eric had arrived at a particularly tense time. After much deliberation and fervent prayer at Peitaiho, the college staff decided to keep moving ahead and sent a "Letter To Parents And Guardians" saying: "The Authorities of the College have decided to open the College as usual in September. They will admit all, whether former students or new students, whose distinct purpose it is to devote themselves quietly to study."

The letter affirmed the college's long-standing purpose of building character through "education of the highest type, permeated with Christian influence, and free from religious compulsion." It stressed the importance of "physical culture and improvement of health through Games and Athletic Sports" and said: "In this connection, The College is glad to announce the addition to the Staff of Mr. Eric Liddell, an International Footballer and World's Champion in Athletics. He is a B.Sc. of Edinburgh University, and will teach Mathematics and Science." No one thought that Eric's presence could quell a student insurrection, but his reputation as an athlete certainly enhanced the school's image.

At the end of August, Eric and his father made the five-hour train journey from Peitaiho, with its cool sea breezes, to the stifling heat of Tientsin. Situated at the confluence of five waterways, including the Grand Canal and the Hai Ho (Sea River) which linked Tientsin to the sea, the "City of the Heavenly Ford" served as the port for Peking, eighty miles to the northwest. Along the bund flanking the Hai Ho as it wound its way through Tientsin, coolies loaded and unloaded cargo from river steamers. Stooped under mammoth sacks of flour, the Chinese laborers hurried with shuffling steps between the quay and the numerous warehouses, called *go-downs,* that lined the streets near the river.

Eric took up residence in the Liddell family home, a spacious two-story brick structure in the LMS compound. The house, No. 6 London Mission, boasted central heating, along with a comfortable sitting room and dining room joined by sliding doors. On the second floor, Jenny, now twenty-two, and thirteen-year-old Ernest each had a room, and there was a master suite for James and Mary. The three Chinese servants occupied quarters attached to the back of the house.

Within a few days Eric had arranged his books and photos of friends in an attic room overlooking the garden and tennis court. Just as he had in Edinburgh, he preferred the highest room in the house. His colleagues back in Scotland, who thought he had gone to the end of the earth, could not have pictured his comfortable digs in a city of nearly a million people.

Tientsin, as a treaty port, was composed of two distinct and unequal parts — the Chinese City and the foreign concessions. In the densely populated Chinese City, most of the 800,000 inhabitants lived in cramped rooms and houses that were little more than shanties. They worked thirteen hours a day in factories weaving carpets, making matches, and hammering tin pots into shape. Thousands of coolies earned a few coins a day doing the harsh physical work of building roads and unloading ships, or the unpleasant task of carrying buckets of night soil out of the city to fertilize the surrounding fields. On the sidewalks, merchants provided everything from haircuts to six-course meals.

Many foreigners never entered the Chinese City except to shop or take a rickshaw tour. Their children were instructed never to eat anything sold by a street vendor.

Life in the foreign concessions was a different matter. Eight nations, including Britain, France, Japan, Germany, Italy, Austria, Belgium, and Russia, had, at one time, been granted areas of Tientsin in which the residents were free to live and carry on business outside of Chinese law. The American Concession had been ceded to Britain in 1902. Each concession operated much like an independent country with its own municipal government, services, churches, and a small contingent of its own troops for protection. Of them all, the British, French, and Japanese concessions were the most modern.

Since the mid-nineteenth century, the dubious practice of "extra-territoriality" had been thrust on China through a series of wars and humiliating treaties, along with a great deal of gunboat diplomacy. As foreign nations forced open the door of trade with China, they produced deep and sustained resentment among many Chinese people. The anger that blazed during the Boxer Uprising of 1900 had been repressed by foreign armies, but the underlying spirit of "China for the Chinese" had not vanished.

The Anglo-Chinese College occupied a plot of ground bordered by Taku Road and Rue de Pasteur in the French Concession. The grey brick, Gothic-style buildings, modeled after Dr. Hart's alma mater, St. John's College, Cambridge, boasted turrets and towers sixty feet tall. The entire school was surrounded by a wall whose battlements seemed more like those of a castle than a college. From the entrance under the South Tower, a wide staircase led up to the chapel and lecture rooms. Everything from the dormitories for the boarding students to the flats for teachers had been planned with a commitment to excellence and quality. But after twenty years of use, much of the physical plant was in need of repair and remodeling.

With only a few weeks before classes began, Eric scoured local shops buying test tubes and beakers for the chemistry laboratory that was now in his charge. In the adjacent British Concession, he walked along Victoria Road, "the Wall Street of Tientsin," past the imposing columns of the Hong Kong & Shanghai Banking Corporation and a dozen other banks representing as many nations. Architecture like that of central London dominated the broad, tree-lined avenue leading toward the massive Gordon Hall, which housed the British Municipal Council Offices. Gordon Hall overlooked Victoria Gardens, where the British Regimental Band played evening concerts during the summer. Across the street, the famed Astor House Hotel hosted the Tientsin Rotary Club every Thursday at 12:30 for lunch.

Two miles southwest, at the end of Race Course Road, the Tientsin Country Club featured swimming, tennis, and horse racing on its spacious grounds. Visiting orchestras and jazz bands kept feet dancing on the hardwood floor of the opulent ballroom. The only Chinese to be seen at the country club were serving drinks, waiting tables, and caring for the flowers. At the time, it did not seem unusual to most expatriates that the "Foreigners Only" policy was also followed at the regular Sunday services of the Anglican Church and the Union Church in the British Concession. Protestant churches in the Chinese City offered services in Chinese for the local citizens.

Six thousand foreign residents representing a variety of lifestyles and purposes lived in Tientsin, most in the concession areas. Some foreign businessmen saw themselves as the economic saviors of a backward and undeveloped country. Educators came to share Western learning, doctors to bring medicine, and missionaries to introduce Christianity. Some people came to exploit the Chinese and others to save them. Many were convinced that with enough time, money, and co-operation, they could put this ancient and troubled country on the path to peace and prosperity. But not everyone agreed on which road was right for China.

A wide social and philosophical gulf often separated those whose enterprise was tobacco or mining from those whose venture was faith. The business community generally viewed missionaries as naive, priggish, and morally judgmental. Members of the mission societies commonly stereotyped Western business executives as affluent, morally corrupt, and unconcerned for the Chinese people. There was behavioral evidence to support both views.

In late September, the political situation in South China had calmed enough for Rob and Ria to depart by train for Shanghai and Swatow. Before reaching Tingchow, they would be carried by sedan chairs over the mountains. Their experience at a remote inland station would be much closer to the prevailing image of missionary work in China than Eric's life at a large private school in a bustling city.

At the age of twenty-four, Eric Liddell was very much the junior member of the British staff at the college. Dr. Hart, a vigorous sixty-seven, had lost his first wife in 1913. Now, this much-admired educator and missionary statesman was ten years into his second marriage and the father of two young daughters. His fertile mind, which had invented the curved front bicycle fork and patented the concept of a television-like device in 1914, was always planning and looking ahead.

At forty-three, Carl Longman had served the college since 1909. High-strung, thin, and serious, he stood a foot taller than his wife, Amy, his exact opposite in physique and personality. Perle and Rosamond, the Longman daughters, may have been the only children who didn't move aside apprehensively when their father strode swiftly down the walkway in the LMS compound.

Gerald Luxon and Roy Peill, both forty and married with children, rounded out the staff currently at the college. The youngest brother of three noted missionary doctors, Peill was pondering his future with the LMS after fifteen years in China. He could not help counting the days until he returned to England to be with his wife, son, and newborn daughter. Luxon, even though he did not possess a university degree, was a well-trained and dedicated teacher who brought world geography to life for his students.

One member of the staff was in England on furlough. A. P. Cullen, thirty-six, had taught Eric at Eltham College in 1912–13. A first-rate scholar with a droll sense of humor, Cullen was so thoroughly at home in the classics that he often talked to the family dog in Latin. He and his family were scheduled to return to China in May 1926. These British colleagues were a congenial lot, but all a generation older than Eric.

Twenty-five Chinese masters (teachers) taught most of the younger boys. Their instruction in the lower grades was predominantly in Chinese, while the older boys were taught by the British staff in English.

On a crisp September morning, Eric walked past the MacKenzie Memorial Hospital and across Taku Road to the college, where he donned the long black gown of a Master and awaited the arrival of his students. With no training as a teacher and only his knowledge of science to rely on, Eric faced the opening of school with a bit of apprehension. Even though all his instruction was in English, the level of student proficiency in the language varied widely.

Much to the pleasure and surprise of the college officials, classes opened without incident, with 350 students enrolled. Dressed in long blue cotton gowns and carrying their books wrapped in cloth, the Chinese students seemed ready and willing to learn. In light of the disturbing events of the previous months, the staff considered it a miracle to be at two-thirds of their capacity.

As the weeks progressed, Eric's humility and good will, both inside and outside the classroom, won the hearts of those around him. A young Chinese teacher at the college watched in amazement as the Olympic champion heartily congratulated a student who had just defeated him in a 100-yard dash. Instead of begrudging the student's large handicap in the race, Eric treated the lad as if they had both started from the same line.

The weeks flew by in a whirlwind of activity. Every school day until noon, Eric taught science classes, and took his turn speaking at the daily assembly for morning prayers. In the afternoon he coached sports, often participating in games with the students. One night a week he led a voluntary Bible study for half a dozen older boys. And twice a week, he met with a tutor to study the Chinese language. Even though Eric had spent his first five years in China, he had retained nothing more than a few words and phrases. It took an incredible amount of study and practice to be able to read, write, and speak Chinese, and language acquisition had always been difficult for Eric. With all the other demands on his time, he found it difficult to find the time he needed to study the language. It seemed he was always being asked to do something.

During a local production of Gilbert and Sullivan's *The Yeomen of the Guard,* with Eric's sister Jenny in the cast, he was pressed into service as prompter. When the Union Church asked him to serve as superintendent of the Sunday school and to teach a class of boys, he accepted without hesitation. And it was not long before the British Municipal Council approached Eric to help design the running track at the Min Yuan stadium being built in the British Concession. Every request came in addition to his considerable responsibilities at the college, but Eric found it impossible to say no.

It would not have been socially acceptable for him to turn down an invitation to address a diverse international audience under the auspices of the Union Church Literary and Social Guild. Even though he found the assigned topic of his own athletic career to be agonizing, he eased into it, as usual, with self-deprecating humor. He admitted to the packed house that his real motivation in addressing them lay deep in his nature as a Scot: by giving a paper before the guild, he became a member free of charge, thus saving himself the two-dollar fee.

For the missionary, the comfort and social opportunities of living in Tientsin were often outweighed by the time-sapping tasks that accompanied life in a port city. In James Liddell's report for 1925, he wrote: "Apart from regular church work, itinerancy, clerical work, one has to use up a lot of time with such things as baptisms, marriages, funerals, committees, boards of management, meeting new arrivals, care of luggage, help to people departing, interviews, letters of introduction, helping Chinese to get work, commissions from the country, obligements to other Missions and other missionaries, correspondence, special addresses, banking, visitors seeking help, etc. etc. These are some of the extras that sometimes hinder one doing the direct work one wants to do, and is here to do. And yet each case seems urgent and needful."

During the weeks just before Christmas 1925, the foreign residents of Tientsin worked, shopped, and caroled to the accompaniment of artillery. A few miles away along the Peking Road, the big guns thundered day and night as two rival warlords fought for control of the city. Panic stalked the residents of the Chinese City, and a steady stream of refugees made their way to safety in the concessions. Finally, on Christmas Eve, the fighting stopped and the guns fell silent as one army emerged victorious. The next morning, for a sparkling moment under the winter sun, there was peace on earth in one corner of China, but little sign of goodwill toward men. Rev. James Liddell ended his report for the year by saying, "One has the feeling that for China 1925 has seen events which are but the prelude of a new order. But whether for the better or the worse is still to be seen."

In April 1926, a young LMS missionary arrived in Tientsin to fill in for a few months at the college. Eric Scarlett, in his late twenties, swept in like a warm spring breeze, and after one term the school was not about to let him go. Full of enthusiasm and good humor, he joined Eric Liddell in the science department, where they developed a course in practical physics to augment the somewhat daunting and theoretical class taught by Dr. Hart. Beyond their knowledge of science and a growing bond of friendship, the two Erics shared a deep commitment to Christ and a mutual desire to reach their students with the gospel.

Like many others of his generation, the disillusionment of wartime combat in France had set Scarlett on a spiritual quest. Through fellow students at the Manchester University of Technology, he became involved in the vibrant and strongly evangelical Student Christian Movement. Then, in the summer of 1920, he had attended a summer convention at Swanick, where, as he said, "for the first time, Christianity became a way of life and ceased to be a department, and the coming of the Kingdom of God the only thing worth striving for."

Before joining the LMS, Scarlett had pioneered the work of the Student Christian Movement among technical universities in Britain. In recommending him to the London Missionary Society, one of his professors at Manchester had written: "He is very easy to work with, very cheerful and rather enjoys difficulties."

Dorothy Scarlett, an accomplished pianist, enjoyed accompanying her husband in his repertoire of comical songs. At parties and summer holiday gatherings at Peitaiho, his music and sense of humor delighted children and adults alike. With their sunny dispositions and zest for living, the Scarletts soon became favorites among the entire LMS family.

And it was a family. In the missionary community, children addressed adults not as Mr. or Mrs. Longman, but as Uncle Carl and Auntie Amy. No one thought it odd that the scholarly Reverend Augustus Pountney Cullen was always known as Uncle Rooper. The nickname had originally been given to Cullen's brother, who could not pronounce his "L's," and once described a caterpillar who "rooped the roop"; but for some reason the nickname stuck to A. P. and followed him all the way to China. Uncle Eric Liddell loved children and was always a favorite of theirs as well.

The missionary children in Tientsin lived in the security of their parents' faith, in spite of the political turbulence and civil war in China. God was not abstract, but very real and present. Family prayers were consistent and sincere, even if a bit too long to suit the children. The annual gatherings at the LMS District Committee meetings in the winter, and during the summer holidays in Peitaiho, were eagerly anticipated by all.

The summer of 1926 brought the announcement of Jenny Liddell's engagement to Frank Turner, a businessman and son of the senior Methodist missionary in Tientsin. A succession of photographs taken at Peitaiho and Tientsin show the foursome of Jenny, Frank, Eric, and Frank's sister, Dorothy, at the beach, in tennis togs, and touring in a canal boat. If Eric had a strong opinion about whether Frank was a good choice for his sister, he kept it to himself. It was his nature and his way not to tell others what to do or try to influence their decisions. A few months later, Jenny decided on her own that Frank was not the right mate for her, and the engagement was called off.

Because both Eric and Jenny were single, they were frequently invited to social functions together. There was no shortage of attractive, eligible young women in Tientsin, but Eric found no one who sparked his interest — no one he wanted to know better, no one who made him laugh freely and forget himself. No one, that is, until the MacKenzie family arrived late in that summer of 1926.

ELEVEN

The Girl in Ringlets

1926–1930

Florence, the oldest of the seven MacKenzie children, was nearly fifteen when her family returned to Tientsin after a year's furlough in Canada. She wore her dark auburn hair in long ringlets that bounced when she talked and laughed, which was most of the time. Standing 5' 6" tall yet without a hint of awkwardness, Flo possessed an air of maturity beyond her years. In a gathering of peers, however, she was very much a fun-loving schoolgirl, always popular and surrounded by friends.

Her siblings were Margaret (13), Norman (11), Esther (9), Finlay (6), Kenneth (2), and four-month-old Agnes Louise. Florence and Margaret covered the walls of their second-floor bedroom with a beautiful arrangement of pictures of flowers clipped from magazines. The artistic Margaret added a number of her own paintings to the bright collage. Each morning after breakfast, they walked with Norman, Esther, and Finlay to the nearby Tientsin Grammar School.

At school, Florence was more athletic than academic, much preferring field hockey to French. If a single word could describe her, it would have been "vibrant." Her best friend, Betty Thomson, always laughed when Flo, for no apparent reason, would jump as high as she could and shout with the sheer joy of being alive.

On an autumn evening at Union Church, James and Mary Liddell introduced Eric to Flo's parents. Hugh MacKenzie, a lanky 6' 2", gripped Eric's hand while his wife, Agnes, instinctively said, "You must come to tea." Their spacious home at 70 Cambridge

Road in the British Concession served as the North China hub for the Honan Mission of the United Church of Canada. Hugh had designed and built the house to accommodate the constant stream of their mission personnel who passed through Tientsin, traveling to and from their stations. With eight bedrooms and an attic that quickly converted into a dormitory with camp cots, the MacKenzie home could always accommodate one more unexpected visitor. In the summer, the children willingly gave up their bedrooms to guests and slept on a screened-in upper verandah. Agnes never knew for sure how many to expect for meals, but her Chinese cook always rose to the occasion. If the work of hospitality ever became a burden for Hugh and Agnes, it always remained a lark for their children. The MacKenzie kids loved the people who stayed in their home, and they had their own favorites among the Canadian missionaries.

Since 1910, Hugh had served the Honan Mission as treasurer and business manager. The family often said, with tongue in cheek, that his "call" to China came while reading a copy of the n magazine that contained two arresting items: (1) an appeal for a business manager in China, and (2) a photo of Miss Agnes Anne Hall who had been appointed to Weihwei the previous year for evangelistic work. Hugh caught the first boat to China, met Agnes in language school, and married her in 1911.

Now, from his office on Race Course Road, Hugh handled the logistics for missionaries and their families scattered from Weihwei to Shanghai. Routing of personal mail, official correspondence, shipments of household goods, dental appointments, currency exchange, and furlough transportation were only a few of the details he took care of on a daily basis. He was a walking railroad timetable for North China, and most of the time he could maneuver deftly around the recurring snarls caused by weather, politics, and war.

Agnes, in her element as hostess of the mission house, supervised a staff of eight servants. She kept the door open to all, lamenting only those of the mission who could not understand why they should pay a small fee for their room and board. Strong-willed and persevering, Agnes could rarely be deflected from a goal until she had accomplished it. As one of her children said, "If mother thought it was right, then it was God's will."

With nine family members and eight Chinese servants, it would have seemed like a full house at the MacKenzies' without any visitors. But there were always visitors, and not just those of their own mission. Young soldiers from the British detachment in Tientsin often came for supper and a game of tennis on the court in the back garden. The fact that two attractive teenage girls lived there was an added draw. It was quite natural for visitors of all kinds to walk unannounced into the friendly home on Cambridge Road.

Eric and Florence first met at the Union Church Sunday school, where he served as superintendent and she played the piano. Very casually and quite naturally, they got to know each other at church, although initially there seems to have been no special attraction between them. Eric hardly had time to shine his shoes, much less ponder romantic possibilities with a girl ten years his junior.

Early in 1927, anti-foreign feeling once again erupted in China, accompanied by a wave of general lawlessness that swept the country. Rob, Ria, and their infant daughter, Peggy, fled Tingchow-fu in a small boat that shot the river rapids to carry them to safety. Just after their escape, marauding bandits destroyed the entire mission property. Villagers in the path of Chiang Kai-shek's Nationalist Army grew more apprehensive as the army began marching northward with the avowed purpose of taking Peking and establishing control.

In early April, acting on a decree from the British and American consular authorities, missionaries throughout North China, including the city of Peking, left their stations and came to live with families of their respective missions in Tientsin. The sudden assembly of people was initially a great reunion, but it soon lengthened into a stressful time. In overcrowded houses, with sick children and dwindling supplies, tempers sometimes became short. Displaced guests as well as their overtaxed hosts missed the usual privacy and sanctuary of home. After two months, the LMS officials sent most of their evacuated missionaries to Peitaiho until they could reoccupy their stations.

Everything in China played out against this backdrop of ongoing civil war, political intrigue, and constant change. While the foreign concessions were relatively safe, everyone knew that the small garrison of troops would not be able to protect them should there be a cataclysmic turn of events.

A. P. Cullen said of those months in 1927: "... the danger passed almost as rapidly as it arose... and the civil war once more resumed its accustomed character of bewildering changes, dishonoured loyalties and indeterminate conflicts, the issue being as far off from solution as ever. The only constant features are the appalling suffering inflicted on the innocent and sorely-tried [Chinese] civilian population, the severing of communications with the resultant famine and utter dislocation of trade in the interior, the unblushing reign of lawlessness in every conceivable form, and the devastating ambition, extortion and corruption of those who are in power. It is the darkest hour of China's long history, and as yet no glimmer of light heralds an approaching dawn."

On May 5, James Liddell wrote to Francis Hawkins, the new LMS Foreign Secretary in London: "We have Rob and his wife with us at present, as he was asked to come and help. He is a bit run down and troubled with small boils in the ear. Perhaps it is that since he arrived [in China] he has had rather trying experiences, and with little time to get at the language he has been rather overwhelmed. Probably you may have heard from him direct. The rest of us are doing quite well, and my wife has recovered considerably, although not yet quite her old self. Eric has done quite a lot in the athletic line, apart from regular work and study, with many etceteras thrown in."

This was James' optimistic and understated way of describing the situation. Rob and Ria were physically and emotionally exhausted after an extremely stressful eighteen months at Tingchow, and their future assignment was uncertain. Mary Liddell had suffered from serious physical ailments for six months of the previous year. After extensive and expensive treatment at Peking Union Medical Hospital, she was better but not completely healthy. And Eric, with all his energy and dedication, was spread extremely thin. Between his work at the college, responsibilities at Union Church, and his involvement in the larger international community, his days and nights overflowed with activity.

Although people in Britain considered Eric's running career over, he continued to be actively involved in sporting events in China. In addition to anchoring the college relay team in local and international meets, he competed against athletes from the various military forces stationed in Tientsin and Peking. In 1927, he broke the Far Eastern records in the 100, 200, and 400 meters, with two British soldiers trailing him in each race.

As the 1928 Olympics neared, some sportswriters wondered why Liddell was not being considered for the British team. The times he posted on rough tracks in China were remarkably close to the qualifying times of athletes in England and America, and he was still the reigning champion at 400 meters. But Eric made no overtures to the Olympic officials, and they seemed to think that he was either uninterested or unavailable.

As the Olympic games were unfolding in Amsterdam, Eric's thoughts were becoming more focused on something else entirely — Florence MacKenzie.

During his four-week summer holiday at Peitaiho, the usual group activities of swimming, tennis, and hikes to the nearby Lotus Hills gave him a natural chance to be in her company. The same missionary culture that made it virtually impossible for the two of them to be alone together provided daily opportunities to be in the same place at the same time. Moonlight sing-alongs beside a bonfire at Rocky Point became more interesting than ever.

When summer ended, Eric continued his deliberate efforts to be near Florence. On the one day a week when Flo came to the Liddell home for a piano lesson from Jenny, Eric managed to be there for tea. If he wanted to take her to Kiessling's for ice cream, he simply invited her brothers and sisters to come along. For the most part, his efforts were so subtle and fumbling that no one, including Florence, had any idea he was courting her. Her younger brother, Norman, was convinced that Eric came to their house to see him.

In October 1928, Eric traveled to Dairen for a track meet during the South Manchurian Railway Celebration of the Coronation of the Emperor of Japan. A capacity crowd of 55,000 witnessed the three days of competition. In describing the event to a reporter, Eric said simply, "The Japanese and French Olympic Teams were there, with their Olympic laurels, fresh from Amsterdam, and it happened, somehow, that I won the 200 and 400 metres."

But it was Eric's mad dash after the race and not his times on the track that became the stuff of legend. After winning the 400-meter race, he had only fifteen minutes to make his boat some five miles away. With a taxi waiting, he stood at attention as the band played "God Save the King" to honor his victory. Just as he was about to dash for the cab, the band struck up "La Marseillaise" for the Frenchman who had come in second. Again, Eric stood still for the anthem. By the time the taxi screeched to a stop at the pier, the boat had already cast off and was slipping away. Eric grabbed his bags and dodged the obstacles along the pier, running in pursuit of his only hope for a timely return to Tientsin. When a gust of wind and a swelling wave pushed the boat closer to the pier, Eric threw his bags aboard then made a running leap for the deck. A reporter who witnessed the event claimed that Liddell cleared at least fifteen feet over water to land safely on the boat. By the time his account had been published in newspapers in the Far East and Britain, the distance had grown until it appeared that Liddell had set a world's record in the long jump. Eric himself said it was just a small leap and that he had done it by imagining that he was a gazelle. His only goal was getting back in time to teach his classes at the college. Or perhaps to see Florence at church.

Nearing her seventeenth birthday, Flo was teaching a Sunday school class of younger girls who invariably giggled when Eric popped in just to see if she needed anything. At picnics, parties, and winter outings, Eric sensed his admiration growing as he watched her with the younger children. They seemed to trust her, while she, in turn, cared for them with creativity and fun, never scolding.

Florence, like most of the other girls, thought the world of Eric. She admired his gentle spirit, his kindness to everyone, and the respectful way he talked to even the youngest children. He was serious about God but never about himself. When he teased or played a practical joke, it was always with a smile and a twinkle in his eye, never intended to embarrass or demean. But even though Flo might have heaved a teenage sigh over his sparkling blue eyes and dimpled chin, the thought of Eric being romantically interested in her was so preposterous that it never crossed her mind.

One Sunday morning during Eric's brief Bible lesson for the younger children, he focused on the word "sincere." "What does it mean?" he asked. "Well, it means genuine, honest, and free from hypocrisy — the real thing. And it comes from two Latin words: sine — without, and sere — wax. Without wax? What's that got to do with anything? Well, I'll tell you.

"Many years ago in the time of the Roman Empire marble was a very popular, beautiful stone. Large slabs were cut out of the ground and skilled craftsmen shaped them into pillars, statues, vases and many beautiful things. Sometimes if the marble was of inferior quality it would develop a crack and consequently became of little value.

"To avoid losing income, some unscrupulous craftsmen would fill the crack with wax, smooth it off, then polish the surface to a high gloss and pass it off as an unblemished piece. Unfortunately, at a later date, the wax would shrink and split and the unfortunate purchaser would realize that he had a worthless piece of marble on his hands.

"Buyers eventually got wise to the fraud, and when purchasing anything made of marble, they demanded assurance that the product was the real thing, namely pure marble without hidden flaws or imperfections filled with wax. The real thing: sine — without; sere — wax. From this we get our English word 'sincere' — being in reality as it is in appearance — real — honest.

"Now then, boys and girls, what about you?

"Are you the real thing? Or do you have some flaws or cracks that you think you have successfully hidden from others?"

It was only a simple story, but Flo couldn't forget it. Nor could she forget the man behind it. If there ever was a "sincere" man, it was Eric Liddell. She had never heard anyone say a word against him.

The passing months also gave Eric a chance to observe Flo. Her reactions to the unexpected revealed the person she was, and despite her youth and immaturity, he saw a young lady he wanted to know much better. At Sunday school parties he found himself thinking less about the logistics of the gathering and more about Flo's peaches and cream complexion and her large, dark hazel eyes.

But beyond her physical attractiveness, he was drawn by her zest for living. She seemed so naturally outgoing and free with people, in contrast to his own quiet nature. After a Sunday school drama in which she played a very ordinary part with a great deal of passion, Eric said to her: "Florence, I didn't realize you had that much fire." She blushed and thanked him, and there was an imperceptible exchange of something more between them.

To Eric, the whole idea of being in love with stern Hugh MacKenzie's daughter was so impossible that it could only exist in the deep places of his heart, where no one but God could know his feelings. The ten years' difference between them loomed large. In time, the gap would seem much less, but it would be years, not days or months, before a deeper relationship between them could exist openly. Still, a settled conviction began to grow in Eric that this was the girl he would marry. And no matter how many years it took, he would leave Flo in God's hands and wait. In the meantime, there was certainly enough to keep him occupied.

Every weekday morning, Eric walked the short distance from the Liddell home, past the MacKenzie Memorial Hospital, then deftly weaved his way through the steady stream of traffic to cross Taku Road. Automobiles, bicycles, produce carts pulled by mules or coolies, and motor buses with tooting horns competed for space along the bustling thoroughfare. The names of other roads changed as they passed into each foreign concession. Rue de France became Victoria Road and then Woodrow Wilson Street. But Taku Road remained the same for its thirty-five-mile length from Tientsin to the port of Taku on the Bohai Sea.

Pausing outside the main gate of the college, Eric watched the boys arriving for school by every means of conveyance, from rickshaws and bicycles to black limousines. Some went purposefully into the school while others lingered outside, purchasing steaming *jiaozis* — the native dumplings — or the sizzling fritters called *jianbing guozi* from a sidewalk vendor.

As he walked across the school quadrangle, a flock of crows cawed a morning greeting from their customary perch in a tall tree. Eric glanced up at the birds and recalled a saying he had heard: "Crows are black the world over." A crow in China was no different from one in Scotland. And the same was true of people. Minds, hearts, and empty places in the soul were the same regardless of nationality, location, or language.

Now into his fourth academic year, Eric felt positive about the Anglo-Chinese College and its philosophy of integrating education and evangelism. The gospel was not tacked on as an appendage, but embodied in everything that happened throughout the day. Dr. Hart considered the classroom and the sports field just as important as morning prayers, the only religious instruction that involved all students. Chinese masters conducted the short service in the native language for the younger boys while Dr. Hart presided in English for those in the upper school. The singing of a hymn was followed by the reading of Scripture and a five-to-ten-minute meditation given by the principal or one of the British teachers.

Eric and each of his British counterparts served as tutor to a particular class, usually for the three years prior to its graduation. Each tutor monitored his class's academic progress, led a voluntary Bible circle once a week, and organized occasional social functions to get to know his boys better. The concept held great potential and often led to deep spiritual change in the students. But it was difficult, at best, to establish casual relationships with the boys while maintaining discipline and the traditional distance between student and teacher.

Results, academically and spiritually, came slowly and with increasing challenges. Less than fifty percent of the students attended the college for more than three years. Each term brought increasing pressure from the Chinese Bureau of Education to conform to their standards. And financial need stalked the school like a heartless landlord threatening to foreclose.

Even within the London Missionary Society itself, critics of the Anglo-Chinese College questioned both its basic premise and the allocation of resources. "The Chinese will educate themselves," said one vocal opponent. "We must go for their souls." Even though the only direct expense to the LMS was the salaries of the five British missionaries, each year there was a call to reduce the number of college staff in order to send a man to rural areas where the need was so great.

At the beginning of 1929, Eric faced a decision about his future. June would mark the completion of his four-year commitment to the Anglo-Chinese College. He had considered returning to Britain with his parents in June, getting further training, then applying to come back to China under the LMS. But by the end of January, with the announcement of Dr. Hart's imminent retirement, Eric had decided to stay at the college through the summer of 1930.

Then, the unexpected changed the situation for the Liddell family again. Early in February of 1929, James Liddell traveled south by rail to Tsangchow for the annual LMS District Committee meetings. Two days later, Mary was shocked to see Dr. Arnold Bryson helping her husband up the front steps of their house in Tientsin. James had suffered a slight stroke, momentarily losing the use of his arm and the ability to speak. Although he was now feeling fine, his colleagues had decided he must return home and rest.

At the age of fifty-eight, James had always been vigorous and healthy, the person others looked to for help in an emergency. During thirty years of service in China, he had missed only ten days of work due to illness, all of it during a spell of stomach flu the previous autumn. Now, however, the doctors told him he should return to Scotland as soon as possible for an extended period of rest. They did not want him to wait until his scheduled furlough in June.

On March 29, Eric accompanied his family to Taku, where his parents, along with Jenny and Ernest, boarded the SS *Sarbrucken* for the eight-week voyage to Rotterdam. Rob had come from Siaochang, where he was now superintendent of the LMS hospital, to say good-bye and help with storing the family goods. James and Mary hoped to see Eric in Scotland in a year, and planned on returning to China themselves when James' condition had improved.

After their departure, Eric moved from the family house into a flat at the college. He had enjoyed the wonderful four years together with his family, and ached at seeing his father leave under a cloud of weakness. They all would have grieved more if they had known that the four who had just sailed would never see China again.

July 1929 marked the first time in four years that the Anglo-Chinese College had not closed early and postponed examinations because of student unrest or the threat of war. The brief lull, abnormal as it seemed, came as a welcome relief after the constant tension of the previous years.

At Peitaiho that summer, Eric became a bit bolder in his pursuit of Florence. After enjoying group activities together during the day, he often turned up after tea on the front porch of the MacKenzie bungalow to ask if Flo would like to go for a walk. During their twilight strolls on the beach, they talked about everything imaginable, and Eric found himself more relaxed and free than he had ever been with anyone. He longed to hold her hand or slip his arm around her waist, but it was not yet time.

On one outing, Eric and Florence joined eight others on a four-day trek into the mountains. Rob Liddell and his brother-in-law, Dr. John Wright, had the group well covered medically. Flo's sister Margaret, her brother Norman, the newly married Howard and Joyce Cook, and two family friends rounded out the party. Their goal was the summit of Pei Niu Ting, where there was an old Buddhist shrine whose priest had not descended for many years. With nine donkeys to ride and one to carry the bedding and supplies, they took turns walking up the dry streambeds and along steep mountain tracks.

During one lunch break while all lay exhausted in the shade, someone asked, "Where's Eric?" One of the girls spotted him on top of a nearby peak. He had used the break to explore a new vista while the others were content to have a nap. It was easy to forget that under his quiet, relaxed exterior there still lay tremendous resources of strength and endurance.

In August, the two Erics — Liddell and Scarlett — teamed up to lead a camp at Peitaiho for poor boys from Tientsin. Thirty-four boys, all but two of them Russians, were sent by the Rotary Club. For a fortnight, the team of Liddell and Scarlett led the boys in fun-filled activities, fed them with nourishing food, and slept with them in large tents. At meals they offered thanks to God, and before the lads fell asleep at night, there was always a prayer to end the day. Whether or not the boys understood what their British hosts said, there was no doubt about their smiles and sincere interest in each of them.

It took two alert and energetic young men to stay a step ahead of the boys who were street-smart and given to saying exactly what they thought. Scarlett remarked: "The language problem was quite interesting, and coping with bursts of anti-Semitism quite exciting. The lads went back looking very fit, and weighing on the average four pounds more per boy. We thoroughly enjoyed it. This Camp is liable to happen again."

By the time Florence MacKenzie celebrated her eighteenth birthday on November 25, 1929, she was becoming anxious about her future. She had always wanted to be a nurse, but knew that entrance to the training school in Canada was very competitive. In a few weeks she would take her final exams at the Tientsin Grammar School and was afraid she would not do well. Eric couldn't help her with French, but he was coming over two nights a week, ostensibly to coach her in mathematics.

One night in late November Flo seemed particularly discouraged, so Eric suddenly closed the math book and said, "Come on, let's get out in the fresh air and go for a walk." For a while, they strolled and talked about what lay ahead for Flo even beyond nurse's training. Did she have any desire to come back to China?

Then, out of the blue, Eric said: "What I've really been hoping for a long time is that you'll come back here and marry me."

Flo was stunned. "What did you say?"

Eric repeated himself.

"I can't believe what I'm hearing," she said. "Are you sure?"

"Absolutely," Eric replied. "What about you?"

Flo could only stammer something about worshiping the ground he walked on and being afraid of what people would say about him robbing the cradle for a bride. Then she stopped in mid-sentence and looked in his eyes: "But, Eric, I do love you desperately... and if you're sure... ."

"Does that mean yes?" he asked.

"Yes, yes, of course," she almost shouted. "I'm so happy I can't even breathe."

With a gentle and very tentative kiss they sealed their commitment to each other. It would have to remain their secret until Eric could speak to her father and they could officially announce their engagement, but both knew that the most incredible thing on earth had happened to them. They were both hopelessly and fearlessly in love with the most wonderful person they knew.

Near the end of March 1930, Eric submitted his application to join the London Missionary Society, also requesting a two-year furlough beginning in July to study at the Scottish Congregational College. He then planned to rejoin the staff of the Anglo-Chinese College. Eric had also written to his sister, Jenny, in Scotland asking her to buy an engagement ring and send it out with friends. He and Florence planned an official announcement after it arrived.

Florence hoped to enter nurse's training in Toronto, and at the end of her three-year course, they would marry. Hugh MacKenzie's permission to wed his daughter had come with the stipulation that Flo must complete her training before the wedding. The time of waiting seemed forever, but at least they had definite plans.

On the morning of April 2, A. P. Cullen and Eric Scarlett boarded a train for Peitaiho with the enviable assignment of checking the LMS cottages to make sure they were in good condition for the summer. Late that afternoon, as they covered the five miles by donkey from the railway station to the seaside town, three young men stepped out of the bushes and blocked their path. When Cullen requested in Chinese that they be allowed to pass, the three men produced pistols and demanded money. As Cullen tried to reason with one of them, he heard a shot behind him and turned to see Scarlett fall from his saddle.

Everything after that was a blur. Panicked, one man pulled Cullen to the ground, took the money from his wallet, and ripped his gold watch and chain from his waistcoat pocket. The other two tore open his suitcase and briefcase, scattering the contents on the road. As the bandits urged each other to be quick about their business, another shot was fired and Cullen felt the bullet whiz past his face. Then the men were gone.

Cullen rushed over to Scarlett, who was lying unconscious on his back, his face ashen and a deep red flow pouring from a bullet wound just above his heart. At first there was a feeble pulse, then no heartbeat at all. Cullen sent the donkey boys to the village for help, then sat down in utter desolation as a curious but unfeeling crowd lured by the sound of gunshots gathered around. Late that night he cabled the devastating news to Tientsin.

On Friday afternoon, Eric Liddell and Hugh MacKenzie were among those of the missionary community who met the train bearing Scarlett's body back to Tientsin. The next day, after a funeral conducted entirely in Chinese at the Taku Road Church, Eric helped carry the coffin of his friend and colleague to the Canton Road Cemetery. Cullen found the strength to conduct the graveside service, and in the midst of all their "Whys?" he focused on the triumph of a life lived fully for Christ.

Eric responded swiftly after the tragedy, and on April 10 sent a letter to Mr. Hawkins, the LMS Foreign Secretary, saying: "Since I last wrote you a good deal has happened so that my plans have had to be altered. The death of Mr. Scarlett means that it would place

CHINA: 1902-1907

Eric's parents, the Rev. James (J. D.) and Mary Liddell (above), were married October 23, 1899, at Shanghai Cathedral.

Eric's father helped oversee the building of these three missionary homes at Siaochang in 1902.

Rev. J. D. Liddell, Mary, Rob (standing), and Eric in Tientsin, 1902.

Eric in typical baby fashion of the day, 1903.

At Siaochang, the Liddell children were never far from the watchful eye of their amah.

CHINA: 1902-1907

Bundled for winter at Siaochang, 1906
(left to right, Rob, Eric, Jenny, Mary).

Ten days on the Grand Canal then 40 miles overland by cart brought the Liddell family to Siaochang in November 1902.

Cart travel was always unpredictable on the North China Plain. *Photo: Council for World Mission.*

The church in the London Missionary Society compound. Siaochang, North China, 1904.

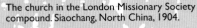

J.D. Liddell took the gospel to villagers in North China.

SCOTLAND: 1907-1908

Siaochang, 1905. J. D. Liddell urges Jenny, 2, to walk toward the camera. Mary standing, left, Eric and Rob appear front and center, left to right.

Eric, Jenny, and Rob, left to right, together in Scotland, 1908.

In 1908, James Liddell returned alone to China while Mary and Jenny stayed to help the boys settle into boarding school.

Happy days on furlough in Scotland soon gave way to the pain of separation.

ELTHAM COLLEGE: 1908-1920

Rob at left, Eric at right, 1908.

Rob and Eric, 1909.

Mary Liddell desperately missed her boys as they grew up without her.

1911, Rob, right, Eric, left.

1918

ELTHAM COLLEGE: 1908-1920

The School for the Sons of
Missionaries, Blackheath.
"The Old Barn."

Eric, second from left, spending
the Easter holiday in quarantine
following the ringworm epidemic
of 1916. *Photo: Arthur Green.*

"Rolling the pitch" at Eltham College.
Photo: Arthur Green.

Jenny and Ernest grew
up in China while their
brothers attended school
in England.

ELTHAM COLLEGE: 1908-1920

Rob, right, loved being in the Eltham College Cadet Corps while Eric, above, tolerated it.

Both Liddells excelled in sports. Rob, captain of the 1917 rugby squad, center, holding ball. Eric, back row, second from left.

In 1918, Eric received the Blackheath Cup as the best all-round sportsman at Eltham College.

EDINBURGH UNIVERSITY: 1921-1924

This 1922 photo shows Eric, second from left, at Craiglockhart —
scene of his university running debut in May 1921.

Above, Eric, second from left, on a bicycle
trip to Ben Nevis, 1921.

Right, by 1923 Eric Liddell was the
most famous athlete in Scotland.
Photo: John Keddie.

Eric, back row, second from right, played seven matches with the Scottish
International Rugby team. Captain A. L. Gracie, holding ball, Ted McLaren, back
row, second from left. *Photo: The Scottish Rugby Union Library and Archives, 1923.*

EDINBURGH UNIVERSITY: 1921-1924

Eric, back row far left, at the Masquerade Ball aboard the SS *Republic* returning from America, May, 1924. *Photo: Sir Arthur Marshall.*

"I run the first half of the race as fast as I can, and then with God's help, I run the second half even faster."

Eric with trainer Tom McKerchar.
Photo: John Keddie.

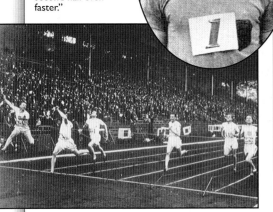

Eric dashed to a bronze in the 200 meters in Paris ...
Photo: John Keddie.

... then shocked the athletic world by striking gold in the 400. Horatio Fitch, USA, silver medalist, right. *Photo: John Keddie.*

400-meter final, Paris, July 11, 1924. *Photo: Corbis.*

Carried from McEwan Hall following University of Edinburgh graduation, July 17, 1924.

D. P. Thomson, Eric's friend and colleague in the Glasgow Students' Evangelistic Union.

Dr. Lavington Hart, founder of the TACC, was a brilliant physicist and educator.

Background:
The Tientsin Anglo-Chinese College towers above *Rue de Pasteur*.

CHINA: 1925-1942

"Lemonade, anyone?" Eric asks at a Union Church Sunday school picnic *Photo: Luby Bubeshko Shutorev.*

The Anglo-Chinese College chemistry lab.

The TACC relay team was hard to beat with Eric Liddell as coach and anchor man. *Photo: Perle Longman.*

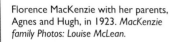
Florence MacKenzie with her parents, Agnes and Hugh, in 1923. *MacKenzie family Photos: Louise McLean.*

Flo, holding sister Louise, was barely 15 when she met Eric in 1926.

CHINA: 1925-1942

Engaged, Tientsin, June 1930.

Toronto, 1932.

J. Gunn, Supt.

H. Locke, Asst. Supt.

F. MacKenzie, School of Nursing, 1933.

Photos: Toronto Hospital archives.

Eric and Flo's wedding was front page news in the *Peking* and *Tientsin Times*, March 27, 1934.

With Patricia at Peitaiho, 1936.

A rare day together, summer, 1937.

CHINA: 1925-1942

L.M.S. missionaries at 1933 North China District Committee meeting. Seated, left to right: Mr. Harold Bate, Mrs. Bate, Edith Owers, Jeana Turner, Gladys Stickland, Mrs. Bryant, Mrs. Rees, Mrs. Busby, Mr. Charles Busby, Mr. Evan Bryant, Ethel Livens, Carol Lenwood, Mrs. Meg Rowlands, Mrs. Minnie Thompson.

Row 2: left to right: Eric Liddell, Dr. Rob Liddell, Ernest S. Box, Mrs. Box, Nancy Edmunson, Mrs. Miriam Milledge, Myfanwy Wood, Janet Evans, Annie Buchan, Mrs. George Luxon, Ivy Greaves, Margery Brameld, Mrs. Jean Cullen, Mrs. Amy Longman, Carl Longman.

Row 3: left to right: Dr. Geoff Milledge, Dr. George Dorling, Alec Baxter, A. H. Jowett-Murray, Mrs. Jowett-Murray, Marjorie Clements, unidentified, Mrs. Ria Liddell, Mrs. Margaret Wright, Dr. John Wright, Arnold Bryson, Mr. Robert Thompson, George Luxon, Will Rowlands, unidentified.

CHINA: 1925-1942

After a harrowing ten-day journey, Rob and Eric reached Siaochang during wartime in December 1937.

Carcant, Scotland, 1940. A golden summer together.

Guard towers, searchlights, electrified barbed wire and machine guns guarded the walls of Weihsien Camp.

A. P. Cullen, Eric's colleague and fellow internee in China. *Photo: Rowena Williams.*

Left, with cameras prohibited during internment, artists recorded their impressions of Weihsien Camp. *Painting by F. Verhoeven, photo: Joe Cotterill.*

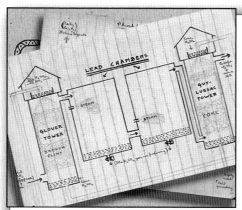

By hand, Eric created a text to teach chemistry without a lab in Weihsien. *Photo: Joyce Stranks Ditmanson.*

Camp life included concerts and programs presented by the internees. *Artwork courtesy of Peter Bazire.*

Shadyside Hospital seen from outside the camp.

American B-29 drops supplies over Weihsien after liberation.

The Salvation Army Band poses for a photograph, August 1945. *Weihsien photos courtesy of Joe Cotterill.*

Heather, left, and Patricia with Flo, holding baby Maureen in Toronto, November 1941.

The children in Weihsien Camp knew him as "Uncle Eric."

Localité-Locality-Ortschaft WEIHSIEN

Province-County-Provinc SHANTUNG

Pays-Country-Land CHINA

Message à transmettre—Mitteilung—Message
(25 mots au maximum, nouvelles de caractère strictement personnel)
(nicht über 25 Worte, nur persönliche Familiennachrichten)—(not 25
family news of strictly personal character).

SIMPLE HAPPY LIFE UNDER PRIMITIVE
CONDITIONS. LIVING WITH JOAN AND BEAN
IN SMALL ROOM. GOOD FELLOWSHIP, GOOD
GAMES. TEACHING IN SCHOOL. GOOD
SUFFICIENT. BOUNDLESS LOVE.
XAMINED BY C. B/

Date-Datum APRIL 18th 1943.

Eric's communication with his family during internment was limited to 25-word Red Cross messages.

The Eric Liddell memorial stone at the Second Middle School of Weifang (Weihsien). *Photo: David Michell.*

the College in a very difficult place were I to go home this year. I have told them that I will wait another year if it will help them out. Would you please cancel any arrangement for deputation that you have made for me. I am sorry to do this, especially as Dad is none too well, but I am sure I am right. Excuse this short note but I wanted to let you know my decision at an early date."

Ten days later the Anglo-Chinese College decided to proceed with the annual baptismal service that included nine young men from Scarlett's class. A letter from Eric to friends said: "This Easter Service, and the seeing of all these students taking their allegiance to our Saviour, was like a ray of light penetrating the darkness of the days we had passed through."

During the next term, Eric taught several of Scarlett's science classes as well as filling in for six weeks as military chaplain to men in the Royal Scots Regiment stationed in Tientsin. "The experience was good for me," he wrote to friends in Britain, "even though it kept me busy from morn till night. I felt during that time that I didn't get enough time for quiet and prayer. Work is prayer, and prayer is work, they say, that is quite true but one needs times of quiet just to be alone with God. However busy one is about His work it cannot make up for the quiet times."

Quite matter-of-factly, he continued in the letter: "On May 18th, there was a large gathering at Mr. and Mrs. MacKenzie's house. There were about forty people present, mostly from the L.M.S. and the United Church of Canada. Just after tea had been served Mr. MacKenzie announced the engagement of their eldest daughter, Florence — to ME. It was a very happy day indeed. After the announcement we adjourned to the tennis court where we watched and participated in several sets. Florence and I had to play one of the sets and we fortunately won. I think the other side must have arranged it like that as they thought we ought to win."

Of his change in plans, he wrote: "I will not say that I will be back next year for I have already said that twice before and both times I've been delayed, but my hope is that a Science teacher will be found and that I will be able to return on furlough next August."

A month after the engagement party, Flo and her sister Margaret traveled with the Ross family to England via the Trans-Siberian Railway. After a look at the sights and a visit with the Liddell family in Scotland, they sailed for Canada.

When school closed for the summer, Eric stayed at the college to study Chinese and managed to pass his exam in Peitaiho at the end of July. After only a week to relax, he left the summer colony to lead another Rotary Club boys' camp. His own description of the event reveals the set of his heart:

"I arrived in Tientsin that night [August 7] and next morning took the boys off to camp at Wo Fo Ssu (The Temple of the Sleeping Buddha). It was a real international camp composed of about sixty boys, Chinese, Russian, American, two Japanese, Jewish, and maybe others. Wo Fo Ssu is on the slope of the hills just outside (10 Miles) Peking. It lends itself to a camp like this, because of the number of interesting places round about. There were hill climbs, the Summer Palace (the place where the Empress Dowager used to live), the Black Dragon Pool, the Hot Sulphur Springs, the old burial place of Sun Yat Sen and many other things. The boys had plenty to do all the time. Although it was not a Christian camp I was allowed to have evening prayers each night. I had a reading then a short talk and closed with prayer. In this way and also by personal work among the boys in which Mr. Hibbard helped considerably we were able to get our message across. The Rotary Club stands for Service and that was a good starting point. We divided the camp into teams, mixing the different nationalities as best we could and before the end we had a fine team spirit. This experimental camp was well worth while.

"On August 19th they all returned while Mr. Band and I stayed on another day to get all the equipment sent back.

"The summer holiday is now drawing to a close. I have not been able to answer any letters you may have sent but you can see that there has not been over much time & I hope you will forgive me if I make this dc [a circular] instead of an individual letter.

"I am well and ready for a new terms work.

Yours in His Service, Eric H. Liddell"

At the time of writing, Eric did not know that the LMS Medical Council had declared his father "permanently unfit to go back" to China. With deep regret, Rev. J. D. Liddell wrote to the Foreign Secretary, resigning from the London Missionary Society. After stating his disappointment at being unable to return to China for another term of service, he concluded his letter with a characteristic expression of thankfulness and good will: "Let me say how much we have enjoyed our years of work, and how much we have appreciated the sympathy and very kind manner in which our Society has dealt with us through you yourself, and others of the Mission House staff. We have never felt that we were other than brethren, and part of a great company, in fellowship with a mighty spiritual power. We expect to continue in this fellowship and do all we can to extend the Kingdom; and the interests of our Society will always have a first call on our time and strength."

When Rob and Eric received the news, it was their sad duty to sort through their parents' belongings, sell the furniture, and ship the boxes of personal items to Scotland for the last time.

❦ TWELVE ❦

A Year and a Thousand Days

1930–1934

As the summer of 1930 drew to a close, it appeared that Florence's age and education might keep her from being admitted to nurse's training at Toronto General Hospital. She was still three months short of her nineteenth birthday, the minimum age for applying. In addition, her academic work at the Tientsin Grammar School did not meet the Canadian standards for matriculation, and she had not taken Latin. However, a sympathetic letter from the registrar noted that even though Flo was educated in China, she had "a general education equivalent to a four-year high school course in Ontario." The letter concluded: "I think I would be disposed to recommend her admission to the School for Nurses if your regulations allow."

If anyone but Helen Locke had received that letter, the outcome could have been very different. But Miss Locke's job as Assistant Superintendent of the School for Nurses gave her the authority to act in the spirit of the law, rather than being bound by the letter. That was precisely why Superintendent Jean I. Gunn had chosen Helen to be her assistant. Miss Gunn's role was to establish and maintain authority, which she did very well. Locke was there to help and encourage the students. Together they were known as Gunn and Locke, "Justice and Mercy," a powerful and compassionate team.

On November 18, Florence began a rigorous three-year course that included nearly 700 hours of classroom instruction in subjects ranging from the Theory and Practice of Nursing to Nervous and Mental Diseases. Her preliminary term was the equivalent of a four-month medical boot camp designed to prepare student nurses to work in the hospital wards, as well as to weed out the unfit and the unwilling. The Calendar of the School for Nurses clearly stated: "This period affords an opportunity of testing the aptitude, physical endurance, application and general fitness of the applicant. It also enables the student to make an intelligent decision in regard to continuing the work."

Once past the initial 120 days, Flo was accepted as a probationer and her real test began. Student nurses spent 58 hours a week in class and at work in the wards of the sprawling 862-bed Toronto General. "The student has two hours off duty daily for recreation and study, one half day per week, and four hours on Sunday," the Calendar continued. "Eight weeks vacation are allowed during the three years." In addition, student nurses were required to make up every day missed because of illness.

Each morning, Flo and the seventy members of her class arose at 5:45 and were expected to be at compulsory morning prayers at 5:55. Breakfast began at 6:30, and from then until lights out at 10:00 at night, there was hardly time to breathe. Students paid no fees for tuition, textbooks, room, board, and laundry, but they earned their education by working in the hospital, where they provided most of the patient care. When Flo began her training there were 315 nurses-in-training on duty at Toronto General and its nearby affiliated hospitals.

In addition to providing direct care to patients and assisting doctors in their duties, student nurses were required to maintain the wards and equipment. This included daily washing of each patient's bed, nightstand, and chair, changing bedding, scrubbing floors, and sterilizing the many medical appliances in a time before disposable equipment. Rubber gloves had to be soaked in a disinfectant solution for twenty minutes, washed, rinsed with hot and cold water, then dropped into boiling water for three minutes. Some student nurses considered themselves little more than charwomen or indentured servants.

Their never-ending, menial tasks sparked this poetic lament:

"A Probationer stood in a ward one day
With a brush in hand and a basin tray.
Her task — beds, tables and chairs to scrub,
And anything else that needed a rub.
'How long will it last?' was the maiden's cry —
'I'll be tired out long ere the day goes by.
Is there never an end to the cleaning that's done?
Must I still do this when my cap I've won?'"

After what seemed endless weeks of being on her feet for twelve hours a day, Flo was taking massive doses of aspirin to ease the throbbing pain in her legs, gulping mugs of strong black coffee to stay awake on night duty, and slipping outside for a forbidden cigarette to soothe her jangled nerves. She knew her parents would be appalled, but it was a way of survival for student nurses. Most of all, she was counting the days until she saw Eric, and praying that his furlough would not be delayed again.

While Flo became proficient with bedpans and bandages, Eric poured himself into life at the Anglo-Chinese College. When school opened in September 1930, he was asked to join the school soccer team as a player/coach. "We have a long way to go yet before we get that spirit into our games that I should like," he said of the situation. But instead of giving lectures on sportsmanship, he much preferred to play alongside the boys, sharing the ups and downs of every game. On a rough rectangle of dirt that bore scant resemblance to a proper soccer pitch in England, he ran and kicked and smiled his way into their confidence. Over time, the boys caught the lessons that could not be taught in the classroom. Eric himself noted the change: "They are learning to put more into a losing game, and also to take the referee's decision in a better spirit" he wrote as the season progressed.

At the opening of the autumn term Eric also became the tutor or advisor of a class of boys in their mid-teens, whom he would guide academically, morally, and spiritually until their graduation. These boys offered a particular challenge because their previous tutor, one of the Chinese teachers, had not been a Christian, and they had done no Bible study during the past two years. They knew nothing of the Old Testament and had heard the Bible read only at morning prayers in the college. When Eric began a voluntary Bible class for these students, he was starting from scratch.

One afternoon a week, nineteen of the forty-three boys came regularly to Eric's flat to study the life of Jesus and the stories of the Old Testament. Several of them, he felt, demonstrated a genuine desire to know the truth. In assessing the value of the Bible classes, Eric said, "We do not have many conversions at this stage, it is usually when a boy has been in a Bible class for two or three years that he is willing to come forward and accept Christ as his Lord and Master. I believe in conversion and also sudden conversion where the Spirit of God so fills a person that he can tell at once what has happened, but I believe that with the appalling ignorance here and the absolute lack of spiritual ideas that a slow reasoned acceptance of Christ is better."

As a means of getting the entire student body into the Bible, Eric prepared a simple daily reading card beginning with the life and teachings of Christ, then moving into the life of the early church and some well-known portions of the New Testament epistles. "My idea," he explained, "was to have a <u>short</u> passage each day, for I wanted them to set apart a time each day for reading and <u>meditation</u>. It was an attempt to introduce the 'Morning Watch' or 'The Evening Quiet Time.'"

Eric and the other missionary teachers had committed their lives to the task of communicating Christ through their work at the college. But in light of the wildly fluctuating political situation, no one knew how much time they had, individually or as an institution. Each year it became more difficult to satisfy the requirements to be a fully recognized school under government registration. Without that official status, they could not hope to attract enough students to remain financially viable and accomplish their mission.

Since Dr. Hart's retirement in 1929, Carl Longman and A. P. Cullen had assumed the arduous task of dealing with the Chinese authorities. Cullen said of the process: "Reams of instructions from the Bureau of Education continue to reach us in a seemingly endless stream; where we can do so, with a clear conscience, we follow these instructions (e.g. in the observance of the 'foreign' New Year rather than the Chinese New Year); where we cannot, we lie low and say nothing."

When the authorities declared that each registered school must have a Chinese principal, the Anglo-Chinese College temporarily satisfied the requirement by appointing an "Honorary" principal. But the experiment ended in failure, frustration, and a catastrophic breakdown in student discipline. The staff began searching for a qualified Chinese educator with deep Christian commitment who could take a full-time position, although they had no idea where they would find either the man or the money for the salary such a person would command.

In the face of all the difficulties and frustrations, the LMS missionaries remained remarkably committed to the original vision of the college. Dr. Hart had given thirty years to the school and Roy Peill had served for fifteen before they both retired; Longman had arrived in 1912 and Cullen in 1916. Gerald Luxon and Eric Liddell were the newcomers with seven and five years of service respectively.

Although living in Tientsin was far easier than serving in a rural station, life in China was still precarious. The Harts and Longmans had both grieved the loss of an infant to disease. Even at the college the missionaries lived with uncertainty and inconvenience, but through it all they showed a resilient optimism and faith in God.

In Eric's report for 1930 he wrote: "The Spirit of our Master slowly works his way into our games, work and services. We do not see, like a builder does, great changes in a week or two, but here and there comes a word of cheer and a sight that makes you sure that the work is slow but sure. Here a boy begins to face life and definitely decides that he will face it, building his life with Christ as its foundation, and there another in the quiet makes his surrender too." He went on to tell of a former student who had recently written from Ch'ing Hua University, saying that he had given his life to Christ.

Eric's report concluded with these words: "The past year has in some ways been disappointing — for one thing, the difficult problem of getting a suitable Christian Principal has not yet been solved — but nevertheless we face this coming year with confidence and cheer, for we hear our Master saying, 'Be of good cheer, I have overcome the world.'"

By January 1931, plans for Eric's anticipated return to England were taking shape in his mind. The previous year he had requested a two-year furlough, knowing this would be his last opportunity for training before a lifetime of missionary service. But now the LMS local committee in China had recommended him for only one year, and as a member of the society he was bound by their decision. His first choice was to take a teacher training course to increase his effectiveness at the college. If he could pick up a few lectures at the Theological College in Edinburgh, that would be a bonus. But by the time the options were sorted out, Eric had decided to study for two terms at the Scottish Congregational College with the goal of being ordained before returning to China. Whether he sensed a definite call to the ministry at that time or saw the handwriting on the educational wall in China, the decision put him on the pathway of new vocational opportunities.

Eric had once quipped to Flo that he would have been happy to make his living playing billiards. She laughed in astonishment at the idea, but it wasn't as absurd as it may have sounded. David McGavin, North China representative for the National Bible Society of Scotland, discovered Liddell's earning potential with a cue when he became the fourth occupant of the college flat in early 1931. After challenging Eric to a game, McGavin stood by helplessly and watched his flat-mate sink ball after ball. With a soft touch and keen eye-hand coordination, Liddell ran the table with ease. Had they been betting men, McGavin's pockets would have been considerably lighter.

"I see now where your misspent youth was spent," McGavin said with a wry smile. The other two men in the flat, Gerald Luxon and

George Dorling, had learned long ago that billiards with Eric was an entertaining but very one-sided pastime. Although none of these men had much time for recreation, they enjoyed the camaraderie of living together, and they got to know one another very well.

Gerald Luxon's wife and two daughters had been in England since the summer of 1929 when he and Eric took up residence together in the flat. After six months as a grass widower, Luxon had taken a whirlwind eight-month furlough to England, returning to the college in September 1930 in time for the new term. A fairly austere man with a brush-like mustache, he was not much for jokes but was a skilled and devoted teacher. He missed his family greatly, but not the obligatory deputation meetings during furlough. In his 1930 report, Luxon remarked, "I am glad to be back once again at my work, which I enjoy much more than running round England to talk about it."

Dr. George Dorling, a brilliant young surgeon, had joined the others in the flat just as Luxon returned from furlough. Three years earlier at his graduation from the London Hospital School of Medicine, Dorling had received an unprecedented five top awards, including the Frederick Treves Prize in Surgery. Now, after a year of language school and some practical experience in the LMS hospital at Tsangchow, he had taken up his duties at the large MacKenzie Memorial Hospital in Tientsin.

At the time, Dorling was, by his own admission, "obviously more enthusiastic about myself and my surgery than about 'my richest gain I count but loss.'" Young in his faith and with little training in practical Christian living, George admired Eric for the depth of his faith and spiritual vitality. He found in Eric a true friend and a man to whom he could bare his soul in complete confidence. "Nothing ever shocked him," the surgeon said of Eric. "His love was too great to be shocked — it was like God's."

Others were not as patient with Dr. Dorling. The local committee in China often found him outspoken, headstrong, and independent. One of the mission society's regulations required men to obtain the sanction of the directors "before completing any engagement with a view to marriage." On every application to join the LMS the final question read: "In the event of your being accepted as a missionary of the Society, are you willing to conform to the regulations appended hereto?" Dorling had answered: "Yes, but I do think you ought to trust me to choose my own wife — you'll have to trust me sometime." One senior missionary chided the head office in London for sending immature candidates who created personnel headaches after they arrived in China. Dorling's name was mentioned as an example. Yet to Eric, George was a young, growing Christian, a flat-mate, and a friend.

As the details of Eric's upcoming furlough continued to ebb and flow, one part of his itinerary remained inviolate — a month in Canada at the beginning and end of his year away. Because Flo's set vacation periods during nurse's training did not coincide with his visit, they would have only her scant time off to be together. Still, it would be two glorious months without depending on letters for news that was always several weeks old.

At the beginning of July, Eric left Tientsin, somewhat amazed that another unforeseen calamity had not again postponed his furlough. During the voyage across the Pacific he shared a cabin with John and Billy Toop, seventeen-year-old twins whom he had agreed to escort to England. In Toronto, the boys would stay with an uncle, then rejoin Eric for the journey to the UK. He had taught the boys in Sunday school at Union Church, and one summer day, to their surprise, had bicycled three miles of rough road under a blazing sun to witness their baptism at Peitaiho. In his flat at the college, he tutored them in chemistry in preparation for medical school. Through Eric, they had learned of the Edinburgh Medical Missionary Society and the financial assistance available for those preparing for such a career. On their father's salary as office manager of the British and Foreign Bible Society in Tientsin, they could not have hoped to attend university.

Each day aboard ship, Eric jogged around the upper deck and maintained a faithful yet unobtrusive regimen of light exercise. The

Toop brothers enjoyed his companionship and repartee, hardly considering him a chaperone. Seasickness was always a topic of conversation, and one night standing at the ship's rail, Eric bid the brothers good night, saying, "I'll be going along to the cabin now." When John said he was going to stay and watch the moon come up, Eric replied over his shoulder, "Oh, is that coming up too?"

Two weeks across the Pacific and three days by train from Vancouver to Toronto brought Eric to Flo's arms. Their year apart had seemed an eternity, and neither of them wanted to think about the time of separation that lay ahead. There was so much to talk about, so much to savor of just being together, they were content to enjoy the present. But in the blink of an eye, the four weeks passed and Eric sailed for England. Flo tried to concentrate on bacteriology but found herself numbering the days until she saw him again.

On a calm August evening, Eric watched Canada slip away as his ship steamed down the ever-widening St. Lawrence and made for the open sea. Ten days later, he delivered the Toop brothers to their destination in London, then dashed for a bus to King's Cross Station and the train to Edinburgh. How strange yet good it seemed to travel through the familiar countryside he had not seen for six years. At Edinburgh's Waverley Station he enjoyed a wonderful, long-anticipated reunion with his parents, Jenny, and Ernest, now a young man of eighteen.

If Eric had maintained any hope that his furlough would allow more time for study than his 1924–25 year of campaigning with D. P. Thomson, the situation became clear soon after his arrival on August 30. The London Missionary Society had committed him to a daunting schedule of deputation meetings. The LMS had ended the previous year with a deficit of nearly £19,000, and with the deepening worldwide depression, it appeared that 1931 would be worse. Eric would be a popular and powerful spokesman to attract missionary recruits and the funds to send them out.

Beyond the LMS deputation schedule, so many requests poured in from sporting groups and churches throughout Britain that the Congregational Church convened a committee to deal with them.

Hundreds, it seemed, wanted the ever-popular missionary-athlete to address their particular group.

Eric himself had asked that half a dozen personal engagements be allowed, including one at the Silcoates School with Professor Sydney Moore, the gifted teacher who had so influenced him at Eltham College. Also, soon after arriving in Scotland, Eric spent a day with D. P. Thomson finalizing plans for meetings they would take together for the Student Campaign Movement. Thomson noted that his friend looked "very fit and happy, a little yellower and balder, otherwise the same old Eric."

On the last day of September, representatives of the sporting and religious worlds joined in a public welcome home meeting for Eric. St. George's West Church in Edinburgh was packed for the Wednesday evening of tributes and appreciation, solid evidence that Eric Liddell's popularity had not diminished during his absence.

Speaking in his usual quiet voice, and with a kind smile, Eric assured the audience that he had come from a place that was not as wild as some people imagined, and from a city that was civilized and had many modern conveniences. Referring to a comment made by D. P. Thomson, Eric recalled a key event of nearly a decade earlier: "When I was at the University, I wanted to help Christ. I wanted to use any talents I had, and I did not feel I could. Mr. Thomson came to me one day and asked if I would not go out to an area to speak. I think the bravest thing I did in my life was to accept that invitation."

Then, in typical fashion, Eric shifted the spotlight from himself to others, saying: "I accept your welcome, not in my own name, but in the name of a great many others. I accept your welcome in the names of those countless men, whose names are almost unknown, who went into places of danger and difficulty and hazarded their lives for the sake of Jesus Christ, and who came back after they had done those things and were never welcomed. In the name of these men and others I accept it. I think we should always remember the men who have made the task we go to far easier than otherwise it would have been.

"In China the evangelists are going out amongst the people. They are going into their homes. They are sleeping in places just the same as the Chinese themselves. They are trying to understand the problems those people have to face, and the greatest challenge there is to every Christian person asks for no great courage, but asks for patience and sympathy that we will be able to sit beside those whose opinions are different from our own, and try to enter into their problems and face them from their point of view.

"Tonight I want to leave a message with you all," he said. "We are all missionaries. We carry our religion with us, or we allow our religion to carry us. Wherever we go, we either bring people nearer to Christ, or we repel them from Christ. We are working for the great Kingdom of God — the time when all people will turn to Christ as their leader, and will not be afraid to own him as such."

In October, Eric began his studies at the Scottish Congregational College under Professor D. Russell Scott and Principal Hywell Hughes. Hughes, fifty-five, and Scott, sixty-one, were outstanding scholars, both possessing two earned doctorates from prestigious universities. In addition, they were congenial men with whom Eric had enjoyed a good relationship during his previous year of study there. From all indications, they devised a rigorous program of study suited to his demanding schedule and did not skimp on his preparation for ordination. When possible, Eric attended lectures on pastoral theology and church history, always considering how what he heard applied to the challenge of taking the gospel to China.

Following another large welcome meeting in Glasgow, Eric plunged into a relentless speaking schedule that brought great joy and reunion with friends while taxing him to the limit. October found him addressing the annual meetings of the LMS in Aberdeen, Dundee, Glasgow, Edinburgh, and Greenock. Most engagements involved a Saturday night open rally and at least three meetings on Sunday, including morning and evening church services and an afternoon meeting for youth.

One of the more difficult aspects for Eric was the constant adulation heaped upon him. He had long ago come to grips with the fact that his athletic celebrity was his platform for the gospel, but the steady stream of hero-worship assaulted his humility. He may have found it refreshing when there was tangible evidence that not everyone thought he was perfect.

The Student magazine of Edinburgh University reported that at the first hymn sing-along of the session, Eric Liddell, "a not obscure alumnus of this University" had given an address on "Modern China And Its Problems." The unvarnished evaluation of the Sunday evening gathering in McEwan Hall was: "Address, not too bad; attendance, considerably worse; conduction, rotten; singing, utterly damnable."

When Eric spoke to an overflow crowd at the Annual Temperance Rally of the Church of Scotland Presbytery of Glasgow, he boldly stated that gambling and intemperance were two of the greatest problems the church was facing; both vices were sapping the energy of their young people. He noted that drink had ruined one of the greatest athletes Scotland ever produced, a man who ended his days begging at the same sporting venues where he used to be cheered.

Eric's remarks on the subject garnered a hostile letter to the editor from a "Moderate Drinker of 74 Years" who bemoaned the fact that Eric Liddell, whom he greatly admired, "has allied himself with narrow-minded, fanatical teetotalers" and adopted "their intolerant language." What the writer didn't realize, of course, was that if he had enjoyed a glass of wine or a pint of beer during a meal with Liddell, he would have received no personal disapproval from Eric.

Later in his furlough, at a rally of the Lord's Day Observance Society, Eric introduced a resolution stating: "That the meeting is of opinion that the increasing use of the Lord's Day for games and recreations, however harmless in themselves, is detrimental to the highest interest of the youth of the country, as well as adding to the amount of unnecessary labour of other people; and calls on all young people's organisations to give full consideration to this aspect of the question."

While it may have seemed to some that he was trying to legislate morality, those who knew Eric best understood that he could hold himself to the highest ideals he proclaimed while never looking down on those who did not share his beliefs. It was conviction, not fanaticism — the same unique blend of integrity and magnanimity that had enabled Eric to congratulate his Olympic teammates who competed on Sunday while standing firm on his own conviction not to run.

As he traveled the country, Eric was often asked to speak about the current situation in China, and he was plied with questions: "Will Britain be forced to return the concession areas?" "Why is there so much anti-foreign feeling?" "What is the place of sport in Chinese life?" "How will the rise of nationalism affect the other nations of the world?"

Eric never dodged the controversial questions, but neither did he pretend to be an expert on China. Whether speaking in the politically charged atmosphere of Belfast, or the safer environment of a Rotary Club in Scotland, he addressed the issues from his perspective and experience at the Anglo-Chinese College. He took a sympathetic view of China's problems in the modern world, once noting that with a ninety percent illiteracy rate among the villagers, the educator must partner with the evangelist.

"Are you satisfied with China?" one listener asked. Eric replied that his attraction to China went beyond the beauty of the country itself. He was returning because he sensed that he was doing a work there that he was meant to be doing.

No matter how demanding his schedule, Eric always found time to write to Flo. Their letters crisscrossed the Atlantic, filled with the news of their lives. Rob and his family were hoping to arrive in Scotland in time for Jenny's marriage to Dr. Charles Somerville on April 20. Eric's father was very involved at Morningside Congregational Church and seemed to be doing well. His mother was much the same, a bit too serious and burdened for her own good. He kept hoping that his speaking schedule would ease, but there was no sign of it.

Flo had missed a week of training in February due to a terrible cold. Her grades were satisfactory, with commendations for good attitude and willingness to work. Her hours were still long, the work demanding, and the behavior of patients during night duty often bizarre. Her mind and spirit were holding up, but her body was ready to quit. She expected her parents and the younger children home on furlough in early summer. Betty Thomson, her best friend from China, planned to enter nurse's training the next autumn.

But beyond the news, each letter affirmed their love and longing for each other. Each exam taken, each deputation meeting completed, brought them closer to the day when they would be together again.

By February, Eric was drained by the demands of his theological study and speaking schedule. Beyond his weariness of body and mind, there seemed to be an ill-defined spiritual unrest as well. He had no peace, no stillness of soul. *Why must it be so hard?* he wondered. If he lacked the sustaining power in his own homeland, where people congratulated him for being a Christian, how could he hope to return to China and serve effectively?

In the midst of his exhaustion, a member of the Oxford Group spoke at an informal gathering in his parents' home. During the meeting, as the speaker focused on the need for complete surrender to God each day, Eric felt his weariness begin to melt away. He knew that the spiritual power he needed would not and could not come from himself. The text from Acts, "But you shall be baptized with the Holy Spirit and with fire," echoed in his mind.

Six years earlier, he had walked and talked with Loudon Hamilton in Galashiels when the Oxford Group movement had just begun. Now it had become the source of spiritual renewal and life-changing power for multiplied thousands of people around the world. Their practical approach to Bible study was: "Read accurately, interpret honestly, apply drastically." One Group member noted that Christianity became practical and vibrant as "absolute standards of honesty and unselfishness were applied not to some pleasant pipe-dream of the sweet by-and-by, but to details of the nasty now-and-now."

Stuart Sanderson and his wife, Bina, understood the freedom and power of following God's guidance, whatever the cost. A lifelong resident of Galashiels, Stuart had taken over his family's woolen manufacturing business when his only brother was killed in the Great War. After meeting Frank Buchman in the early 1920s, the Sandersons opened their home for gatherings of people seeking to find spiritual reality in Christ.

A few years later, the tweed industry faced a time of crisis, with some mills laying off workers and others closing. Stuart and Bina were advised to cut their losses and get out. Instead, they decided to ask God what He wanted them to do. The thought kept coming: "Dismiss nobody. Keep the mill going. Put all your resources into doing it." To the shock of their neighbors, the Sandersons sold their stately home and moved into an unoccupied cottage adjacent to the mill.

They were still living in that small cottage when Eric visited them in May 1932. The three enjoyed a refreshing time of laughter and sharing together, but during the conversation a question from Stuart seemed to put a finger directly on an issue hidden deep in Eric's heart. He sidestepped the question, put Stuart off, and blatantly lied about the matter. But God would not let him forget. Back in Edinburgh a week later, the question came to Eric's mind, and he dismissed it as trivial. Finally, on a Sunday morning, Stuart's question and his own dishonest reply again confronted Eric. He knew he must put it right immediately. Eric telephoned Sanderson, then drove the thirty miles to Galashiels. He told Stuart the truth, and they had an honest talk.

Eric related the entire incident to the people gathered for a monthly meeting of the Oxford Group in Edinburgh. The minutes do not reveal either Sanderson's question or the deeper issue in Eric's life, but they document the importance of the incident to Eric. He wanted to associate himself with the group, he told them, because its members had challenged him to a keener faith and practice. He was going back to China leading a fuller Christian life than when he first went out. A brochure for a September House Party in St. Andrews carried the following statement from Eric: "The Group has brought to me personally a greater power in my own life, discipline without the thought of discipline, and a greater willingness to share the deepest things in my life. In my time in this country I have met no body of people who are so vitally active and through whom the Spirit of God works so clearly as the Oxford Group."

On Wednesday evening, June 22, 1932, in the chapel of the Scottish Congregational College, Eric Liddell was ordained as a minister of the gospel. During the service, attended only by family and a few close friends, Principal Hughes put the questions to the candidate, D. P. Thomson gave the ordination prayer, and Professor Russell Scott delivered the charge. With joy and tears, they all commended him to the service and the care of Almighty God.

The next day, with his furlough in Scotland drawing to a close, Eric took time to write Gerald Luxon's sixteen-year-old daughter in boarding school at Walthamstow Hall:

My dear Pixie: I quite understand about the present to your Daddy—thank you so much for the card. I like the words very much. Your Mother sent on a gift from Dick [her younger brother] which I am to take with me. If Dick made it all himself I think he has done very well.

Today I have been to the Dentist! He is a kind chap isn't he? He pulled one of my teeth out after playing about with the nerve for a bit, fortunately it is round near the back.

These last days have been gorgeous, no rain for 24 days.

You'll be swatting at English while I write this and then arithmetic tomorrow. All the best of wishes — do well Pixie.

Have you come across this verse?

"I would be true, for there are those who trust me;
I would be pure, for there are those who care;
I would be strong, for there is much to suffer;
I would be brave, for there is much to dare."

Why not make it your aim all through life? It is such a fine aim to have.

> With lots of love, from Uncle Eric.

At the end of June, a final family good-bye brought Eric's furlough in Britain to a bittersweet end. Rob and Ria would be back in China the next year, but Eric knew it would be at least six years before he saw Jenny, Ernest, and his parents again. He embraced his mother and shook hands with his father, acutely aware that now they must stay and he must go, as the call to China put half a world between them once again.

Aboard the SS *Duchess of York*, Eric's thoughts became a mixture of memory and anticipation. The sheer exhaustion of speaking at hundreds of meetings began to fade while the fond recollections remained. There was the blustery Saturday in March when he had presented the medals and trophies during the Annual Athletic Sports Day at Eltham College. And his father's great enjoyment of the April weekend in Drymen when Eric preached in East Church, which three generations of Liddells had attended. In the Foresters' Hall, next to Auntie Lizzie and Uncle Robert MacFarlane's house, Eric had addressed a lively meeting of the Scottish Women's Rural Institute. Powerful reminders of his boyhood in the Scottish village had flooded Eric's memory at every turn.

And then there was dear Jenny, now married and a mother to three young-adult stepchildren. The ten years separating Eric and Flo seemed slight compared to the twenty-six years between Jenny and the widowed Dr. Charles Somerville. But Jenny loved him, and Charlie seemed to be a good and stable man, a long-time family acquaintance going back to his years in China as a missionary. Eric hoped they would have many happy years together.

But he could not dwell long in the past as he sailed toward Flo in Canada and then on to China.

Two weeks after leaving the port of Liverpool, Eric sat on the porch rail at Mrs. A. E. Thomson's house on Rose Park Drive in Toronto. On that summer afternoon he laughed easily with Mrs. Thomson and her daughter Betty, Flo's longtime friend from

Tientsin. But his eyes and heart were focused on the street down which Flo would walk after her shift ended at the hospital. He was in mid-sentence when he saw her in the distance, and without an apology he swung over the rail and ran to meet her, sweeping her up in his arms. The electricity between them seemed to crackle through the air like the sizzle of lightning before a thunderclap. They embraced for a long time without speaking, trying to make up for the yearnings of a year apart. Then he kissed her quickly and they walked back toward the house, arms around each other's waists, as if they had just met for a stroll along the beach at Peitaiho.

Betty turned to her mother and said, "I don't think I've ever known two people so much in love."

For a month, Flo and Eric spent every hour they could find just being together. This time, however, the entire MacKenzie family was present to stake their claim on Eric. Flo's brothers and sisters treated him like a long-lost older brother, and her mother seemed ever-present when they thought they might have a few minutes alone.

With Flo near the beginning of her final year in nurse's training, they could almost set a date for their wedding. Christmas of '33 sounded wonderful but overly optimistic. Perhaps the next spring. It was still too early to talk about where they would live and how to decorate the rooms. So much remained to be done before their hopes could approach reality. But it was wonderful to sit outside on a summer evening and dream together.

But part of the current reality was Eric's status as a celebrity, even in Canada. One afternoon at a Toronto sports ground, Eric met up with members of the British Olympic team, taking a few days of rest and training on their way to the games in Los Angeles. The worldwide Great Depression and the expense of travel to California had forced nine countries to withdraw and reduced the number of participating athletes to half the total that had competed in Amsterdam four years before. Eric had a word of advice and encouragement for the runners and bid them good-bye with a request: "Remember me to my friends in Scotland."

During Eric's time in Toronto, R. E. Knowles, a well-known Canadian journalist sought him out for a story. The eccentric

Knowles, who specialized in celebrity profiles, had already interviewed such notables as Babe Ruth, Bertrand Russell, and U.S. presidential candidate Franklin D. Roosevelt. If the writer expected an athlete ready to boast about his success, he clearly had the wrong man. Relaxed and smiling as usual, Eric downplayed everything, including his 1929 races in Tientsin against Dr. Otto Peltzer, the great German runner. Peltzer had set world records at 500, 800, and 1,500 meters, and had once beaten the incomparable Paavo Nurmi at the Finn's best distance.

"How did you come out?" Knowles asked.

"Oh, I won the 400 metres. Peltzer won the 800."

Liddell, of course, did not mention that after the race Peltzer had told him that if he would train for the 800, he would be the world's greatest at that distance.

After getting Eric to admit that he had won the North China Championship in 1930, Knowles, a former Presbyterian minister, turned to another theme.

"Do you ever preach on the text, 'So run that you may obtain?'"

"Actually," Eric replied, "I'd rather preach on 'The race is not to the swift.'"

Knowles continued to probe. "Are you glad you gave your life to missionary work? Don't you miss the limelight, the rush, the frenzy, the cheers, the rich red wine of victory?"

Eric answered: "Oh well, of course it's natural for a chap to think over all that sometimes, but I'm glad I'm at the work I'm engaged in now. A fellow's life counts for far more at this than the other. Not a corruptible crown, but an incorruptible, you know."

A few days after Knowles' article appeared in the *Toronto Star*, Eric and Flo said a more hopeful good-bye than ever before. Even though their next meeting was some eighteen months away, God willing, it would be in China, only days before their wedding. And that would be something worth cheering about.

On the train from Toronto to Vancouver, Eric again marveled at the vast open spaces and endless fields of ripening wheat slipping past his window. For long stretches across the Prairie Provinces of

Manitoba, Saskatchewan, and Alberta, hardly a person was to be seen. It was so unlike the densely populated North China Plain. The city of Tientsin contained more people than the provinces of Manitoba and Alberta combined.

And what would he find when he returned? During his absence, Japan had conquered Manchuria, renamed it Manchukuo, and established the hapless Pu Yi as a puppet ruler. Chinese outrage at the aggression had sparked street fighting with Japanese troops in the old city of Tientsin, forcing a five-day closure of the Anglo-Chinese College. Early in 1932, Japan had provoked "the Shanghai incident," during which they bombed portions of that city to rubble, killing thousands of Chinese civilians.

Of all these events, Cullen had written: "It is well to remember that the whole situation in the Far East is pregnant with dark possibilities for Japan as well as for her present victims."

What next? Eric wondered, but it was impossible to know.

On the ship from Vancouver to Yokohama he enjoyed the company of friends, yet took time each day to think, pray, and gather strength for the months ahead. The past year had done him good, not just by being away, but by bringing him face to face with the depth of his own need to live in complete surrender to God. In many ways, he was returning a different man.

THIRTEEN

The Burden Is Light

1933–1935

Eric returned to Tientsin with a lighter spirit and heavier responsibilities than ever before. In addition to his teaching duties, he became secretary of the college, a task that required him to attend meetings of the Board of Governors, record the minutes, and handle much of the official correspondence for the school. With Cullen gone on furlough and no one yet sent to replace Scarlett, the work of five British missionaries fell to Liddell, Longman, and Luxon.

Eric also served as chairman of the Games Committee with the oversight of all sports activities. Some of the Chinese teachers coached the boys in various sports, but the ultimate responsibility belonged to Eric. He saw this role as a key element in the Christian mission of the college, but it required a great deal of time. Every Saturday afternoon he took the field as a member of the college soccer team to play alongside the boys. In the spring, weeks of planning and coordination went into the annual sports day held each May.

As if that were not enough, Eric had been placed in charge of the religious activities of the school, including Sunday services in the chapel and morning prayers for the students where he took his turn as one of the speakers. Seventeen students came regularly to his voluntary Bible class. Eric designed a daily Scripture reading card that he gave to every boy along with the hearty encouragement to read consistently at home. "By this I hope to get them into the habit of 1. Quiet morning prayer. 2. Expectation that the Bible has a message for them which can be applied to their own lives day by day," Eric wrote. "I cannot claim any great success but there are one or two beginnings."

Like every teacher, Eric found it difficult to meet individual academic needs while teaching large classes. Creating two sections of senior mathematics helped to address the wide differences in ability among boys in the same class, but it provided only a partial solution. In addition, cultural differences, laziness, cheating, and disruptive behavior taxed his resourcefulness and patience each day.

"The class has not been an easy one," Eric reported, "and it has driven me to a deeper life of prayer myself. There was one boy who was especially irritating so I put him down for special prayer. After several months I came to know one of his big problems and should have pressed my advantage especially as I had passed through a similar difficulty but I'm afraid I missed the chance. This year he has been much better and for a time joined the Bible class, but there's a long way to go with him yet."

Outside the college, Eric taught a class of boys each week at Union Church and continued as superintendent of the Sunday school. But he did not confine himself to English-speaking activities. At the request of Ernest Box, a fellow LMS missionary and former schoolmate at Eltham College, Eric began meeting each week with a group of men at Ku Lou Hsi Church, a Chinese congregation near the Drum Tower in the old city. Although Eric had passed the written exams required by the mission society, his conversational Chinese remained weak. Nevertheless, he plunged in, seeing it as yet another avenue of helping.

"Ku Lou Hsi has been and still is a difficult problem," Eric later reported. "There is no ordained Chinese Pastor in charge and I think the evangelist feels his hands tied by one or two of the deacons who have been there for many years. In the class, we have the Evangelist, a man who has started a Christian book shop, one or two of the Sunday School teachers, and some others. We have banded ourselves together to pray for one another daily for power, for we feel that we must start with ourselves. We want depth in ourselves first. I have tried to incorporate some of the Oxford Group principles which made such a difference to my own life."

At the heart of those principles was the importance of having daily, intimate contact with Jesus Christ. A morning quiet time, Bible reading, prayer, honest sharing with others, and seeking God's guidance were not required activities, but simply the means of pursuing a dynamic spiritual life. The goal was a vital faith expressed in practical ways that drew others to the Savior. In this circle, Eric was not the teacher, but a fellow traveler with his Chinese colleagues.

At the Taku Road Christian Church, where James Liddell had invested much of his life in Tientsin, Eric served as an advisor to a Saturday night group led by Chinese youth. After his weekly soccer game at the college, he had just enough time to bathe and eat a quick meal before walking to the church for that meeting.

Eric and Flo missed each other desperately, but they had little time to feel sorry for themselves. While Eric taught chemistry and marked papers, Flo endured a rigorous three months of duty in a psychiatric hospital. Her supervisor noted that she adapted rather slowly to the work there, even though she was always patient and sympathetic. By the end of January 1933, Flo was exhausted and spent two weeks in bed recovering from anemia. At times she wondered if she would live to marry Eric in another year.

Mercifully, her next assignment took her to the Hospital for Sick Children where her spirits revived. She loved the children and felt as much as home with them as she had in caring for her younger brothers and sisters. But her highest marks and warmest commendations came in obstetrics and gynecology. "Excellent, very interested, efficient and understanding," wrote her supervisors. The only thing more fun than children were babies, and Flo couldn't wait to be the mother of Eric's children.

In May, Flo went through graduation exercises with the Class of 1933, even though she had six months of work remaining. By now, she and Eric could see the end of their long separation. Flo's father and her brother Finlay returned to China while her mother and the younger children remained in Toronto, planning to sail back together for the wedding.

Ten thousand miles away at the Anglo-Chinese College the usually tense "days of humiliation" associated with the anniversary of the Shanghai incident of 1925 passed without student protests or the threat of a strike. Eric noted that "the whole spirit of the student classes seems to have changed within the last year or two."

And there had been a deep and lasting change in him as well. The receipt of a booklet about the sudden death of a missionary wife prompted a rare written expression of Eric's own spiritual journey. In a letter to the LMS Foreign Secretary, Mr. Hawkins, Eric wrote:

"To think that she was at the May meetings being farewelled and then that within a few months God wanted her. I have read the booklet with interest — it is strange how so many go through a spiritual struggle of a similar kind to Lucy's — what a wonderful thing it is to pass through and then come to a greater light and experience because of it. During my time at home last year I too was passing through a greater struggle than I had ever had before. It has brought me back here with a clearer message than before and a more personal Christ."

No one knows whether it was Eric's new spiritual freedom, his pragmatic approach to life, or the stifling summer heat that caused him to appear in the Union Church pulpit dressed in white shorts. His attire caused more of a stir than his Sunday sermon, and led to something of a reprimand from the very proper members of the British community. Eric valued meaningful traditions, but had little use for pomposity or unnecessary discomfort. But out of respect for the feelings of others, he didn't wear his shorts in the pulpit again.

The autumn arrival of the SS *Rawalpindi* brought the welcome return of Rob and his family to Siaochang, where he resumed his duties as hospital superintendent. During his absence, Dr. Geoff Milledge, an Eltham College teammate of Eric's, and Annie Buchan, a small but determined Scottish nurse, had held things together at the rural station. A fearless woman of great energy and dedication, Annie reigned supreme over the nurses, and most doctors, at Siaochang.

A month later, as Eric preached on Sunday at the Union Church, he had the unusual sense that his father was very near him. The next morning, as he ate breakfast, a cable arrived saying that the Reverend J. D. Liddell had died suddenly the day before. There were no details of how or when or where. Overwhelmed, Eric sat alone for a few moments, then slowly walked from the flat to his first class of the day. Two weeks later, a letter reached him with the details. His father had gone to Drymen for "Remembrance Day." On Saturday, November 11, he had returned to his sister Maggie's house after spending the morning talking with friends in the village. He sat down in a chair, suffered a massive stroke, and was gone at the age of sixty-three.

In his last letter to his son, James had proclaimed himself "full of energy," a phrase so characteristic of his optimism and zest for living. Now, tributes from friends and colleagues poured in with grateful thanks for what James Liddell had meant to each of them. Eric wrote to his mother: "I have just kept straight on with my work here. It has been the best thing possible for me."

During the next few weeks, Eric wrote often to his mother. It seemed almost callous to speak of wedding plans in the wake of death, but he knew she would want to know what was happening. In early December he reported that Flo had finished her exams the week before. She was tired and anxious to leave the hospital, but had to make up the sick days she had missed during her training. She and her mother hoped to sail February 10 from Vancouver on the SS *Empress of Canada*. A description of getting their flat painted and furnished rounded out his news.

When the college closed for the holidays, Eric left for Siaochang to spend Christmas with Rob. There, where they had played as boys, they talked of their life, their family, and their father as only brothers can. How much they had admired their father, yet how little time they had spent together. When expressing his disappointment at Rob's initial assignment to Tingchow-fu in 1924, James had written the foreign secretary saying: "Since Rob was eight years of age, apart from this last furlough, I have only seen him for six months." And then there had been their parents' years apart from each other as Mary returned early and stayed late on furloughs to be with the boys. In a new way, Eric and Rob realized what their parents had been through during their years of missionary service. Now both of them faced the same dilemma.

A few months earlier, Rob and Ria had left their seven-year-old daughter, Peggy, in Britain to enter the School for the Daughters of Missionaries. As their train pulled out of Waverley Station, little Peggy stood on Platform 19, waving goodbye and sobbing uncontrollably. She would be thirteen before they saw her again. This was a wrenching experience that neither parents nor child would ever forget. Peggy would be fine at Walthamstow Hall, they had assured themselves. It had to be done. It was part of missionary life. But deep in Eric's heart, he questioned whether he could ever leave his children in boarding school.

As Flo's arrival drew near, Eric wrote to his mother: "There isn't much time for reading: it always seems to be giving out rather than taking in; a bad thing, I know, but perhaps safer than erring on the other side. I'm still on the subject of the Holy Spirit at Ku Lou Hsi. How I long to see us all get a real great baptism of Him." He was glad to hear that she had received his letter asking her to look up the words to the hymn, "Be Still, My Soul."

"I often play it over," he added, "a calm, restful, beautiful tune."

Near the end of February, he encouraged his mother to visit Jenny and spend some time in the garden. The snowdrops would be out, soon followed by the crocuses and daffodils. He was glad he could picture her at home on Marchmont Road, and at Jen's house a few miles away in Bonnyrigg.

But most importantly, he was free to talk about his father. "On Sunday I took the address at Ku Lou Hsi. My Chinese is really a bit better than it was but what a long way I have to go yet. Today at tea-time, three old students came in. In the conversation it came out that two of them had been baptised by Dad in the College Chapel. Again at Ku Lou Hsi, they all knew Dad… and can remember the way he came amongst them. It's fine to be able to leave an impression like that everywhere."

On March 5, Eric, Hugh MacKenzie, and fourteen-year-old Finlay caught a late morning train for the thirty-mile journey from Tientsin to the port of Taku. The boat bringing Flo, Agnes, and the younger MacKenzie children from Kobe, Japan, was due sometime that afternoon. As the day progressed, Finlay had never seen Eric so nervous. Usually the picture of calmness, Eric paced the floor, drummed his fingers on the table, and kept glancing at his watch. A strong offshore wind kept the boat out of the river until nearly 6:00 in the evening. After two tries at the pier, the vessel finally docked and the years of waiting ended.

Eric and Flo sat up half the night talking, then caught a 5:30 A.M. train to Tientsin, with three weeks left to finalize plans for their wedding and get their flat in order. Part of the fun included unpacking the many prizes Eric had won during his running career in Scotland. Clocks, cutlery, vases, and other decorative items adorned their flat, courtesy of the Scottish Amateur Athletics Association and others.

They were married on Tuesday, March 27, 1934, and news of their wedding appeared on the front page of the *Peking and Tientsin Times*:

> There was a large attendance of foreigners and Chinese at the Union Church this afternoon when the Rev. Eric H. Liddell, the well-known Olympic champion, was united in matrimony with Miss Florence Jean MacKenzie, the daughter of Mr. and Mrs. Hugh MacKenzie, well known and much respected residents of Tientsin.

The Anglo-Chinese College had declared a half-holiday for the wedding, and Eric wanted the Chinese staff included. That must have raised a few eyebrows since only the foreign community, and not Chinese, attended the services at Union Church. But Eric and Flo would have it no other way.

Flo wore her mother's wedding dress and Jenny's veil. Her large bouquet of pink carnations was almost the size of her youngest sister, Agnes Louise, who beamed with pride as her flower girl. Eric looked nervous but distinguished in his wedding garb of necktie, morning coat, and top hat.

Eric's flat-mate, Dr. George Dorling, and his fiancée, Gwyneth Rees, served as best man and maid of honor. They carried on gamely through the day, even though their own year-long engagement was unraveling. How often George had sought Eric's listening ear and wise counsel during the previous months.

It seemed odd but understandable that Rob was not a member of the wedding party. Circumstances at Siaochang and transportation to Tientsin were so unpredictable that the most important plans could be thwarted.

After a reception at the MacKenzie home, Eric and his bride left for a ten-day honeymoon in one of the LMS cottages in the Western Hills outside Peking. From their verandah, they drank in the breathtaking view of the surrounding countryside. Below them, the plain stretched toward the ancient city of Peking ten miles away. Elevation gave them an entirely different view of the world, and that's what they sought for their life together. Wherever they went, whatever they did, they wanted to see things from God's perspective.

The reality of being husband and wife sank in slowly but deliciously each day. They now belonged to each other for a lifetime. They laughed and walked and talked and loved freely, savoring their oneness and all that it promised for the future. For Eric, Flo brought completion and a new beginning. With her, his mind and heart were open—with nothing held back. In her company, his natural shyness and reserve melted away in the warmth of her acceptance and love.

Before returning to Tientsin, they spent a day in Peking with Myfanwy Wood, an LMS missionary and long-time family friend, who had served alongside Eric's parents at Siaochang and Peking. During the years when Rob and Eric were at Eltham College, she had been like an older sister to Jenny. Still lithe and energetic at fifty-one, Myfanwy was an attractive, capable, and highly respected woman in what was essentially a man's missionary world. An astute observer of China and the enterprise of foreign missions, she had a deep love for the Chinese people combined with a dynamic faith in Christ. Besides all that, she was great fun. A day with her never failed to enlarge the life and vision of her companions.

Myfanwy took them all over the city she knew so well, having lunch with one friend and tea with another. Late in the afternoon, the newlyweds left by rickshaw for the Western Hills. "Eric was radiantly happy," Myfanwy later wrote to her family, "and I like Florence very much. She reminds me somewhat of Mrs. J. D. Liddell. She has the same colouring and the same shy quiet manner."

While in Peking, Eric developed a sore throat that progressed into tonsillitis. He returned to the college weak and unable to teach for two weeks. It was the first time during his ten years in China that he had missed work due to illness. Carl Longman was philosophical about it all, saying, "When you marry a nurse I suppose you must keep her in training."

Eric, who had inherited his father's robust constitution, quickly regained his strength, and he and Flo settled into the routine of life together. However, it soon became obvious that Flo's mother so enjoyed having them close by that she could not resist dropping in for tea almost every day. Though Eric loved his mother-in-law, he quipped to a friend that his favorite hymn might soon become "Peace, perfect peace, with loved ones far away."

With the arrival of Mr. and Mrs. Robert Thompson in January 1934, the college had its full complement of five British teachers for the first time since Eric Scarlett's death nearly four years before. Thompson's wife, Minnie, was also an experienced teacher, giving the college, in effect, two for the price of one.

With new regulations flowing from the Chinese Bureau of Education, it required endless patience and readjustment to cope with the changing demands. The college added new courses to prepare students for the nationally mandated achievement exam known as the "Group Test." College officials also assembled the entire student body twice a day to raise and lower the national flag. But the foreign staff felt there was a larger agenda than the stated goal of developing "pride of country and feelings of national loyalty and unity." Their apprehension was well founded, for the process of "developing nationalism" soon took an ominous turn.

During the summer of 1934, the first-year class in the senior middle school was required to attend two weeks of military camp. The training continued during the autumn term at the college, with twice-weekly drill outside school hours. This was accommodated with little disruption to the school, even though Cullen, a committed pacifist, was appalled by the government's obvious steps to prepare a ready supply of young men for military service. But he knew, as did the other staff members, that the college must either comply with the order or close down.

Eric expressed his view in a letter to friends: "By orders from the Government one of our classes has to take military drill and although I hate war, and feel the attitude of Christian people to it is going to be one of the greatest challenges in the future, yet it has smartened up some of the lads quite a bit."

But the government's next decree was an educational nightmare. The next April, in 1935, one class would be required to suspend their studies and attend three months of intensive military training in camp at Paotingfu. Eric equated it to the students "missing half a year's work." In addition, the college was ordered to provide Boy Scout uniforms and training for all the junior middle school students. Far from being a wholesome opportunity to learn outdoor skills, this was simply another step in early military preparation.

In the midst of the escalating spirit of nationalism, however, another Spirit was quietly and powerfully at work in China. At Siaochang, Will and Margaret Rowlands, along with Edith Owers, decided to incorporate some Oxford Group principles into their annual autumn retreat. Led by Gardner Tewkesbury, who had been born in China and educated at Nanking University, the gathering of Chinese pastors and Bible-women, along with foreign missionaries, met each day as equals before God. They began with quiet time alone for prayer and Bible reading, followed by a time of sharing what they had discovered from the Scriptures. No one was quite prepared for the dramatic results. The reports of the LMS missionaries, written months later, all spoke at length about the retreat's impact and the impossibility of conveying in words what they had experienced. It was not the surface emotion, but the deep spiritual change that had left them wonderfully amazed.

Alec Baxter, a new missionary on a temporary visit to Siaochang, realized his own spiritual inadequacy as he saw people enjoying an experience of the risen Christ that he, with his "mental reservations and personal dislikes," was quite unable to share. "I can never be sufficiently thankful," he declared, "for the steps which led to a complete re-surrendering of my life to God, and for the new life and vitality engendered by this in my own spiritual progress."

Edith Owers described the unusual result among Chinese pastors and evangelists who gathered in twos and threes between meetings to dissolve old misunderstandings and differences of years' standing. "All this time," she said, "I had the privilege of living with the Bible-women in their new quarters, and none of us will ever forget that week. Life and work ever since has been on an entirely different footing."

Tewkesbury, fluent in Chinese, made himself available day and night for personal talks with the pastors and evangelists. Will Rowlands concluded his report on the retreat by saying: "There are many in Siaochang today who owe their release from besetting sin and new power in service to these heart-searching talks."

The Oxford Group had many critics and detractors, but the people who received help through it always spoke of a new spiritual vitality gained from a personal surrender to Jesus Christ. The underlying dynamic was not emotional manipulation but spiritual consecration. From its small beginnings in 1921 at Loudon Hamilton's "Beef and Beer Club" to its present worldwide impact, the group had maintained the simple belief that Christ brought dramatic change to people everywhere who gave their lives to Him.

Eric's contact with the Group in 1932 had helped rekindle his love for Christ. In the wider missionary community, many others were being touched in a similar way, as the walk of faith, which had become burdensome, was transformed into a lighthearted journey of joy. Bible study and prayer ceased being obligations and became, instead, opportunities to enjoy the presence of the living God. And in the midst of a world that seemed hurtling toward war, this renewed their confidence in God's power to change people. Their job was to sow the seed and trust God to make it grow.

An event preceding the Siaochang retreat stood as a vivid metaphor of the future of Christianity in China. The previous spring, Will Rowlands had hired a gardener, "a lame old man of over 60 with a love for flowers," and turned him loose to work his will on the mass of tangled bushes and ragged grass that had overgrown much of the LMS compound. The man dug up the ground, planted seeds, and grafted trees just before the summer heat engulfed the North China Plain. For months, there appeared to be no result. But the late summer rains came, and when the missionaries returned from holiday, the compound blazed with flowers and blossoming trees. They stood awestruck and wondered aloud if this was really Siaochang. "It came to me very strongly," Rowlands wrote, "that this was a symbol and a sign that before long the spiritual desert round about us should also blossom as the rose."

During the autumn term, Eric began a voluntary morning meeting for the college staff. "I've been glad that for the first time I've been able to gather some of the teachers each morning for prayer and thought before the day's work started," he wrote in his report for 1934. "It has meant a deeper fellowship with a number of them as we sought to try to find and follow God's will for us during the days. One of the (Chinese) staff who hitherto did no Christian work has started a Bible Class in a lower form. I hope this will grow and that we will steadily find the Will of God a clearer thing in our lives and also obedience to it a greater delight and joy."

With the Longmans on furlough, Eric and Flo took over their practice of inviting the forty college boarders into their home every other Sunday evening. Both knew how much some tea, cakes, and lighthearted games in a real home could mean to a boy whose parents were far away. And sometime near the end of 1934, Flo surprised Eric with the news that they were expecting a little boarder of their own. Whoever it was should arrive the next summer!

When Flo married Eric, she inherited two servants, a houseboy and cook, whom Eric had employed since his parents left China in 1929. Yu Kwan, the houseboy, had worked for Mary Liddell since Eric was born. He was very loyal to Eric and looked on the newlyweds as mere children in his care. Flo stood in awe of his ability to keep everything in the household running efficiently.

The cook, a quiet man who hated emotional conflict of any kind, came to Eric one day distraught. His family in Siaochang had decided that he needed a wife and was sending a girl who was due to arrive in Tientsin the next day. Years before, his family had sent him a wife who made it her goal to spend all his money. He had torn up the marriage certificate and sent her away, a response quite permissible under Chinese law. Now he was afraid the same thing would happen again. Eric encouraged him to wait and see what the girl was like.

The chosen bride turned out to be a quiet country girl some thirty years younger than the cook. He was quite taken with her and decided to proceed with the marriage. Eric and Flo liked her as well and agreed to take her on as their amah when the baby was born.

Eric never took for granted the privilege of coming home each evening. Having lived with a crowd of boys in a boarding school dormitory for so many years, he found life with Flo far more fulfilling than he had dreamed it could be. Both of them valued hospitality and considered their home in the college flat a place to include people rather than a hide-a-way in which to avoid them. Their door was always open to students, strangers, and friends. When visiting missionaries came to Tientsin, the greatest treat for a child was staying with the Liddells. It was never the furniture or the food that the children remembered, but the warmth and love that emanated from Uncle Eric and Auntie Flo. They were fun!

Their colleagues at the Anglo-Chinese College and their many friends in the community hoped Eric and Flo would spend a lifetime of service in Tientsin. But not everyone in the London Missionary Society saw it that way.

FOURTEEN

Storm Clouds

1935–1937

At the annual college baptismal service in April 1935, three members of Eric's class publicly declared their faith in Christ, along with eight others from the college. Even though the Christian influence of the Anglo-Chinese College was widely acknowledged within the LMS, there was a growing feeling that it commanded a disproportionate share of the resources in North China. With the crying need for help in the rural areas, the Executive Committee passed the following resolution on May 16, 1935: "Owing to the smallness of the N. China evangelistic staff during the next few years and its consequent inadequacy to meet the needs of the country fields, a situation which is made more difficult by the proposed loan of Mr. Box to meet the serious emergency that has arisen in Central China, the Executive Committee asks Mr. Eric Liddell to consider whether this does not constitute a Call to him to give temporary help, for a period of say two years, to the country evangelistic work. The Chairman and Secretary are asked to consult with Mr. Liddell and the T.A.C.C. staff with a view to arriving at a decision at the forthcoming meetings of the District Committee."

At the time of the resolution, Eric and Flo had been married just over a year and she was seven months pregnant. They discussed the request for days, praying and wondering what to do. Were they willing to leave Tientsin and take their newborn to a country station? Was the decision theirs or would the District Committee simply post them to another location? Most important, what did God want them to do?

On July 13, Patricia Margaret Liddell was born in Tientsin, and for the moment everything else was forgotten. She had her father's blonde hair, Flo's hazel eyes, and the tiniest fingers Eric had ever seen. He was instantly smitten.

Ten days after his daughter's birth, Eric traveled alone to Peitaiho to discuss the matter of his possible transfer with his LMS colleagues assembled for the annual District Committee meetings. The staff at the TACC offered a heartfelt plea that Eric be allowed to remain at the college. During this very difficult time, his departure would create a real hardship for the school. Those on the other side of the issue called for help in the understaffed country field, where Chinese pastors needed help and encouragement. Finally, the committee turned to Eric.

He had weighed the matter carefully, trying to sort out the most important issues. For one thing, he felt that his Chinese was not adequate to launch immediately into the rural work. And although the transfer was temporary, he wondered if it might not mean a permanent change to country work. If so, he did not feel a definite enough call to do that.

The committee concluded "that inasmuch as Mr. E. H. Liddell himself does not feel the call to the country evangelistic work to be of such a nature as would warrant his transfer to that work, it is resolved that the matter be not proceeded with."

But this was not the end of it. The committee went on to say: "We venture to suggest that the time has arrived when the whole policy and work of the TACC should be considered in the light of the above needs and other new conditions, with a view to carrying out, as soon as circumstances will allow, its recognized policy of gradual reduction of its L.M.S. supported foreign staff."

With the meetings over, Eric brought Flo and two-and-a-half-week-old Patricia to Peitaiho for a month's holiday. On August 9 he wrote to Thomas Cocker-Brown, the foreign secretary, saying that he was enjoying the coolness and the freshness of the air. "We are not visiting so many of the meetings here as usual but once again we are having a very helpful time in that direction," he added. "New vision and new power."

"You will have seen by now what was the result of the suggestion of my temporary transfer to Siaochang. I personally feel that we came to the right decision and I believe all the others in the D.C. did too."

Then, referring to Patricia, Eric concluded, "We certainly hope that this added joy will enrich our fellowship one with another and with God." And she did. He and Flo often stood beside their daughter as she slept, unable to take their eyes off her. Together they whispered, "How did we ever manage to produce such a beautiful child?"

The longer Eric lived in Tientsin, the more he appreciated Peitaiho. In the morning, instead of being greeted by the noise of city traffic, he sat on the porch of the bungalow listening to the songs of birds and the sound of waves gently breaking on the beach below. Breathing deeply, he could feel strength flowing back into his body and spirit.

Eric had been the advisor for the graduating class of 1935, but expressed disappointment that he had been unable to forge a strong relationship with them. "I never felt I gained their loyalty or obtained any deep friendship," he said. He knew that he exerted an influence that could not always be seen, but added, "I do feel that I should be able to see more direct results from my work."

Back in Tientsin, with the issue of his assignment settled, Eric began the school year with a new determination to "put more into all that leads to a greater interest in all parts of the boys' lives and a deeper fellowship with the Staff." He began by hanging pictures on several classroom walls to brighten them up. The drab and sparsely furnished staff room, which had remained largely unused for several years, found new life as a common room after Eric rounded up some comfortable chairs and a few tables. Soon he tackled the task of finding new furniture for the boarders' rooms as well.

Just as Will Rowlands had planted flowers in Siaochang, Eric and Flo planted the seeds of brightness and beauty for the Chinese teachers and students around them. Eric seemed to bond more quickly with the boys in his new class, getting to know them personally and praying for many of them by name each day. He closed his report for 1935 by saying, "Greater discipline, deeper fellowship and the baptism of the Holy Spirit is what I seek and pray for in the coming year."

The year 1936 unfolded much like a spring day filled with light and promise. But the spring weather in Tientsin was as volatile as the political situation in China. A day that dawned sunny and bright could suddenly be plunged into near darkness at noon by a howling dust storm sweeping down from the Gobi Desert. From the Drum Tower to the Gordon Hall, the dry air fairly crackled with static electricity as people rushed for shelter holding handkerchiefs over their faces. Lamps were lighted in the old city, and electric lights turned on in the concessions. Servants hurriedly closed windows and stuffed rags under doors in a futile attempt to keep out the swirling dust. Soon a layer of grit covered everything inside even the finest houses. The storm would pass, but only after leaving its mark on everything and everyone in its path.

Everyone in China knew that political storm cells brewed on a dozen fronts, gathering strength for the day when they would unleash all their fury. The Communist forces under Mao Tse-tung had escaped extermination by Chiang Kai-shek's Nationalist Army and found refuge in a northern province after their "Long March" of 6,000 miles. Though diminished in numbers, their goal of dominating China had not changed.

In the capital of Nanking, Generalissimo Chiang Kai-shek played a dangerous game of political chess, trying to keep discontented students and domestic enemies at bay while maneuvering to avoid being overcome by the more powerful and aggressive Japanese. In the middle of it all, hundreds of millions of people awaited the next move, completely powerless to influence the outcome.

A few weeks before Eric and Flo's second anniversary, a remarkable return to winter froze nineteen ships in an ice field off Taku and blew them out to sea. Photos taken from airplanes sent to drop food to the stranded sailors appeared in local newspapers.

"It looks like the Arctic," Eric remarked to Flo. A glance outside the frosted windows of their flat revealed a city bundled against temperatures hovering at three degrees below zero.

In the College House, formerly occupied by Dr. and Mrs. Lavington Hart, Carl Longman labored over his memorandum on the college staffing question. When the issue again came before the Executive Committee, he hoped that the document would argue persuasively for the retention of all five foreign missionaries. If the appeal failed, he knew they would lose Eric Liddell.

The fact obvious to everyone was that Eric was the only member of the college's foreign staff suited for country work. A. P. Cullen was ordained, but his frail health could never stand the strain of rough travel and poor food. Longman had already given twenty-five years to the college and was an academic, not an evangelist. Luxon's gift was teaching, and by his own admission he was "not good at learning a language." To send Robert and Minnie Thompson away would cost the college two teachers. At the age of thirty-four, Eric was young, strong, and adaptable.

The spiritual work at the college was flourishing, with over 300 students enrolled in the voluntary Bible circles. A special series of messages at the Sunday services in the college chapel brought a strong response from the members of the senior middle classes. Eric brought the first message, titled "The Divine Lover," and Longman concluded the series six weeks later with "The Great Decision." During April and May, a total of fifty-six students were baptized, a bold step in which they made a public expression of their Christian faith. Each signed a covenant in which he declared his belief in Jesus Christ as his Savior, promised to follow and serve Him as his Master, and vowed to seek to learn of Him daily, as well as try to extend His kingdom among men.

A few students sought baptism because they thought it would bring preferential treatment and better grades from the British teachers. The long-time problem of "rice Christians," who professed faith to get a handout, was no stranger to the college. But most of those baptized were sincere believers who, after personal talks with their tutor, had genuinely given themselves to Christ the Lord.

On the heels of a successful year at the college, the LMS community was stunned by the death of Dr. John Wright, superintendent of the MacKenzie Memorial Hospital. After a short illness, Dr. Wright had succumbed to typhoid fever a week before his fortieth birthday. This was a hard blow to the Liddell family. John Wright and Rob Liddell had been medical students together at Edinburgh and had married sisters, Margaret and Ria Aitken. Like everyone else, the Wrights had looked forward to a month that summer at Peitaiho and long years of service in China. As friends grieved with Margaret and the two children, all were sobered by the reminder that they could always depend on God, but never on tomorrow.

At the end of July, the annual meeting of the North China District Committee convened in Peitaiho. Of particular interest was the committee's consideration of the Tientsin Anglo-Chinese College staff issue. After discussion, the committee agreed that "the present moment is not opportune for the transfer either of a man or a salary from the T.A.C.C." However, the college must plan, within three years, to reduce the number of LMS-supported staff to four.

The committee further recommended "that the T.A.C.C. be asked to loan the services of Rev. E. H. Liddell to the country evangelistic work for a period of not less than four months, either Autumn 1937 or Spring 1938. This would give Mr. Liddell a chance of getting experience in such work, on the basis of which he would be able to form a decision as to his future sphere."

The decision, a compassionate one for all involved, allowed Eric to stay at the college for another year. Then, after several months in the country field, he would have a year's furlough during which to decide whether he sensed God's call to continue. Myfanwy Wood clearly expressed the intention behind the official resolution: "We want him to test himself at country evangelistic work beforehand, so that if he feels it is God's will for him he will gladly give the rest of his life to it."

The month in Peitaiho, as always, was a tonic for Eric. "Here in the quiet of P.T.H.," he wrote to friends, "you feel all the world should be at peace; certainly there seems no place like this for me. Patricia can walk by herself, and trots all over the place. Just before I left she did twelve yards on her own but now she can do ever so much more." Each day on the beach, Patricia increased her range and pace, trotting along the sand until she fell with a surprised plop. The summer sun browned her legs and bleached her golden curls even whiter.

Eric, as always, wore a hat to cover his bald head, except when swimming. He might well have considered wearing the hat in the sea after a missionary colleague smacked his bald pate, thinking it was a large specimen of the stinging jellyfish so prevalent there. Eric surfaced and shocked his friends with a display of temper they thought didn't exist in him.

Every evening, with Trisha under the watchful eye of her amah, Flo and Eric walked the beach below East Cliff, talking of people and places and the future. Flo was expecting their next child in December, and they had already discussed names. If it was a boy, they would call him James Hugh, after both grandfathers. But when it came to choosing a girl's name, the agreement ended. Flo favored Carol since the baby was expected near Christmas. But Eric was set on Heather in honor of his native Scotland. For once, Eric's mediating skill failed to produce a resolution.

By mid-December they still had not agreed, so Eric suggested a drawing. He placed two slips of paper in a hat and gave Flo the honor of selecting the name. She unfolded the slip and read "Heather." A few minutes later, Eric confessed that he had written "Heather" on both slips. Flo threw a sofa cushion at him, but let the decision stand. It was hard to argue with a man who was laughing so hard.

When her December 19 due date passed and the days dragged on into January, Flo became quite concerned. One afternoon she said in a somber tone, "There's something I want you to promise me."

Sitting down beside her, Eric took her hand.

"If anything happens to me," she continued, "I want you to promise me you'll marry again, and I do hope you marry one of these girls nearer your own age." Flo went on to mention the names of two women she considered suitable candidates.

Eric pondered her solemn words for a few moments, then said: "Now, Flo, you know I'm always happy to do whatever you ask. However, since you chose my first wife for me, I think it would only be fair if this time I was allowed to do my own choosing." There was not the hint of a smile on his face, but his blue eyes twinkled with fun. Flo laughed too, then found herself crying and hugging this remarkable man who loved her so much. She knew she was the most fortunate woman in the world.

When Heather Jean finally arrived on January 6, 1937, Eric's Chinese colleagues at the college once again had to moderate their planned celebration. In Chinese culture having a son was paramount, and they found it hard to believe that an Olympic champion had failed twice in a row. They offered polite congratulations and discreet presents, but the plans for a congratulatory dinner were quickly scrapped. Eric didn't mind a bit and was once again awed by the second little princess who had come into his life.

A few weeks after Heather's birth, Rob and Ria arrived in Tientsin, bringing seven-year-old Ralph for X-rays at the MacKenzie Hospital. The doctors there confirmed Rob's fear that his son had developed tuberculosis of the spine. Because no adequate treatment was available in China, they booked the earliest available passage for Ria and Ralph to return to Britain. With Ralph encased in a plaster body cast, he and his mother sailed for England on March 2 from Shanghai. The prognosis for his recovery was good, but it meant they would be apart until Rob's next furlough in the summer of 1939.

As Eric's letters reveal, the spring of 1937 passed in a blur of activity.

"May 2, 1937: Every day this last week I have been at the Min Yuan for the heats of the North China Championships, and yesterday we had the finals. This has been the finest sports we have had as regards records, but there have been many points brought up which needed tact and quick decisions. Throughout it all I have been very conscious of the power of God to keep and help in the clarity of thinking. I find the standard of absolute honesty clarifies one's thinking.

"On Thursday, the Italian onlookers disagreed with my decision on the tug-of-war and ran in at the close. But with the book of rules in my pocket and my foot on the spot where the mistake had been made, it was quite easy to convince them of their error. I'll enclose the piece from the paper about it, which sounds much worse than it really was."

The article headline read: MR. ERIC LIDDELL NEARLY MOBBED.

His letter continued by telling of one member of his class for whom he had been praying for over a year. "He is captain of the football… but difficult and quick in temper. Last summer he turned sick, and I've kept my eye on him closely since. It was a great joy to have him come along on his own like that. Either to-day or to-morrow I see him particularly about the step [of baptism] he wishes to take.

"To add to this week's work, on Tuesday and Friday the staff have had volley-ball games from 7:30 to 8:30 a.m., before classes; and before that, from 6:30 to 7:30, I've had times of sharing with the Anglican minister. It's been a great time, and I feel quite fresh after it all."

Mid-May found Tientsin's British Concession glowing like a fairyland after dark as businesses and homes wrapped themselves in strings of red, white, and blue lights to celebrate the coronation of King George VI. On May 13, several thousand people gathered for the trooping of the colors, followed by a church service in Victoria Gardens and a reception at the home of the British Consul. To conclude the celebration, a British warship anchored in the Hai Ho River fired a twenty-one gun salute, those assembled drank the health of their new monarch, and the band played "God Save the King." Through the late afternoon and evening, people gathered around their wireless sets as the BBC relayed the coronation cere-mony from Westminster Abbey to listeners around the world.

The following day, Eric wrote to his family: "A resolution has gone round that Flo and I should go to Siaochang as from September so that if it is accepted by the Synod we shall be down in the south by the autumn."

With his class away on military drill, Eric found time to complete a study and teaching guide on the Sermon on the Mount for the Union Church Sunday school teachers. Scattered throughout its twenty-three typed pages were thoughts and quotations from some of Eric's favorite books, including *The Christ of the Mount* by E. Stanley Jones and Maude Royden's *Christ Triumphant*. But it also revealed his longing that the children grasp the meaning of Jesus' words. For the lesson on "Blessed are they which do hunger and thirst after righteousness; for they shall be filled," (Matthew 5:6), Eric wrote: "Try and see if the children know what it means to hunger and thirst. How long have they gone without food? One day? Two? Three? Describe what it is like — re-read some story of intense hunger so as to have a vivid picture in your mind or better still describe a poor beggar boy in Tientsin with his face close to the window of a shop with food in it."

"The Kingdom," Eric often said in Sunday school, "is where the King reigns. If He is reigning in my heart, then the Kingdom of Heaven has come to me."

When the college closed for the summer holidays, Eric again joined Flo and the girls in Peitaiho. "After a week or two at the sea-side we were all as brown as berries and as fit as could be," he reported.

On July 22, he returned alone to Tientsin to conduct the college entrance examinations for prospective students. For a week, Eric and the boys broiled in the 100-degree heat until the exams were completed. After marking the papers and posting the results, his thoughts turned to Peitaiho and a return to his family. Walking along Rue de Pasteur next to the college, he thought it odd that the concession barriers had been closed. He paused, and in the distance heard what sounded like firecrackers, but he knew of no reason for a celebration.

In a matter of minutes the sinister boom of heavy artillery and the whine of diving airplanes overwhelmed every other sound as the demons of war broke loose in North China.

FIFTEEN

Siaochang and the Rising Sun

1937–1940

Eric rushed across the street to the MacKenzie Memorial Hospital, where he and Carl Longman and old Dr. E. J. Stuckey climbed the stairs to the open roof. From that vantage point, sixty feet above the ground, they watched Japanese airplanes bomb the old city, just over a mile away. Diving and wheeling, the invaders rained destruction on sites suspected of harboring Chinese soldiers. Puffs of smoke were soon followed by hungry flames that spread through whole tracts of wooden structures. In an act of deliberate and wanton destruction, the planes reduced Nankai University and the nearby middle school to piles of rubble. Machine guns rattled incessantly through the afternoon, and artillery continued to boom long after the airplanes had departed. Longman wrote: "The firing sounds as if it were coming from our garden. No one knows what is really happening."

Soon it became clear that both sides were carefully avoiding the foreign concessions in Tientsin. The Japanese had no desire to provoke other foreign powers, and the Chinese army resisted any temptation to seek refuge in the foreign enclaves. The fighting lasted only three days before Tientsin fell to the superior Japanese forces on July 30. Resistance in Peking was even less. Tensions had been high since the July 10 clash between Chinese and Japanese forces at the Marco Polo Bridge, near Peking, but no one had expected a full-scale invasion. Now it appeared that Japan might try to overpower all of North China, just as it had taken Manchuria six years before. News on the wireless described the Japanese advance on several fronts.

The immediate problem for Eric and his colleagues was the growing flood of Chinese trying to enter the concessions. With the entire city in a state of emergency, Eric volunteered his services as an interpreter and also helped with police duties at the barriers leading into the British Concession. Carl and Amy Longman turned their attention to the 350 refugees who were soon camped in the college quadrangle, with an additional 150 housed in the hospital and the Taku Road Church. Hundreds of others caught in the crossfire sought treatment for their wounds.

For a week, Eric had no way to communicate with Flo and the children in Peitaiho. Slowly life in Tientsin, now under Japanese control, ebbed toward normalcy. Those Chinese who had been displaced by the fighting left the concessions. Foreigners were able to go about their business, except in areas where the armies of the Rising Sun pursued the retreating forces of Chiang Kai-shek.

In late August, Eric rejoined his family at the coast for a brief respite. With the railway cut south of Tientsin, and fighting in the countryside, their plans to move to Siaochang had been upset. It was rumored that if the Chinese Nationalist Army returned to fight the Japanese in Tientsin, all British subjects might be evacuated to Singapore.

Each day brought new and unsettling reports, and the LMS Emergency Committee in Tientsin met frequently, trying to cope with the chaos caused by the military situation. Missionaries on holiday and at conferences were scattered from Kuling to Kobe, with no reliable means of communication as they tried to return to their posts. At the end of August, the committee decided that Eric should remain at the college during the autumn term until it was safe to go to Siaochang. But no one knew how long that would be.

Remarkably, the Anglo-Chinese College opened in September with a record 575 students. Along with teaching classes, Eric spent considerable time overseeing the repair and renovation of the college buildings, a process that had been underway since early summer. With great satisfaction, he managed to equip the boarders' rooms with new beds and wardrobes. But it was hard to concentrate on life at the college when so many people in the country were suffering.

Will Rowlands, whose wife and children were in England, had returned alone to Siaochang in late September to find the countryside devastated by floods. Instead of the normal one day of travel from Tehchow, the forty-mile journey took him three days, the last two of them by boat across fields where only the tops of the ruined grain remained visible. In a letter that miraculously reached Tientsin, Rowlands said that two-thirds of the hospital had been destroyed and many other buildings heavily damaged by the flood. The missionary homes, the school, and the church inside the compound wall were intact, but that was all. Rowlands said he would remain there with his Chinese colleagues, but he appealed for Dr. Rob Liddell to return as soon as possible. British consular officials, however, forbade travel into the area, and not even a Chinese courier could get back through with a reply to Rowlands' message. Will carried on as the only missionary at Siaochang, relying on a Chinese doctor's wireless set for news of the outside world.

In November, the college released Eric, and he, along with others, began attempts to reach Siaochang. He traveled with Dr. Geoff Milledge and a small group to Tsangchow, halfway along the railway line to Tehchow. The Japanese allowed Milledge to remain but sent Eric and the others back. A week later Eric and Charles Busby reached Tehchow but were not allowed to travel to Siaochang. The Japanese politely returned their railway fare while firmly dispatching them back to Tientsin. There seemed no way to reach Rowlands.

As Rob and Eric sought God's guidance, another plan took shape in their minds. Since the Japanese controlled the railways and main roads, why not try a different approach? With the sanction of the Emergency Committee and the permission of the British Consul, they concocted a bold plan. It was not without risk, but worth a try.

On the morning of November 29, Eric kissed Flo and the girls good-bye and made his way with Rob through the British Concession to the bank of the Hai Ho. Along with three Chinese colleagues, they boarded a boat captained by a genial man who called himself "The Chief of the West River." His craft, 110 feet long, boasted a towering mast and weathered sail. From Tientsin, it was 275 miles upriver to their destination. The first day they covered only half a mile before being stopped by a Japanese sentry and held for twenty-four hours until a customs official arrived and cleared them to continue.

Since they could walk as fast as the boat was moving, each day Rob and Eric trudged endless miles along the muddy river bank to keep warm and relieve the boredom. On occasion, they helped pull the boat when there was no wind. At night they slept in their clothes, bundled against the cold. The price for avoiding the Japanese army was encountering groups of armed bandits and irregular forces who relieved the Chinese passengers of money and goods, while leaving the foreigners alone. Interrogations at bridges along the way were always unpredictable and usually conducted at gunpoint. Rob gave great credit to his colleagues, Ma and Liu, for saying the right thing in polite Chinese fashion whenever they met these irregulars.

After 120 miles on the West River, they said good-bye to "The Chief" and found "a round-faced, fat and jolly-looking fellow" who offered them a place on his boat traveling up the Fu Yang Ho toward the town of Heng Shui. A few days later they encountered another memorable character when they stopped for the night at the inn of a Chinese woman called Ta Chiao (Big Feet). Rob later described her as "a woman of large dimensions, very businesslike and capable of holding her own at any time, voluble and fond of repartee and fearless in what she said." She reminded him of a hurricane, and he reported that "after she had spoken for five minutes on end at a terrific speed without either punctuation or a pause for breath, we were left in the same state as the rustics in Goldsmith's 'Deserted Village':—'And still they gazed and still the wonder grew.'"

In late afternoon on December 7 Rob and Eric reached Heng Shui and decided to spend the night before traveling overland to Siaochang. They found the hospital of their friend Dr. Wu a mass of wreckage, and in one of the storage sheds Rob discovered the motorbike he had left there, now with tires flat, tool box missing, and enough screws removed by the Japanese to make it unusable.

The next day, with no carts available, the brothers covered the final ten miles to Siaochang on foot and walked through the front gate at 4:00 in the afternoon. Will Rowlands was in the middle of a meeting for the election of new deacons when the gatekeeper entered, bent close to his ear, and said in a hoarse whisper, "Li tai-fu lai la!" ("Dr. Liddell has come.") Will thought there must be some mistake since he knew it was impossible for anyone to reach Siaochang. He excused himself from the meeting, walked quickly to his house, and encountered two scruffy men in Russian fur hats who had not shaved or bathed for ten days. He hugged them both and laughed with joy after eleven weeks of isolation on the station.

Rob downplayed the dangers of the trip by saying: "We thoroughly enjoyed the whole affair, had plenty of fresh air, long sleeps and a healthy amount of exercise." The next Sunday a great service of thanksgiving was held in which he, Eric, and two of their Chinese colleagues spoke gratefully of the goodness and protection of God throughout the journey.

With the surrounding countryside in a state of near-anarchy, Will, Rob, and Eric met each morning to pray and seek God's guidance for their next step. If Christianity had a word of light and power for people in the grip of fear and despair, how could they best make it known? The thought that came was "Why not begin at home?" Nearly eighty people were living inside the LMS compound. Some had been Christians for many years while others had little knowledge of the gospel.

After several days of planning and organization, Will and the Liddells began a week of special meetings. Their goal was to offer a warm and joyous gathering with a clear presentation of the message of Christ. Each afternoon, Rob gave a brief talk on an Old Testament passage. When the main gate closed for the night, the compound residents had little to do, so in the evening a choir of local mission workers trained by Rowlands led the singing of evangelistic hymns, followed by an address in Chinese from Will, Rob, or Eric. And just as the flowers had blossomed after the autumn rains three years before, so new spiritual life burst forth amid the devastation of flood and war. "What rejoiced us most of all," Rowlands wrote, "was the way in which a number of those who had been nominal or cold Christians for many years heard Christ's call to full surrender and came out definitely on the Lord's side."

Three weeks later, with the countryside relatively quiet, Rob remained at Siaochang to man the station while Will and Eric traveled the road to Tehchow and then went by train to Tientsin. All along the rail line, charred buildings and overturned railway cars bore mute testimony to the recent fighting. But, for the present, the war had moved south, and after an uneventful journey the two men arrived in time for the annual meetings of the North China District Committee.

Because of the unsettled conditions, Eric and Flo decided that she and the children would remain in Tientsin. They dreaded the weeks of separation, but Eric's duties would bring him back to the city every month or so. When the military situation eased, they could join him in Siaochang.

With Will Rowlands scheduled to leave on furlough in the summer, Eric volunteered to delay his own furlough for a year so that the Siaochang district would not be without a country evangelist. Rob would become superintendent of the MacKenzie Hospital in Tientsin, but would visit Siaochang regularly to supervise the Chinese doctor until one of the new LMS physicians completed language school.

Eric's report for 1937 summarized his feelings after six weeks at Siaochang: "It has been good for me that in a year of unprecedented hardship and suffering for the people, I should be sent away from the city and that the journey down here (Siaochang) should have given me such an opportunity of seeing some of the hardest hit places between here and Tientsin.

"The floods have caused much havoc, but the loss sustained by them forms only a small part of the sorrows of the people. Fear reigns in all their hearts. Bands of irregular soldiers, bandits, etc., are all over the countryside. They settle on a village and live off it and the surrounding villages. Repeated demands are made to the villagers to supply grain, money, rifles, and food and they must supply these as best they can. Fear reigns everywhere and the bitterest thing of all is to think that this trouble comes to them from their own people in the midst of a great national tragedy. No year would have given me a better chance than this one in the country 'to sit where they (the common people) sit till their sorrows become my sorrows.'"

It was difficult for anyone outside North China to grasp the enormous suffering resulting from the Sino-Japanese war. Perhaps the most telling image was the widely published newspaper photograph of a Chinese baby sitting alone, crying, amid the charred bodies and smoking rubble of the Shanghai railway station. Later, when the capital city of Nanking fell to the invaders in December 1937 and the Japanese army was turned loose to wreak havoc on the city, the reports of the ensuing horror seemed unbelievable. The stories sickened those brave enough to read the eyewitness accounts given by foreigners who saw young women raped and murdered in the streets. Men were tied to posts and used for bayonet practice; thousands of captured Chinese soldiers were machine-gunned to death by Japanese troops, some of whom wept and vomited as they carried out the sadistic orders. Incredibly, the world stood idly by. British business interests continued to flourish, and American salvage firms sold shiploads of scrap iron to Japan at soaring prices. As the war wandered across China like a drunken man, atrocities by one side led to revenge by the other.

Chiang Kai-shek, accused by many of abandoning his people to the invading army, avoided every Japanese attempt to lure his forces into a decisive battle. The Chinese Nationalists and Communists set aside their differences long enough to resist the Japanese with a common strategy of attrition:

Enemy advances, we retreat;
Enemy stops, we harass;
Enemy withdraws, we attack.

For the next six months, life for Eric and Flo fell into a pattern of long separations punctuated by his sudden, unannounced arrivals in Tientsin. He came to purchase medical supplies for the hospital or handle a myriad of other logistical matters for the rural mission station. Often, the days in the city evaporated with little time for his family. Sometimes he received an urgent summons to return to Siaochang because of trouble there. After a hurried good-bye to Flo, he would board the train, hoping he could cross the Japanese military lines and dodge the ragtag bands of marauders without losing the precious goods in his care.

At any station on the railway journey, a third-class carriage might be invaded by Japanese smugglers transporting manufactured goods or narcotics. In full view of the cowed Chinese railway officials, they forced the occupants to leave their seats and go elsewhere. Talking loudly and placing their carefully guarded wicker baskets on the seats next to them, the smugglers arranged everything to their own liking.

Eric had seen evidence of the drug trade for years before the present hostilities broke out in 1937. Within a few blocks of the Anglo-Chinese College scores of drug manufacturing plants and retail shops operated openly under the privilege of extra-territoriality in the adjacent Japanese Concession. Some observers claimed that a deliberate policy of introducing and selling drugs in China was part of Japan's policy of subversion. Sales to international syndicates, including those in Europe and the United States, generated vast sums of money to fuel the war machine.

In the areas of North China under its control, Japan had banned the use of Chinese currency and introduced its own paper money. But in the places still under Chinese control, the Japanese scrip was worthless. One of Eric's recurring tasks was to obtain Chinese currency in Tientsin and bring it to Siaochang to pay the hospital staff, teachers, and mission workers. It was Flo's idea to hide the money in a hollowed-out loaf of French bread, which Eric carried in plain view, sticking out of the top of his knapsack.

In a letter to friends, he described the challenge of travel between Siaochang and Tientsin: "There are two main railways, one running from Tientsin to Shanghai, and the other from Peking to Hankow. These two lines are not quite parallel and pass, one forty miles to the east of us, and the other fifty miles to the west. The railway lines have been in the hands of the Japanese, but the land in between in the hands of the Chinese. With every visit to Tientsin we pass from the Chinese controlled part to the section occupied by the Japanese, the place of crossing being the ferry at Tehchow.

"Sometimes it has been easy passing the sentries and sometimes it has taken a long time. I think I have had nearly every type of experience. They have searched my shoes to see if I had secret letters hidden in them. On seeing my compass once, they said, 'May I have this, please,' or something to that effect. I told them it was of more value to me than to them. Once when I was at Sang Yuan waiting in the Inn, the Japanese Military came in to inspect all luggage. As I opened mine, the man's eyes fell on the New Testament. In slow and broken English, he said, 'Bible — you Christian?'; held out his hand and shook mine, then turned and went."

"And so it is as we go on these journeys we never know what kind of reception we'll get, but it's a good thing to take it all with a smile and to make sure that however troublesome things may be they aren't going to make one annoyed."

Eric carried photos of Patricia and Heather next to his identification papers and often showed both together. Many Japanese sentries were quickly disarmed by the smiling little girls, while others reached for pictures of their own children and showed them to Eric. Smiling and nodding, they allowed him to pass and saved their long interrogation for another traveler.

Eric's evangelistic forays to the villages around Siaochang took him into a veritable no-man's land inhabited by a hodgepodge of military forces. On any given day he might encounter Chinese Nationalist regulars, members of the Communist Eighth Route Army, local village militias, Japanese troops, or armed bandits posing as whatever they considered convenient for that day. On a regular basis he was questioned, detained, searched, and shot at. But his inconvenience and danger were overshadowed by the joy he experienced in his task.

In May, Eric and Will Rowlands traveled forty miles northwest of Siaochang to the market town of Hsin Chi. Along the way, Will told Eric the history of the church there and how the spiritual fire kindled during the autumn retreat at Siaochang five years earlier continued to blaze among the people. Eric was amazed to find a group of Chinese believers meeting each morning for prayer and a sharing of ideas on the Scripture passage for the day, then holding evangelistic meetings each evening in the church. On their own, these local Christians had commenced an outreach, roughly translated as "tea and talk," where friends were invited to come for tea, cakes, and conversation. In a very natural way, as the discussion turned to deeper matters, the believers of Hsin Chi told what the Savior meant to them.

"The place was alive," Eric wrote. "People were coming all the time for talks on all subjects but most of all for talks on spiritual matters, for, they said, their hearts were thirsty. It was specially busy for we were only to be there three or four days, and many who knew Mr. Rowlands wanted a time with him before he left for furlough. This trip showed me the vitality there was in this Church and the wide influence it is having on the neighbourhood besides introducing me to them and preparing the way for my next visit in December."

Not every village brought the same encouragement. In some places they found large church buildings built with money from the Boxer Indemnity Fund, but only a handful of timid believers. "The whole thing is too big a burden for the small number of Christians," Eric observed, "and I often wish we could scrap the whole lot and start again with Churches growing in the natural way, starting in a small way and as the life of the church increases so additions could be made."

Soon after their return to Siaochang, Will Rowlands went on furlough and Rob left to take up his responsibilities in Tientsin. Eric became "Acting Superintendent" of the hospital, responsible for completing the repairs and new construction.

In a late summer letter to D. P. Thomson in Scotland, Eric described his month at Peitaiho with Flo and the children as "a glorious holiday." The peaceful days and nights by the sea gave them more time together than they had had during the previous eight months. With Heather and Patricia in little seats fitted on Eric and Flo's bicycles, they had great fun pedaling along the beach and through the town. There were unhurried moments on the verandah when Tricia could rub her hand across Eric's bald head and announce, "Daddy, your hair has gone back."

Before bedtime, Eric entertained the girls with stories and rhymes. One little song always sent Trish and Heather into gales of laughter:

> "Little fly up on the wall
> Ain't you got no clothes at all?
> Ain't you got no shimmy shirty?
> Ain't you got no petti-skirty?
> Little fly?
> Ain't you cold?"

Yang Nai Nai, their amah, was intrigued by all the laughter and asked Eric to repeat the rhyme in Chinese. Upon hearing it, she smiled politely, indicating that the humor did not translate.

And every evening, with the girls sleeping under the watchful eye of Yang Nai Nai, Eric and Flo slipped out for a walk. They strolled the beach, savoring the fresh, clean air and the moments alone.

In conversations with fellow missionaries, Eric expressed his desire that Flo and the children should join him at Siaochang in the autumn. He felt they would be as secure inside the compound as they were in Tientsin, and it would completely relieve the stress of being separated. A few weeks later, the Executive Committee agreed. But before the move could be made, Arthur Chirgwin, General Secretary of the LMS, visited China for a firsthand look at conditions there. While he and Eric were traveling south of Tientsin, their train journey was interrupted because a portion of the track had been blown up by guerrilla forces. When they parted company, Eric casually encouraged Chirgwin to hide his money in his shoes as a safeguard against soldiers or bandits who would surely search his pockets. Before leaving China, Chirgwin suspended the Executive

Committee decision, concluding that the countryside was definitely "not safe." Flo and the girls had to remain in Tientsin.

Summarizing his first year at Siaochang, Eric wrote, "The scenes have changed so quickly and the problems been so varied that I almost wonder if I have been looking through a kaleidoscope." Many of the experiences mentioned so briefly in his annual report would each have required several pages to do them justice:

— Bicycle travel over roads that were intact one day would become impossible the next, after local residents were ordered to dig trenches across them to hinder Japanese trucks.

— In September, with the soaring price and growing scarcity of local coal, Eric contracted for sixty tons of hard anthracite in Tientsin, planning to take it back to Siaochang by barge. "People said it couldn't be done," Eric recalled, "which is always a good starting point." Creeping up the West River at two miles per hour on the barge, he was robbed twice by armed bandits, detained for a day and a half by the Japanese, then on two occasions forced by ragtag military groups to pay exorbitant "taxes." With his money exhausted, he left the barge and journeyed back to Tientsin for a fresh supply of currency. After a mutiny by the crew and a half-day's interrogation by members of the Communist army, he and the coal finally reached Siaochang.

— Just before Christmas, he returned to Hsin Chi to baptize a number of new believers. Rumors of an impending attack kept the congregation small, and in the middle of his address to the candidates, Japanese artillery shells rained down on the town, with two falling near the church. Soon after, thirty-one truckloads of Japanese soldiers rumbled in to search the town, including the church. "I don't think any who were baptised that day will easily forget the accompanying circumstances."

His annual report for 1938 concluded with a tribute to the grace of God, and the words of a poem received from a friend:

"HAPPINESS is to have enough for the day's needs with
always some to spare for those who have not.

"IT is to possess the love of friends and to have the knowledge
that all is well with them.

"IT IS TO LIVE IN PEACE WITH ALL MEN.

"HAPPINESS is to have the strength to face with courage all
that the day may bring.

"IT is to cherish the gift of laughter, to be quick to note all
that is lovely and of good report.

"HAPPINESS is to find our joy in the common things of life
for so will youth abide in our hearts till the end of our days.

"Thank God for the gift of happiness."

The minutes of the District Committee meetings held in February
1939 in Tientsin include the following entry. "Rev. E. H. Liddell's
Future Work: Mr. Liddell having expressed his conviction of his
call to Evangelistic work, the D. C. appoints him to this work and
informs the Synod of this action."

The minutes also indicate that the meetings had scarcely begun
when Eric and several of his colleagues were summoned back to
Siaochang to handle an emergency situation created by the growing
menace of Japanese troops and an expected influx of 2,000 refugees
from the adjacent village.

One of the men accompanying Eric was Dr. Ken McAll, who
had been in China just over a year. Young and outspoken, he was
regarded as somewhat of a loose cannon by the LMS officials in
Tientsin. He and his fiancée, Frances Aldridge, had been greatly
influenced by the Oxford Group and were both keen seekers of God
and His will. However, when the personal guidance Ken received
didn't coincide with the directives of the LMS, he freely made his
displeasure known.

After reaching Siaochang with Eric and the others, Ken's
baptism of fire as a missionary doctor came as the usual heavy load
of illness and injury among the local people was compounded by

increased military activity in the area. Especially heartrending were the many cases of innocent bystanders who simply could not get out of the way.

Ken and Dr. Keith Graham, another first-term missionary, were at the hospital on a cold winter day when a cart trundled through the front gate followed by Eric on his bicycle. Inside the cart lay a man with a serious gunshot wound, and riding unsteadily on the shafts was another Chinese man whose neck was swathed in dirty rags. The victim of a botched execution by the Japanese, he pressed the rags against a deep sword gash extending from the back of his neck to his mouth. Eric had picked up both men while traveling between Tehchow and Siaochang.

Within a few days, the man with the bullet wound died, while the one who had narrowly escaped decapitation began a slow recovery. During his convalescence, the doctors learned that he was a trained artist, so they supplied him with some materials of his craft. In gratefulness for the care he had received and the message of Christ he was hearing, he painted a number of beautiful watercolors. One, of a red peony rose, became Eric's favorite. Inscribed on it in Chinese characters were the words: "She (the peony rose) is the most beautiful in the city. Her (China) modesty and manner come from God."

As summer neared, each of Eric's hurried visits with Flo in Tientsin increased their anticipation of the furlough that lay just ahead. During his long absences the girls had become accustomed to waking early each morning and climbing into bed with their mother. One morning after Eric had slipped in quietly late the night before, Heather toddled in from her room and, upon seeing another head on the pillow, said, "Who's this, the cook?" Eric roared with laughter. "I knew the cook was like family," he said, "but I didn't know it had come to this!"

On a sweltering day in late June, Rob Liddell and A. P. Cullen stood at a Japanese barricade in Tientsin, hopelessly delayed by red tape. If they missed the train that afternoon, their chance to reach England via the Trans-Siberian railway would evaporate. When all seemed lost, a burly taxi driver approached them and said simply, "Follow me." With Rob and Cullen in tow, he moved to the head of the line waving a passport and shouting, "Deutsche! Deutsche!" The Japanese guards, believing him to be German, waved them through. Only as they drove to the station in the man's taxi did they discover that he was Jewish, not German, and his passport was expired. Who he was and why he had come to their aid they never knew. Two weeks later they were back in England.

Eric and his family were also scheduled to leave in June, but increased harassment from the Japanese forces around Siaochang caused him to delay their departure until the end of July. When he volunteered to stay even longer, the Executive Committee practically ordered him to leave on furlough. If the situation in China continued to deteriorate, his colleagues would need him back rested and refreshed in a year.

In mid-August, they said good-bye to Hugh and Agnes MacKenzie in Tientsin, then sailed for Canada, looking forward to a month in Toronto where they would visit with Flo's brothers and sisters before traveling on to Britain. Their one hope was for time together as a family, free from the dangers and uncertainties of hostile armies. But just as they reached Toronto, Hitler invaded Poland, and two days later Britain and France responded with a declaration of war. Within hours, a German U-boat sank the passenger liner SS *Athenia* off the Irish coast, leaving 118 people dead and throwing the Liddells' plans into confusion.

On September 5, Eric wrote to the LMS Foreign Secretary, Cocker-Brown, trying to sort out their options. Eric felt that taking Patricia and Heather to Britain right now would be "most unwise." Travel across the Atlantic was risky, and there had been talk of evacuating women and children from cities in Britain in case the Germans invaded. "I would like therefore to suggest," Eric continued, "that I take my furlough here and that arrangements be made between the L.M.S. and the United Church of Canada for the year or part of the year that I am here."

Cocker-Brown replied with understanding, while stressing that the Deputation Department was counting on Eric's being in England for the next year. "Our problem of maintaining the Society's income is not going to be an easy one, as you may imagine, and we are going to make special efforts to make good means of approach to churches which are being cut off by war conditions." In the end, the foreign secretary put the ball compassionately but squarely in Eric's court: "We shall have to leave the final decision with you, but we are anxious on the one hand to have you in England and, on the other, to avoid unnecessary risk of travel to your wife and family."

But with more than a week's turn-around time between airmail letters, Eric and Flo had to take action before Cocker-Brown's reply had arrived. They decided to rent a house in Toronto where Flo and the girls would stay while Eric traveled to Britain.

Much of Eric's next letter concerned a request for special financial arrangements necessary during their months of separation. "The fact is," he wrote to Cocker-Brown, "to cover expenses for the family here and myself elsewhere I shall have to call upon all I have.

"I should arrive in Liverpool about November 3rd," he continued, "am feeling fine and fit and will be ready for deputation work at once. You can make it as heavy as you like, for my family being here, I shall have no home ties except to spend time with mother. The winter is the heavy time for deputation. I would appreciate it if by May I could be released and allowed to return here for some time with the family."

By early November Eric had reached Edinburgh and was living with his mother. With war raging in Europe and goods rationed at home, life was far different from his visit eight years earlier. There were no large "welcome home" meetings this time and little fanfare in the press. But once again, people were hungry for news of China. Along with his observations on the war with Japan, Eric sought to bring before people the church in China and the suffering it was experiencing. Eric rarely spoke in public of his dangerous encounters with bandits and military forces, but one listener recalled the profound impact of a talk that was "just a simple portrait gallery, in words, of some of his Chinese friends and contacts."

One of Eric's great joys was a visit with D. P. Thomson, who at the age of forty-three had married for the first time only a few months before. When Eric met the woman who had married the irrepressible D. P., he saw in quiet Mary Rothnie the perfect counterpoint to the rousing melody of Thomson's life. As a wedding gift, Eric gave them a beautiful watercolor painting from China and told them the story of the artist who had found healing of body and spirit at Siaochang.

By late January of 1940, it was clear that the LMS wanted Eric to stay for their annual meetings, which had been moved from May to June. Once again he was faced with a decision about Flo and the children. If he could not return to Canada until July, it would mean only a month together before their furlough ended. In addition, he was unsure if the mission would allow wives and children to return to China. He needed to let Flo know something before April 17 when the lease for the house in Toronto had to be terminated or renewed.

Flo had been pleading with Eric for weeks to let them come to Scotland and be with him. With the prospect of having to work until June, along with the deceptive lull in military action known as "the phony war," Eric decided it was time for them to be together again. Elated, Flo and the girls boarded the Cunard White Star Liner *Scythia* in New York for the ten-day journey. The ship could accommodate 2,200 passengers but carried only 147 brave souls on this wartime voyage across the Atlantic.

When they reached Liverpool on March 23, Flo cabled their arrival to Eric, who was in Ireland for LMS meetings. But their journey wasn't over yet. They had safely crossed the U-boat infested North Atlantic, only to have their train to Edinburgh involved in a collision that shattered windows throughout the car, threw everyone in their compartment to the floor, and left them groping to find each other in the dark. Amazingly, neither Flo nor the girls were among the scores of passengers injured in the accident. After the train was pulled back to the station in Carstairs, some friendly sailors home on leave treated them to tea and entertained the girls.

Meanwhile, Rob's wife, Ria, and Jenny's husband, Charlie Somerville, waited anxiously at Waverley Station, knowing only that there had been an accident and the injured were being treated. Eric had phoned earlier in the evening from Ireland and had no idea anything had gone wrong. His family finally arrived in Edinburgh just after 1:00 in the morning.

Safe at home with Eric's mother, Flo poured out the story over a steaming mug of Horlicks malted milk before they all went gratefully to bed. The next day, Flo wrote to her own mother, "We're just fine this morning — a bit stiff and a few bruises but isn't it a miracle? The children seem none the worse. I'm going to phone Eric tonight. He'll be home Wed. morning.

"It's grand to be here. The weather is perfectly heavenly and there are crocuses in the garden. I must fly now. I'll write soon. Your loving, Florence."

When Eric arrived home, it was hard to tell who was most excited, Flo or the girls. He swept them all up in his arms and held them tight until Patricia and Heather wriggled free. They had so much to tell him and so many things they wanted to do. Being together again after four months apart seemed too good to be true.

Mary Liddell doted on the granddaughters she had never seen and gladly watched them while Eric and Flo slipped away to be alone.

"The other evening," Flo wrote to her sister Margaret, "Eric and I started out to see Deanna Durbin in "First Love." We went to one place and found a queue about a block long — so we took a car down to Princes Street to another theatre that was showing the same picture — and there we found a queue two blocks long. We didn't feel like standing around so we bought a paper and looked over the shows. We found "Mad About Music" at a theatre not far from here. Eric has never seen Deanna so we went there. A snappy little theatre, very modern — good machines."

Later, they made their way home through the darkened streets of Edinburgh, blacked out against the threat of German air raids. Walking arm in arm with her husband, Flo didn't mind a bit. With him she felt completely safe.

Her letter to Margaret continued:

"Mrs. Liddell is fine and we get along very well together. She has failed a lot since we [Flo and Marg] saw her ten years ago but she is really very energetic. She thinks I underclothe the children but we haven't come to blows yet!!

"The grass is ever so green and the snowdrops, crocuses and daffodils are all out in full bloom. It really is gorgeous. I'm still wearing my fur coat and I'm glad I wasn't here all winter.

"Eric goes away again this Sat. and then I'll try and get some work done!! The children will hardly let Eric out of their sight. We're all having the time of our lives and enjoying life immensely.

"I hope you're all well and flourishing. Give my bestest love to Esther and Fin. Tell Jeff I got the letters she forwarded — for which many thanks. Cheery-bye for now. Try and find a minute to send me a scratch.

"Your ever loving sister, Flo."

After they had stayed with Eric's mother for several weeks, Eric and Flo were graciously given the use of a bungalow at Carcant by Charlie and Jenny Somerville. At this family retreat twenty miles outside Edinburgh, in a valley surrounded by the Moorfoot Hills, Eric and Flo found the tranquillity they had sought for so long. The loudest sound was the bleating of the sheep grazing on the hillsides, or the sputtering engine of a small truck bringing Adams the butcher from Dalkeith or Forsyth the baker from Innerleithen.

Each morning, Patricia and Heather walked by themselves to the shepherd's house and carried back metal pitchers of warm, fresh milk. To further encourage their developing self-reliance, Flo let the girls dress themselves, adding to the general amusement of everyone when Heather appeared in unusual combinations of colors and clothing. Afternoons found them swimming with Eric and Flo in the small lochan, basking in the pockets of shallow water warmed by the sun. Because several families had cabins at Carcant, the girls always had playmates and the freedom to roam the valley with friends. One afternoon Eric was walking with the girls when a rabbit ran down the fence-row in front of them. With a burst of speed, Eric ran the bunny down and picked it up by the hind legs. Heather and Patricia hardly had time to express their delight before their father snapped the rabbit's head against the fence and killed it. They were horrified and immediately began to cry. Eric had been so intent on bringing game home for "rabbit pie," to supplement their meat ration, that he hadn't reckoned on the little girls' reaction. Their grief was quickly forgotten, however, when he told them they could catch a bunny if they could put salt on its tail. Trish and Heather spent many happy hours with salt shakers in hand, one step behind the local hares.

In June, Rob came for a visit and told Eric that after an agonizing time of heart searching and seeking God's direction, he had decided not to return to China. His son, Ralph, still required hospitalization for his spinal condition, to be followed by a long process of convalescence and therapy, and Rob didn't feel it would be right to leave Ria to cope alone, especially during wartime. Earlier, he had expressed his struggle in a letter to the LMS General Secretary: "I never thought of anything but a whole lifetime spent on the mission field till recently when events and circumstances forced it upon me. My heart, my spirit, my desires and will all tend towards the one end and the one place, but these are not always the guiding lines or principles."

On June 12, Rob had written Arthur Chirgwin, regretfully informing him of his final decision: "In many ways it would be much easier for me to go back to China, even if it were only for another term of service and to complete 20 years, but with the responsibilities that are clearly mine at this time I see no alternative but to resign from the Society, and start some form of work in this country."

With sixteen years of service under the LMS, Rob needed four more years to be eligible for a retirement allowance. But his family needed him now. The society regretfully accepted his resignation, but hoped that he might be able to return to Tientsin when his circumstances were different. Words were inadequate to convey the mutual sense of loss experienced by Rob at the prospect of leaving the work in China and by his colleagues there, when they heard that he would not return.

The war seemed so distant from the little valley in Scotland, but it was very real and pressing. At Carcant, they listened to Winston Churchill tell the people of Britain that he could offer only "blood, toil, tears, and sweat." They followed the miraculous escape of more than 300,000 British, French, and Belgian troops from Dunkerque, and agonized over the fall of France. And then there was Hitler's chilling boast that he would march into London by September. In July, the Luftwaffe began to blast British airfields and ports.

Eric and Flo continued to take their future one step at a time. They planned to return to China in the autumn, but realized how quickly things could change in the uncertain climate of the deepening world conflict. After a visit with friends, Mary and George Cameron, Eric sent them a thank-you note, saying: "I only hope at some future date you'll be able to visit us; but where or when that will be it is rather difficult to know! Canada? China? Perhaps here?"

As July ebbed into August, they treasured each day at Carcant. Local folk who had lived in the area for a lifetime could not remember a golden summer like that of 1940 when warm, sunny days followed each other for weeks. At night, Eric seldom needed to light the little coal fire in the sitting room where they talked and read and played endless games of Snakes and Ladders with the girls. A glass of cold, pure spring water from a pipe in the kitchen still seemed luxurious after years of boiling their drinking water. And no one came at night to summon Eric away to deal with the aftermath of a flood or a marching army.

When their time at Carcant came to an end, everyone was sad to see them go. Eighteen-year-old Alie Somerville sensed there was something special about Eric and Flo. They were so easy to talk to, so enjoyable to be around, they seemed to raise the level of thought and conversation just by their presence. Everyone from the Big House to the shepherd's cottage commented among themselves about the kindness and personal interest Flo and Eric showed them.

But inevitably the time came, on a late summer day, that the Liddells loaded their things into the Baby Austin that Charlie and

Jen had loaned them and slowly motored back to Edinburgh to say good-bye. A few days later, Jenny drove them to Waverley Station. She hugged Eric, kissed the little girls, and handed Flo a large bag of sweets, precious in those days of rationed sugar.

And then they were gone.

❧ SIXTEEN ❧

Accelerating Uncertainty

1940–1941

Tight security and repeated inspections of luggage greeted the Liddells as they boarded the ship on August 12, 1940, in Liverpool. Announcement followed announcement: "All cameras must be turned in and will be returned on landing in Canada." "Life boat drill will be conducted in one hour." "All passengers must put on life belts when the signal is given." Even the ship's name had been painted over on the hull to keep enemy agents from collecting information about sailings.

But none of the three hundred passengers and crew complained. Like a metal duck in a shooting gallery, their ship had to steam across the Atlantic where scores of Hitler's U-boats lay submerged, awaiting their arrival. Once out of port, their small ship took its place in the center of a fifty-ship convoy, flanked by cargo vessels and escorted by warships of the Royal Navy. But even that could not guarantee their protection.

Just off the Irish Coast, the hunters began to stalk their prey. Tricia and Heather were asleep at 8:30 in the evening when Eric felt a thud against the side of the ship, followed by a loud bang. They had been hit by a torpedo whose cap exploded without detonating the warhead. Immediately the ship began a zigzag pattern, signaling the convoy to follow suit. In spite of sleeping in their clothes and hearing constant alarms, Eric and Flo tried to make a game of it for the girls. If they couldn't shield them from danger, they could at least guard them from fear.

The next day, the "all clear" signal allowed the passengers to gather in the dining room, only to be sent away during the first course by another alarm. That night they lost a ship near the back of the convoy, and the following morning, with everyone standing by the lifeboats, a ship exploded and sank just a quarter of a mile away. A day later, the naval escort reluctantly pulled away, leaving the convoy to complete the crossing unguarded. When the total of lost ships reached five, the convoy commander gave instructions to break the formation and disperse. Day and night, through rough seas, the engines throbbed above their normal limit, racing across the open water.

On Sunday, August 18, at the request of the passengers, Eric conducted an evening service of thanksgiving for their escape. But before they sighted the coast of Nova Scotia, the Germans had struck again — this time hitting Patricia and Heather with measles "of the unpatriotic variety." Besides discomfort for the girls, this meant that they might be held in quarantine.

When the ship docked at 9:00 in the evening, Eric and Flo were told they must go through immigration that night. Fortunately, since their immediate destination was Toronto, they were passed medically. Unfortunately, all the hotels were full. So while Eric loaded the heavy luggage to be sent ahead, Flo took the children to a Red Cross shelter for some refreshments. With no place to stay, they took a taxi back to the ship, arriving after midnight. The beds in their cabin had been stripped, so they slept in their clothes and left the next day for Toronto.

For a brief time in September, the Liddells were between the war in Europe and Asia. As they enjoyed a quiet lakeside picnic with Flo's family, German bombs rained down on London, and Japanese troops took over the village next to the LMS compound at Siaochang. But they willingly left the peaceful surroundings in Canada, and by the end of October they were back in China.

After settling Flo and the children in Tientsin, Eric traveled the familiar route to Siaochang. A hundred miles south of Tientsin, the train passed through Tsangchow, where the LMS had recently been forced to close its hospital and withdraw its missionaries. Dr. Geoff

Milledge, the superintendent there, had gone to Siaochang, where he and the rest of the missionaries eagerly awaited Eric's arrival. During the past months it had become more apparent that the Japanese wanted them out of Siaochang, and soon. In July, the Japanese had imprisoned Mr. Ma, one of the teachers, on trumped-up charges of collaborating with the Communist Eighth Route Army. Continued reprisals against the Chinese staff left the missionaries wondering whether their presence was helping or hindering their colleagues.

A letter from Eric written in early December said: "No home letters have come through yet, though we have been back here over a month. The missionaries here with children at home are just longing for news of them. As you know, this place is a garrisoned village now. As I look out of my bedroom window, in the east house, the south village looks like one of the outposts of the Empire. The last few days we have watched rather depressed and dejected men going out on forced labour, to prepare a motor road to pass to the east of Siaochang."

He had recently spent the weekend in a village where he held services, welcomed new members into the church, and performed a wedding. "After the bowing was over and the benediction pronounced," Eric wrote, "we turned and went to where the bridal dinner was prepared. And so, in the midst of all the fears and alarms, the world goes on as if all were calm and quiet. The heavier guns could be heard that evening only a mile away, as they fired in the direction of the people who were cutting up the road. But in Huo Chu we just met together for a service of prayer, praise and thanks, thinking about our contribution to a better world; and the bridal pair spent their first night with the sound of gunfire in their ears, but love and joy in their hearts."

Of his travels throughout the district to the various churches, Eric said: "When I am out it is giving, giving, all the time, and trying to get to know the people, and trying to leave them a message of encouragement and peace in a time when there is no external peace at all."

Eric was able to spend two weeks at Christmas with Flo and the girls, and again came back to Tientsin at the end of January for the annual District Committee meetings. But the sessions had hardly begun when an urgent message arrived from Milledge in Siaochang. It appeared the Japanese were making their move. Eric and Ken McAll left immediately, arriving at the compound on January 28. Before Will Rowlands arrived three days later, the Japanese had interrogated the Chinese headmaster and several teachers, accusing them of anti-Japanese teaching in the school.

The missionaries did not want to abandon their friends, the station, or the work, but their Chinese colleagues unanimously agreed that nothing would be gained by their remaining. The time had come for the missionaries to evacuate Siaochang. Eric sent a message to the Japanese Officer-in-Charge saying they had decided to leave, but wished to discuss several important matters with him, including their departure and the arrests of their workers. The officer arrived with a cadre of troops, repeated the accusation of anti-Japanese teaching, and gave the missionaries two weeks to get out. Eric shuttled back to Tientsin to inform the committee, then traveled south once again to help with the evacuation.

As the Japanese Officer-in-Charge inventoried the furniture and equipment in the compound, Eric walked alongside him through the missionary houses. Eric did not tell him that his father had helped build the homes nearly four decades before. Nor did he speak when they paused for a moment in Jenny's room, then walked downstairs to the place where he had jabbered with Yu Kwan and learned his first Chinese words. On the verandah, only Eric noticed the hook that had held the rope swing on which, their amah had protested, Rob and Eric would break their necks. Memories were strong, but there was no time for nostalgia.

On February 13, the Officer-in-Charge sealed the hospital, school, and foreign residences. He took the keys from Will Rowlands and gave him a list of the inventoried items, which none of the missionaries expected to see again. Eric cycled alongside the last cart out of the compound, confident of God's goodness yet deeply distressed by the unchecked cruelty of man. By February 18 everyone was back in Tientsin, and a cable was sent to London: "SIAOCHANG SAFELY EVACUATED."

Two days later, word came that the headmaster and a woman teacher at Siaochang had been released. The Japanese had achieved what they wanted — the missionaries were gone. But across the North China Plain the ground had been tilled and the seeds of faith planted. They would blossom and grow as God gave the increase.

All the Siaochang missionaries received temporary assignments, with Eric being appointed to the country field of Tientsin. With little opportunity for work outside the city in the current conditions, his immediate concern was for his family. Flo had just given him the wonderful news that she was expecting a baby in September, which added a new dimension to their deliberations about the future.

The LMS went on record that "the present situation does not warrant any general withdrawal of L.M.S. missionaries from North China. We should aim at maintaining the work until conditions render this impossible." The mission was not pressing for the evacuation of wives and children, as were the American and Canadian societies, but the LMS fully supported any of their members who wished to send their families home.

It was not a clear-cut decision for anyone. Flo's best friend, Betty Thomson, was now back in China, married to Dr. Godfrey Gale and expecting her first baby in mid-summer. In February the Gales had requested passage home for Betty, but later reconsidered. Betty packed and unpacked three times before they finally decided they would stay together in China. Everyone balanced the difficulty of separation against the safety of those they loved most.

For nearly three months Eric and Flo went back and forth on the issue. She just couldn't bring herself to leave after being separated for most of the previous four years. Finally, in April, they decided she and the girls should go back to Canada. She could live with her parents for a time, have the baby in September, and stay in Toronto until Eric could join her. Both of them felt he would be back in a year, certainly not more than two. Something had to give in China, and when it did, the foreigners would simply be told to leave. The British consular officials would give them ample warning.

Eric believed Flo and the girls would be safer to cross the Pacific on a Japanese ship, so they booked passage on the *Nita Maru*, sailing from Kobe in May.

A few days before their departure, the Tientsin Grammar School, where Patricia attended kindergarten, held its annual sports day. Eric and Trish entered the Fathers and Daughters Race, and for obvious reasons were favored to win. But after Patricia ran her portion of the race, she wouldn't give the handkerchief to her father. By the time Eric persuaded her to let him take it, the race had been won by someone else. Eric didn't mind losing, but later that evening he used the experience to have a word with Patricia. "It doesn't matter if you win," he told her, "but no matter what you're doing, it's important to always do your best."

A few days later, the Liddells traveled together across the Yellow Sea to Japan, feeling the strangeness of being in the land whose aggression had so altered their lives. Patricia, nearly six, seemed to sense the importance of their journey, but to four-year-old Heather it was simply a lark, and their four days in a Japanese hotel a wonderful family holiday.

Then, on a bright sunny day, it was time to say good-bye. They boarded the *Nita Maru*, a beautiful new ship that was making only its third Pacific crossing. Eric took them to their cabin and after stowing their hand baggage, he picked up Patricia and set her on his knee. Speaking softly and with a smile, he told her that she was getting to be a big girl and he wanted her to help Mummy, help take care of Heather and help with the new baby that was coming. Would she promise to do that for him until he got back home?

She nodded and hugged her daddy. Of course she would take care of everyone. "I promise," she said.

Outside their cabin, a voice crackled over the loudspeaker, first in Japanese and then in English: "All visitors must now leave the ship. All visitors must please now leave the ship."

Flo placed a hand on her churning stomach, not knowing whether being six months pregnant or leaving Eric was making her feel so sick.

Eric scooped up the girls, giving each a fierce hug. He held Flo gently, kissed her, and closed the cabin door behind him.

Flo kept her composure just long enough for Eric to ascend the stairs; then she burst into tears. Patricia, who had just promised to take care of everyone, rushed to her mother's aid, asking if she could bring her an aspirin and a drink of water.

Heather had seen her father come and go so often that this day seemed no different from his traveling back to Siaochang. "Let's go see if they have a swimming pool on this boat like they did on the last one," she said blithely.

Patricia scolded her for even thinking of such a thing when Mummy was feeling so badly.

Hearing her four-year-old rebuked by her older sister for "bothering Mummy" was too much for Flo. Taking a deep breath, she pulled herself together. "All right," she said, "that's enough of that. Come on, we all go look for the nursery and maybe we can see Daddy on the pier."

On the upper deck they made their way to the rail and Patricia shouted, "There he is!"

Eric, in his characteristic white shorts, sport shirt, and knee-length socks was striding quickly away from the ship along the pier. Suddenly he turned, scanned the ship, and spotted them.

Flo and the girls waved furiously. "Good-bye, Daddy," they shouted. "I love you. I love you. Come home soon."

Eric stood motionless on the pier as the tugs eased the *Nita Maru* out of her berth and into the harbor. In three weeks, Flo and the girls would be in Toronto.

"It's better for them," he said to himself. "They'll be safe until I get home."

Back in Tientsin, Eric continued in his rather ill-defined role as evangelist to the Tientsin country field. When possible, he made brief visits to the outlying villages to establish contact with Chinese pastors and to encourage the local congregations. But the unsettled military situation kept him in the city most of the time. There, his duties seemed to be nearly as much administrative as spiritual.

During the previous year, the LMS had been forced to abandon its country fields in Tsangchow and Siaochang. Now, it seemed prudent to place property deeds in the British Consulate in Tientsin, and to make photographic copies for the mission safe. Authorities in the French Concession were consulted about their willingness to operate the MacKenzie Memorial Hospital if mission doctors had to be withdrawn.

But the most pressing questions involved personnel. If evacuation from North China became mandatory, some missionaries might be sent home while others could be voluntarily reassigned to the parts of western China not under Japanese control. But it was all guesswork until circumstances demanded a change.

When a request came through from the Chinese Church of Christ in China asking that Eric Liddell be permanently reassigned to the far southwest in Yunnan Province, the Executive Committee unanimously agreed that he should remain in Tientsin. The fact that Eric had now served in North China for sixteen years made him a highly respected member of the LMS during the turbulent days of change.

In the midst of all this uncertainty and contingency planning, life followed a familiar pattern. At the end of June, Eric moved into the upper college flat with A. P. Cullen, whose wife and children had remained in England after their last furlough. Cullen was glad for the company and remarked that they had no disagreements over what kind of food Yen Chih prepared because Eric "seems to like everything."

Although he desperately missed Flo and the children, there is no evidence that Eric spent a lot of time second-guessing the decision to send them to Canada. They had prayed, asked God's guidance, and by faith had chosen the path they felt right for them. Other missionary colleagues with pregnant wives, including Dr. Godfrey Gale and Dr. Ken McAll, had decided to remain together in China. To its credit, the LMS had supported both courses of action, giving its missionaries great freedom in matters related to their families. In July, Betty Thomson Gale and Frances McAll both safely welcomed their firstborn, both daughters, in Tsinan. Eric rejoiced when he heard the good news, knowing that Flo would be pleased when she heard of Betty's safe delivery.

He spent the month of August at Peitaiho but found the situation there markedly different from other summers. The number of people from the international business community had decreased dramatically, and most of the foreigners seemed to be missionaries. As he walked the beaches, often by himself, he noticed very few American women and children. Many of the British men, like him, were there without families. The entire foreign community had dwindled, and only a few people were staying for the entire summer season. On Rocky Point, children still posed for photos and shouted as the sea spray drenched them. But their mothers and fathers wondered if this would be their last summer of cool breezes and carefree nights in their cherished sanctuary of Peitaiho.

One of the most noticeable consequences of Japanese authority in the town was that the whole system of garbage collection had collapsed. At the urging of doctors, housewives in the foreign community began burning and burying their own rubbish to lessen the threat of contamination and disease. It was another reminder that the freedom and efficiency achieved by a cooperative international community was a relic of the past.

Eric returned to Tientsin on September 1, 1941, with his thoughts focused on Flo and the impending arrival of their third child. Whether the baby was early or late, he could expect a cable anytime. During the four months he and Flo had been apart, the letters that had managed to get through had been a lifeline to them both. He could picture his wife and girls so clearly in Toronto, living in a house on Rathnally Avenue with her parents, now home on furlough. Patricia, just as she had promised, was helping Flo in many ways. Heather had been to church with her granny and was very well behaved. As he read of Heather's good manners in church, Eric smiled, wondering who would dare behave otherwise sitting next to the imposing Agnes MacKenzie. Flo's father was thinking of returning to Tientsin, in spite of the deteriorating situation. The mission wanted Hugh MacKenzie back, and he longed to go.

On September 10, Eric wrote Flo with all his news from Tientsin. He had received two letters from her in one day and was glad to hear she had received five of his. But now it appeared that the mail might leave Tientsin only once every three weeks, so he would make this letter a long one.

The intimacies they shared by mail belong only to them. But the day to day events of their lives open a window of understanding into the sustaining power in their lives. Eric reported that in preparation for a series of special meetings at which he was to speak, he had been studying Divine guidance. Whom does God lead? What are the obstacles to His guidance? What means does He use? Circumstances? The enlightened Christian conscience? His Word? The inner voice? Prayer, thought, and meditation? Perhaps all of these. In addition, he had been pondering the Sermon on the Mount and the work of the Holy Spirit in a Christian's life.

Along with his study of the Bible, Eric often read the books of E. Stanley Jones, jotting down passages. In *The Christ of the Mount*, Jones had said: "The first three Beatitudes strike at the aggressive attitude to life, preparing us for the most amazing offensive of love."

In his present circumstances, Eric's meditations were far from theoretical. When passing through Japanese checkpoints — being questioned, searched, and often endlessly delayed on the whim of an arrogant soldier — the truths he studied became realities. A person either came home at night frustrated and fuming, or filled with the peace of God. Eric had concluded that in every daily contact he had, whether with British, Japanese, or Chinese, he wanted to be part of God's "amazing offensive of love."

Through quiet times of prayer and Bible reading, Eric gained assurance that God would sustain him during the days and months to come. He knew that confirmation of the Lord's guidance would come only by faith, not by whether the resulting circumstances were good or bad.

Eric jotted down the following thought about God's presence during difficult times: "When thou passest through the waters, (the wide, wide waters that demand perseverance, the unseen, unsailed waters that demand faith and confidence, the cruel, pitiless waters that demand patience and courage and unfailing love), I will be with thee."

Many afternoons, Eric and A. P. Cullen went for a long walk together through the French or British Concessions. Occasionally they took in a movie at the Empire Theater or one of the less expensive Chinese establishments. Walt Disney's *Pinocchio* provided an evening of diversion, while *Susan and God*, starring Joan Crawford and Fredric March, sparked a lively discussion about the Oxford Group Movement. During the Siaochang days, Eric had planned so many times to take Flo to a movie or a concert, only to have his visits to Tientsin consumed by work, then abruptly ended by an urgent summons to return to the station. Now he had endless time and no family to fill it.

September 19 brought a cable with the long-awaited news that Nancy Maureen had been born on September 17 in Toronto. He cabled back immediately. "Wonderful news! Love, Eric."

A few days later, he and Cullen celebrated Maureen's birth, along with half a dozen other family birthdays and anniversaries, with dinner in a restaurant, followed by a movie. With little extra money, the evening could not have been considered lavish, but it was festive, leavened with laughter and repartee. Later, they tuned in the wireless to catch the BBC news relayed from Shanghai. Cullen preferred that station over Hong Kong because the Shanghai broadcast always concluded by playing at least a few bars of "There'll Always Be an England."

In spite of the few touches of normalcy on the surface, the situation in North China was clearly unraveling at the deepest level. One of the most discouraging disruptions involved delivery of mail. In past years, a letter that caught the Siberian mail would usually reach England in two weeks. Now, postal communication had become completely unpredictable, with weeks or months elapsing between letters from home. Cullen went for three months with only a smattering of news from his family, then received thirty-two letters in two days. This feast or famine system could take people to heights of elation or plunge them into depths of depression, depending on what arrived — or didn't arrive — in the mail.

In October, Eric made a brief foray into the countryside, taking along J. Edwin Davies, a young LMS recruit from Cambridge. College friends had dubbed Davies "Bear" because of his affinity for A. A. Milne's *Winnie the Pooh*. The nickname followed him to China and quickly became his title throughout the missionary community. For a week, Eric and Bear bicycled to villages in the plain some twenty miles outside Tientsin, where they stayed in Chinese homes and ate the humble food offered them. Their conversations with their hosts were about Christ the Savior, with Eric often leading those gathered in the singing of a hymn.

At night the two of them slept side by side on a *k'ang*, the traditional Chinese bed, consisting of a platform about three feet high made of mud bricks. Every morning at six Eric gently shook Bear awake for their quiet time with God. Sitting in the cold room, by the light from a candle or small lamp, they listened to the Lord, sought His Spirit, read the Bible, shared their thoughts, and prayed together. Eric never varied his practice of beginning each day with a full hour devoted to fellowship with God. Davies returned from the journey confident that prayer was the center and the secret of Eric Liddell's intimate relationship with the Almighty.

Throughout the autumn, the LMS missionaries in Tientsin pursued the opportunities at hand. Cullen, Longman, and Luxon had a full complement of students at the college. Dr. Geoff Milledge and nurse Annie Buchan led the medical work at MacKenzie Hospital, along with initiating a special evangelistic outreach among the Chinese staff and patients. Eric pitched in wherever he was needed while waiting for another opening to visit villages in the country field. But no one knew how long the tenuous situation would hold.

A letter written November 3, 1941, from Geoff Milledge's wife, Miriam, to their family in England summed up the feelings of many missionaries in China: "You, like ourselves, must wonder what the future holds for us. It is useless to try to prophesy, but on the whole we are optimistic. One thing that is pretty clear is that at this stage, we must accept whatever comes, as it is rather late in the day to take safety measures. To put it quite simply, we feel that we are here under authority. This is where God sent us, and we don't feel that we have had any orders from him to leave for anywhere else. I feel sure that we would have had a distinct leading to do so if this was God's plan for us. When work is closing down in many places, one feels the greatness of the opportunity here."

Early in December, Flo's father said good-bye to his family in Toronto and began his journey back to China. Agnes and Flo, perhaps more than any one, understood why he felt compelled to go. The Honan Mission was his life and he loved the work. His colleagues in China needed him. During a time of crisis, who better to have in Tientsin than Hugh MacKenzie? He knew who to call, what to do, and how to deal with everyone from rickshaw pullers to government officials. If anyone could get it done, it was the man who had so ably managed the mission's business affairs in North China for the past thirty years.

But on Sunday, December 7, 1941, while walking on a fog-shrouded dock in San Francisco, Hugh was struck by a car and knocked unconscious. He was taken to a hospital, examined, and soon released, only to be stunned with the news that the Japanese had attacked the American naval base at Pearl Harbor and declared war on the United States and Britain. Hugh's ship, scheduled to sail the next day, would not be leaving port. All travel across the Pacific had been indefinitely suspended.

America was going to war.

SEVENTEEN

House Arrest

1941–1942

It was 2:30 in the morning, December 8, 1941, in Tientsin when the Japanese strike force began raining destruction on the Hawaiian island of Oahu. As Eric Liddell slept, the dive-bombers bore down on Wheeler and Hickam airfields, destroying rows of American fighters and bombers on the ground. Torpedo planes swept in low over Pearl Harbor, turning the shallow waters of Battleship Row into a raging inferno of burning ships and dying men. By the time Eric awoke at his usual hour, it took only a glance out his window to know that everything had changed.

Barbed wire and truckloads of Japanese soldiers were everywhere. Before dawn, they had closed the gates connecting the French and British Concessions and erected machine-gun emplacements in front of Gordon Hall. The hopelessly outnumbered foreign military forces left guarding the concession areas had surrendered without firing a shot. The Japanese were now in complete control.

As the day wore on, news of the attack on Pearl Harbor swept through the Chinese and foreign communities in Tientsin. In the face of conflicting reports and wild rumors about what Japan intended to do, people simply had to wait and see what their fate would be. But one fact was immediately clear. No one would be leaving China now without permission from the Japanese.

Three days later, on December 11, all the students at the Anglo-Chinese College were sent home, and a band of eleven Japanese inspectors sealed the classrooms and all the doors into the college except one from the Longmans' residence. They made a cursory search of the living premises, including the flat occupied by Eric and Cullen. After impounding their radio set, the inspectors moved across the road, where they examined the hospital and the houses in the LMS compound.

During the next few days, all British and American nationals had to register at Japanese military headquarters, giving detailed information about themselves, including a list of their personal property and bank accounts. Most people knew better than to ask questions, having learned that they would receive further information when the Japanese decided to give it.

After the initial flurry of orders and restrictions, life settled into a quiet but uneasy routine. For a time, Chinese were allowed into the concessions to visit their foreign friends, bringing news of the city and the outside world. Eric and his colleagues could move freely within the French Concession which housed the LMS compound, but could not cross into the adjacent British sector. With snow covering the ground, they celebrated Christmas together with a roast beef dinner and a party for the missionary children.

In Toronto, the MacKenzies welcomed Hugh back home, tired and discouraged after his failed attempt to reach China. His persistent cough, stemming from a serious respiratory illness many years before, seemed deeper, but he assured them it was a passing matter. Of greater concern to Agnes and Flo was the noticeable difference in his eyes. With a look of deep sadness, he returned the recent photograph of Flo and the girls that she had sent with him for Eric. The closing of the door to China had taken something out of Hugh, and Flo could only hope that a new task in Canada would bring back her father's characteristic determination.

And what of Eric and the others in China? How she longed for a word from someone, letting her know that everyone was safe. But that could be a long time coming. In the meantime, she would give herself to caring for her three daughters and entrust everyone to the loving hands of God.

On January 15, 1942, the Japanese ordered all British and American nationals in Tientsin to move into the British Concession. Day after day, long lines of people with their possessions passed through the barricades and into the homes of colleagues and friends. Eric was everywhere helping others pack, load household goods, and relocate in the bitterly cold weather. A. P. Cullen moved into a flat with the Lewises near Union Church. The Longmans found refuge with the Earl family on London Road. Eric, along with the Luxons and Gwen Morris, were taken in by the Howard Smiths at the Methodist Mission Compound. The foreign medical staff of MacKenzie Hospital was allowed to remain in the LMS compound for a few weeks before they, too, were sent packing. Geoff and Miriam Milledge set up housekeeping in the ornate library of the Masonic Hall.

New rules and regulations flowed in a steady stream from military headquarters. All "enemy aliens" had to wear armbands when they were outside their houses. The British wore bright red bands with the word "Ying" — from *Ying Kuo* (England) — printed with a Chinese character on them. Some people proudly embroidered the black ink to make it stand out because the character *Ying* meant "noble and brave." It was a small act of defiance when other forms of resistance proved futile. Any surly Britisher who refused to bow to a Japanese sentry at a checkpoint was likely to be sent to the end of a long line and endlessly delayed before being allowed to pass.

The greatest change for the missionary community was their complete removal from the work for which they had come to China. Restricted to the British Concession and now prohibited from contact with Chinese, except for shopkeepers and servants, they could no longer teach, preach, or practice medicine. Some appreciated the initial respite from the continual round of demanding responsibilities, while others struggled with their inability to perform the task to which they felt God had called them. They had become missionaries without a mission.

But to their credit, most soon set about other tasks. With the Tientsin Grammar School closed, Gerald Luxon and Howard Smith organized classes in various homes for their own children and others.

Cullen and Longman joined the team and began teaching several classes a week in science, Latin, and English. Missionary wives assumed greater responsibility for cleaning, cooking, and laundry – and a few communal kitchens were organized as some combined their resources. By economizing and pooling their money, the LMS group felt they had enough to sustain them for six months.

The situation was difficult, but not impossible. Church services continued at the various houses of worship. On Good Friday, April 3, an ad hoc choir performed Stainer's "Crucifixion" to a packed house at Union Church. Easter Sunday services drew crowds as well. On weeknight evenings, friends gathered in various homes to listen to gramophone records, discuss books, or play bridge. Birthdays or anniversaries were celebrated by bringing out a few carefully conserved delicacies.

Perhaps the greatest hardship for everyone was the almost complete lack of communication with loved ones at home. The trickle of mail they had been receiving before Pearl Harbor had virtually dried up. Letters were taking three to six months to reach China from Canada or England, if they arrived at all. Families at home often wept upon opening the post box and finding a stack of letters they had sent to China months before, now returned unopened. In April, Cullen noted that it had been four months since he heard from his family, and that their last letter had taken three months to reach him. His most recent news of his wife and children in England was seven months old.

With the usual communication channels clogged, it didn't take people long to become creative. Since western China was not under Japanese control and the Chinese postal system still functioned, people began sending letters to contacts in "Free China," who in turn posted them on to their final destination. In early April, Flo was thrilled to receive a letter from Eric and amazed to see that it had been posted from Chungking. The letter was short, assuring her that everyone was well. He didn't bother to explain the letter's unusual routing via Chiang Kai-shek's western capital. She immediately sent the letter on to LMS headquarters in London so they would have an official word about their people in Tientsin.

A few weeks later, an envelope postmarked California arrived at the United Church Office in Toronto. It contained a typed message for Florence Liddell with the heading: "This message was transmitted by the Chinese International Broadcasting Station, VGOY of Chungking." It had been picked up by a radio listening-post in Ventura, north of Los Angeles, transcribed, and forwarded to Canada. The message read: "No need to worry on behalf of me or my colleagues. We are all in good health and spirits, nicely housed with Methodist Mission friends in Port city. You are constantly in my thoughts. My love to all family circle especially Patricia, Heather, Maureen and yourself." Clearly, Eric was using every means possible to assure the home folk that the missionaries were alive and well in Tientsin.

In Chungking, Clara Preston, a United Church of Canada nurse, and Perle Longman, daughter of Carl and Amy, both became one-woman mail-forwarding services. Because Perle worked for the British Embassy, she could send items via diplomatic pouch by air over "The Hump" to India and on to her younger sister, Rosamond, a nurse in England. Ros typed the news into circular letters that were sent out to families of the LMS missionaries. While letters sent through conventional channels struggled to cross the oceans, the Chungking connection provided a lifeline of news to people longing to know the fate of family and friends in China.

On their eighth anniversary, Eric wrote Flo saying he had been reliving the wonderful days surrounding their wedding. When the letter finally reached her, she could picture her husband's serious gaze for the camera that day as they stood together outside Union Church. It was so unlike the characteristic broad grin that had shaped his face into a kind of perpetual smile. And back in China, whenever Eric looked at a photograph of Flo, he still saw the vivacious young girl who had stolen his heart and brought such surprising joy into his life.

✣

After two months of close quarters in Tientsin, it would have been natural for some friction and misunderstanding to develop among the missionaries crowded together. But just the opposite was true in the Howard Smith household, where "Uncle Eric" lived out the Sermon on the Mount in his typical understated way. When Howard's wife, Mary Jane, mentioned that the shops were often sold out of bread by the time she reached them, Eric volunteered to go at five each morning and buy for the entire household. After a powerful spring dust storm left everything inside the house covered with grit, Mary Jane walked downstairs at six the next morning to begin sweeping up, only to discover Eric just finishing the task. He had begun at 4:30 in the morning with broom, dust pan, and dusters, working quietly to avoid waking anyone.

Howard was aware of the Oxford Group's influence on Liddell, not because Eric talked about it, but because the Four Absolutes of honesty, purity, unselfishness, and love undergirded all he did. "The remarkable thing about Eric," Smith remarked, "was the way in which he was never too busy to accommodate himself to the wishes of others, and the way he could accept trivial things and trivial duties."

If a group of boys wanted to play cricket, Uncle Eric was ready. When the grownups needed a fourth for bridge in the evening, he joined in with gusto. He spent hours helping the Smith's daughters — Jean, twelve, and Frances, eleven — arrange Chinese stamps in their albums. He answered their endless questions about various dates and issues, and he seemed to have more fun than anyone. Smith also marveled at Eric's stamina as he taught the girls to play tennis in summer heat that registered 100 degrees in the shade.

In the face of the sweeping changes and growing unpredictability of the war, the constant in Eric's day was his early morning hour with God. Those who lived with him and knew him best understood that the secret of his life was not a habit or a routine, but personal fellowship with Almighty God and complete surrender to Him.

A booklet of prayers, which Eric had compiled during the previous months of restricted missionary activity, was printed by Union Church early in 1942. Titled *Prayers for Daily Use*, it offered a guide for private worship that bore his unmistakable mark. Eric began his introduction with the words of a familiar chorus: "Be like Jesus, this my song, in the home and in the throng; / Be like Jesus all day long, I would be like Jesus."

After acknowledging the book *Morning Prayers for School and Family*, arranged by Mrs. Guy Rogers, as the source of many of the prayers included, Eric's personal preface continued: "I have tried to bring before you certain thoughts which I have found helpful in the Christian Life. The aim is that we should be like Jesus, thoughtful, kind, generous, true, pure and depending entirely on God's help, seeking to be the kind of man or woman He desires us to be: seeking, in all things, to do His Will and to please Him.

"These prayers are not intended to take the place of your private devotions but to be read over slowly, meditated on, with ever this question in your mind, 'How can I help God to answer this prayer?'

"Arranged by Rev. Eric H. Liddell for the use of the Union Church, Tientsin."

On the first few pages, under the heading "The Key to Knowing God," Eric offered suggestions on how to have an effective daily prayer hour. They reveal not only what he believed, but also what he sought to practice each day.

"One word stands out from all others as the key to knowing God, to having his peace and assurance in your heart; it is OBEDIENCE.

"To OBEY God's Will was like food to Jesus, refreshing His mind, body and spirit. 'My meat is to do the Will of Him that sent me.'

"OBEDIENCE to God's Will is the secret of spiritual knowledge and insight. It is not willingness to know, but willingness to DO (obey) God's Will that brings certainty.

"'If any man will do (obey) His Will, he shall know of the doctrine, whether it be of God, or whether I speak of Myself.'

"OBEDIENCE IS THE SECRET OF GUIDANCE.

Every Christian should live a God-guided life. If you are not guided by God you will be guided by something else.

"The Christian that doesn't know this sense of guidance in his life is missing something vital.

"Take OBEDIENCE with you into your prayer hour, for you will know as much of God, and only as much of God, as you are willing to put into practice.

> When we walk with the Lord,
> In the light of His Word
> What a glory He sheds on our way!
> While we DO HIS GOOD WILL
> He abides with us still,
> And with all who will TRUST and OBEY."

The prayers Eric selected ranged from "A Prayer for Absent Loved Ones" to "A Prayer for Animals," which were so often underfed and overworked in China. The booklet concluded with this "Prayer for Thanksgiving":

"O Lord Jesus Christ, Who art one with the Father, we thank Thee because, wherever we are this day, Thou wilt be lovingly watching us. We give Thee thanks for a life made stronger through conflict, more joyous through thinking of others, nobler through companionship with Thyself.

"Grant us perfect rest; and as we rest with Thee so may we rise with Thee, strong to bear our part in the coming of Thy glorious Kingdom.

"We thank Thee for those who work and make life easier for us; for servants who give us greater time for more congenial work; for books that inspire us; for music that thrills us; for games that train our bodies and teach us to be generous in victory and magnanimous in defeat; for work,

without which the temptations of life would be too
great for us; for friendship and all the joy it
brings; for the sacrifices of those who stood for
truth, laboured for better conditions, took the
part of the downtrodden and lived lovingly and
unselfishly to make this world more like the
Kingdom of God. Father, teach me to live in the
same self-sacrificing spirit. AMEN."

Summer in Tientsin arrived with a vengeance, as if to mock the
fact that there would be no holidays this year in Peitaiho. For two
straight weeks in July, daytime temperatures exceeded 100 degrees,
with one torrid afternoon sending the mercury to an oppressive
114. People sweltered and swore, but there was little to do but
endure.

During the heat wave, two developments set the foreign
community a-buzz. First, the rumors of possible repatriation became
reality. Then, as if to quell the surging spirits, the Japanese issued an
order forbidding church services in the British Concession. It was a
crushing blow, spiritually and socially, but with the hope of an early
departure, its initial impact was softened.

Concrete repatriation plans began to take shape through the
neutral Swiss Consular authorities. All "enemy aliens" were asked
to register and indicate whether they wished to stay in China or
be sent to their home countries. With thousands of civilians of
Japanese descent being held in "War Relocation Authority Centers"
in the United States, it was to the advantage of both countries to
reduce their burden of surveillance and cost through a series of
direct personnel exchanges. British and Canadian citizens would be
included in the quotas. At first Eric felt he should remain in China,
but when he learned that many other missionaries had opted to stay,
he put his name on the list for evacuation.

Early in August, representatives of six mission agencies, including
the LMS, signed over their properties to local authorities in Tientsin.

Hospitals and dwellings went to the Chinese Church; schools were given to the local municipal authorities to be controlled by the Chinese Bureau of Education. Like a ship cut from its moorings and drifting away in a fog, this tangible evidence of the work to which missionaries had given much of their lives began to recede from view. For thirty-three years, Carl Longman had poured his heart and soul into the Anglo-Chinese College, and now it was gone. After signing on behalf of the LMS, he wrote to Cocker-Brown, the LMS Foreign Secretary in London: "You will note what has happened to our beloved institution, and of course we wonder just what it will mean as to its future and especially the future of missionaries in schools." With that done, Longman felt there was no reason for him to remain in China. He was ready to go home.

On August 9, Eric wrote to Flo saying he had put his name on the repatriation list. He asked how she would feel if he volunteered for a pioneer home mission assignment in Canada. It would mean hard work in a rural area and sacrifices for her. And, of course, they must consider the children. But he felt the need was so great in the unreached areas that he might want to respond.

Just as his letter reached Flo, another envelope arrived for her from Foreign Secretary Cocker-Brown. He had been informed of the repatriation scheme and wondered where Eric might go if he was able to leave. Would he head directly for Canada or for the UK? Did she know what his plans might be? The secretary seemed so confident that Eric would be leaving China that he concluded with "Best wishes to yourself and to Eric if he has by any chance turned up yet."

Flo wanted to share his optimism but carefully guarded herself against assuming that Eric was on his way home. It was the first of November before she answered Cocker-Brown's letter, having had no further communication from Eric since his letter of August 9. She had no idea where he might go, but she was concerned that since the repatriation ships seemed to take people only as far as South Africa, he might become stranded there unless the LMS or the United Church of Canada could wire money for his fare onward from Durban. She tried to keep her hopes subdued by adding, "it will probably be quite a while before Eric actually gets out."

She continued her letter by passing along the most recent news reaching Toronto: "Mrs. Thomson has just had a letter from her daughter Mrs. Godfrey Gale. It was dated August from Shanghai and they were waiting for the next ship. They were in very cramped quarters and it was hot, but they were well and looking forward to sailing for home."

But even as Flo wrote those words, the missionaries waiting in Shanghai knew that things had gone terribly wrong. With high hopes, the Milledges, Gales, McAlls, and some 300 other Britons and Americans had embarked by train for Shanghai in mid-August, assured by the consular officials that they had a berth on the first ship to sail. But as they waited day after day, housed in the Columbia Country Club on the outskirts of Shanghai, the truth became clear. Yes, their names had most assuredly been on the list, but many of the wealthy and influential foreigners in Shanghai had bribed officials to put them first. After the first ship sailed, hundreds of people were left in the country club, with the men sleeping on camp beds in the bowling alley and in the bar while the women and children were crowded together in separate areas. As October gave way to November, their hopes of going home ebbed away.

Eric Liddell, along with Carl and Amy Longman, had not been included on the first repatriation list in Tientsin. But Mr. Joerg, the Swiss Consul there, told Carl he felt confident that all who had asked for repatriation would get away. For weeks, Amy and many others held out hope that they would be in England by Christmas. But gradually it became evident that any chance for leaving in 1942 had come and gone. Even more disquieting was the persistent rumor that the Japanese were planning to place all enemy nationals into internment camps.

With a renewed sense of urgency, Eric labored to complete a project on which he had been working for several months. He titled it simply "Discipleship" and organized it as a book of daily readings for an entire year. As he wrote, he pictured members of the dynamic church at Hsin Chi and his former college students. With them in mind, he designed a guide to help young Christians develop spiritually, hoping it would someday be translated into

Chinese. For the month of January, Eric developed the theme of "Surrender." February focused on "God's Moral Law and the Sermon on the Mount." Each month had a list of thematic daily Bible readings, preceded by a brief introduction and followed by "Suggested Reading" — usually one or two books that had been significant to Eric.

In the section titled "Victorious Living" Eric wrote: "Victory over all the circumstances of life comes not by might, nor by power, but by a practical confidence in God and by allowing His Spirit to dwell in our hearts and control our actions and emotions.

"Learn in the days of ease and comfort, to think in terms of the prayer that follows, so that when the days of hardship come you will be fully prepared and equipped to meet them.

"Father, I pray that no circumstances however bitter or however long drawn out, may cause me to break Thy Law, the Law of Love to Thee and to my neighbour. That I may not become resentful, have hurt feelings, hate or become embittered by life's experiences, but that in and through all I may see Thy guiding hand and have a heart full of gratitude for Thy daily mercy, daily love, daily power and daily presence.

"Help me in the day when I need it most to remember that:

— All things work together for good to them that love the Lord.
— I can do all things through Him that strengtheneth me.
— My grace is sufficient for thee, for My strength is made perfect in weakness.

"'Now unto Him who is able to keep you from falling, and to present you faultless before the presence of His glory with exceeding joy, to the only wise God our Saviour, be glory and majesty, dominion and power, both now and ever, Amen.'"

On November 5, in a letter to Flo, Eric referred to this book of daily Bible readings: "If it never comes to anything it will have been useful for my own thinking. And to me will always be a companion booklet to the Daily Prayers which I got out. It would be so easy to let this time go by with nothing done; nothing really constructive, and so have the days frittered away."

By the time Christmas arrived, the extended MacKenzie family was living in a three-story house at 21 Gloucester Street, just east of Yonge Street, a busy north-south thoroughfare in Toronto. Every evening, Flo and the girls repeated a familiar pattern. They would sing a song or two together, read a story, and talk about Eric. "When it's night time here," Heather said, "it's morning in China. The moon we see tonight, Daddy will see when we wake up tomorrow."

If something had frightened them during the day, Flo encouraged them to talk about it. Patricia, with a photo of Eric in hand, told fifteen-month-old Maureen that this was their daddy. Then before Flo turned out the lights, they would pray together.

"Dear Heavenly Father, bless Uncle Ken in the Air Force and Granny and Grandpa and all the soldiers and Mother and Auntie Margaret and Auntie Esther and Uncle Fin, and Uncle Norman, and Auntie Louise, and help Daddy to come home soon. Amen."

"Amen," Flo added softly. "Amen."

PART III

THE FINISH LINE

1943–1945

Be still, my soul: when dearest friends depart,
And all is darkened in the vale of tears
Then shalt thou better know His love, His heart,
Who comes to soothe thy sorrow and thy fears.
Be still, my soul: thy Jesus can repay
From His own fullness all He takes away.

☙ EIGHTEEN ❧

Weihsien

1943

At the dawn of 1943, rumors were as plentiful as rats in the streets of Tientsin. Throughout the native city and the foreign areas, gossip about the world and the war scampered from shop to shop and house to house, always finding a way in, sometimes greeted with a cry of alarm, but never ignored. The most persistent whisper claimed that the Japanese were preparing to intern all enemy nationals living in North China. According to one source, British and American citizens would be shipped to Tokyo and held there to discourage the Allies from bombing the city. Other versions had foreigners being sent to Hong Kong or the Philippines to rid occupied China of the threat of enemy agents. Some believed internment was merely the prelude to mass executions.

Despite the wild speculations, people in the foreign community recognized that, from the Japanese point of view, the idea of internment made sense. Keeping thousands of people under house arrest in the major cities of North China required too much time, money, and effort for the occupying forces. Soldiers were needed in battle far more than at the barricades separating Rue de France from Victoria Road in Tientsin. Gradually, talk of being moved to some kind of prison camp began to change from "if" to "when."

On January 6, Eric's mind was focused on his family in Toronto. It was Heather's sixth birthday, and he tried to picture the little girl who had been only four the last time he saw her. What would she be doing today? Of course, Flo would have a party for her, and many of the MacKenzie family would be there. He prayed it would be a good day for his daughter, and he longed more than ever to be there and hold her in his arms.

During their usual afternoon walk through the British Concession, Eric and Cullen talked of their wives and children, even though there was nothing new to report. Cullen had not seen his family since September of 1940, and letters were now as scarce as unbiased news reports. They paused for a moment and stepped out of the biting wind while Cullen filled his pipe. The headaches that had plagued him for years were worse than usual, and he was down to the last pouch of his favorite Blue Nun tobacco. He touched a match to the bowl and, as the smoke curled away, smiled and told Eric a favorite memory of Heather as a toddler. They laughed together, bolstered by the recollection and by a stalwart confidence that God would bring them all together again in His time. As the sun dropped toward the horizon, they started back along London Road toward the Methodist Mission Compound.

In Toronto, Flo tucked the girls into bed, then began a letter to Eric. Even though Heather was still recovering from a mild case of the mumps, she had been quite a grown-up little lady all day.

"I wish you could have seen Heather's eyes when the tray of presents and a big chocolate cake with candles came in," Flo wrote. "We gave her a few very inexpensive presents, just the things she loves, a box of paints, two pencils with rubbers on the end and a big fat exercise book, two hankies, two bows for her hair and painting books. She was so thrilled she didn't want any cake. She just wanted to go right up to her room and play with them. Trish wanted to go too but she took her cake with her."

After saying everything she could on both sides of a thin sheet of paper, Flo sealed the letter with a prayer that she wouldn't find it returned to her post box in six months.

Eric served as "postman" for the LMS missionaries in Tientsin, so the sight of him with a packet of envelopes in his hand was always greeted with great enthusiasm. Late on the night of March 12, however, he made the rounds bearing bad news to all his colleagues. At 10:30, his knock at the door awoke Carl and Amy Longman from their sleep. With a word of apology for the lateness of the hour, he handed them a letter and said, "I thought you'd want to know as soon as possible," and then was on his way.

Over a late cup of tea, the Longmans read the confirmation of all the speculations of the previous two months. The letter from the British Residents Committee stated that all "enemy nationals" in Tientsin — including British, Americans, Dutch, and Belgians — were to be transferred to the Civil Assembly Centre at Weihsien, Shantung Province. They would go in three separate groups on March 23, 28, and 30. Each person was allowed to send ahead four large pieces of luggage, one of which was to be a single bed and mattress. Two suitcases could be carried as hand luggage on the journey. Eric and the Longmans were listed among those in the last group scheduled to leave Tientsin.

In Peking and Tsingtao, other foreign nationals received similar letters and began scrambling for additional information to help them prepare. Where was Weihsien? To what kind of place were they going? What things would be provided in the camp and what items must they take for themselves? Would they be able to send and receive mail there? Who was in charge and how would they be treated?

In Peking, Brigadier Ken Stranks, a Salvation Army officer, rode his bicycle around to scores of homes, urging everyone who had a musical instrument to take it. "However long we're there," he said, "we'll need music." Through official channels, the future internees obtained permission from the Japanese to ship two grand pianos and several gramophones to Weihsien, along with four refrigerators, some sewing machines, and athletic equipment for games.

Before leaving, Eric signed a required declaration stating that he had been a paying guest in the home of Rev. D. Howard Smith, that he had no personal servant, and that he had no key to the house in which he had left all his things in one small room on the top floor. The complete inventory of his possessions read:

1 Blackwood book case
1 Chest of drawers
1 Typewriting table
1 Carpet (12x4)
1 Blackwood mirror
1 Box of books
1 Box of Clothes, cushions, pillow, etc.
2 Corries of kitchen utensils.

As the groups departed at their appointed times, people reluctantly left behind nearly everything they owned, convinced that they would never see their belongings again. Everyone had packed only what they considered essential for their personal needs and the good of the community. Doctors brought their medical bags and some vital medicines; teachers included instructional materials; those with specialized skills brought tools. And everyone brought a plate, cup, and eating utensils. But in spite of all their planning and organizing, no one was adequately prepared for what actually lay ahead.

At 7:00 in the evening on March 30, Eric joined a group of nearly 300 persons at the old British military barracks in Tientsin. For the next hour and a half, Japanese guards carefully searched everyone's allotted two suitcases. Then at 9:00 they were required to carry their belongings through the streets for a mile to the railway station. Along the route, Japanese photographers recorded scenes of the "humiliated" foreigners leaving the city that had once been their fortress of financial and political power. Onlookers, many of them sympathetic Chinese, lined the route, silently watching their friends and former colleagues depart.

After crowding themselves and their luggage into third-class railway cars, they sat down on straight-backed wooden seats for the 300-mile journey to Weihsien. Shortly before midnight, the train rumbled out of the station into the darkness. As it wound its way slowly south through Tsangchow and Techow, Eric thought about the towns and villages they were passing. He knew them by heart, having traveled the route so many times on his way to Siaochang. Throughout the long night, the elderly groaned with discomfort, while fitful children and those near them could not find the relief of sleep. Their only food and drink was what they had brought with them.

At 10:30 the next morning, they reached Tsinan and were told they must change trains. After transferring all their baggage without the accustomed help of coolies, they traveled toward the sun across the northern maritime province of Shantung, whose eastern half forms a large promontory jutting far out into the Yellow Sea toward Manchuria and Korea. At 3:30 in the afternoon, the train lurched to a stop at Weihsien station, where the transfer of people and luggage began again, this time into Japanese trucks and buses for the final three jolting miles out of the city to their new home.

As the camp came into view, they saw a large compound surrounded by a tall gray wall, whose corner turrets served as guard towers, with searchlights and machine guns. With barbed wire curling along the top of the wall, it was obvious that the Japanese didn't want anyone to leave. Over the main gate, Chinese characters proclaimed this to be the "Courtyard of the Happy Way."

As the last arrivals, Eric and his group brought the total camp population to nearly 1,800. After a brief orientation and assignment of quarters, they sat down to a supper of leek and potato stew. Listening to the stories of those who had preceded them, the new arrivals tried to grasp the broad picture of where they were and what was happening.

During the previous ten days, the Japanese had brought six groups from three different cities to Weihsien. When the first contingent arrived from Tsingtao, they were shown a dirty building with a pile of vegetables outside and told that food preparation was up to them. After cleaning the kitchen, they managed to prepare a meager meal. Because their trunks and beds, sent four days before, had not yet arrived, they slept in their clothes on the floor of whatever empty rooms they could find.

Each day, the camp became more organized, but it was still slow going. Those in Eric's group, like all their predecessors, found that their beds had not yet reached Weihsien. But at least the later arrivals had been welcomed by sympathetic friends, who loaned them blankets and quilts in which to sleep on the thin bamboo mats separating their aching bodies from the cold floor.

The Civil Assembly Center at Weihsien occupied a former missionary compound established in 1883 by American Presbyterians. Inside an area of about one city block were school buildings, a church seating nearly 700, some 400 individual rooms, and a hospital. The five large Western-style missionary houses were now occupied by Japanese officers and guards.

The buildings were structurally sound but had been stripped by successive, marauding bands of soldiers. The hospital, a gift from Shadyside Presbyterian Church in Pittsburgh, Pennsylvania, had been one of the finest in North China before the war. Now, the heating system with its steam for sterilization, along with all the water pipes, had been ripped out, leaving gaping holes in the walls. The X-ray machine, operating tables, and every item of surgical equipment had been removed. Dirt, plaster, and filth covered the floors.

The pathways throughout the compound were littered with broken furniture, bricks, and other debris. But those things could be dealt with in time. The immediate crisis centered on the camp latrines. With water pipes torn out and no means to flush, they had become cesspools whose stench initially repelled even those in greatest need. After three days of talk and suggestions about how to solve the problem, a group of Catholic priests and nuns, along with a few Protestant missionaries, donned rubber boots and armed themselves with buckets and mops. With handkerchiefs tied as masks on their faces, they waded in and cleaned out the latrines.

Weihsien Camp was under the control of Japanese Consular officials who expected the internees to organize their affairs and perform all the labor necessary to keep the camp functioning. The only Chinese workers allowed inside were coolies who came to remove night soil from the open cesspools. The Japanese would provide enough food to maintain the health of those held there, but everything else was up to the internees themselves.

The commandant, Mr. Tsukigawa, spoke little English, and quickly came to be regarded by the internees as indecisive and incompetent in practical matters. Unfortunately, he had been serving as a Japanese Vice-Consul in Honolulu on December 7, 1941, and he still considered his expulsion at the hands of the outraged Americans very undiplomatic. Under the commandant, four department heads monitored camp activity while thirty to forty consular policemen acted as guards.

The internees immediately set about making the buildings and facilities livable. Fifteen doctors and a group of volunteers worked to clean and equip the hospital. Within two weeks they had a ward of beds, a working laboratory, and the capability to perform surgery. In other areas of camp life, those with experience and skills trained others to cook, bake bread, repair plumbing, and build furniture out of what they found in the rubbish pile. Nine committees — Education, General Affairs, Engineering, Quarters, Medical, Food Supplies, Finance, Employment, and Discipline — each headed by a man with business experience, looked after the day to day details of life. The committee chairmen became known as the Council of Nine.

Every able-bodied person in camp, including women and older teens, was assigned a job and expected to work at least three hours each day. Businessmen and their wives, who had previously been waited on by a cadre of Chinese servants, found themselves pumping water and peeling vegetables. Captains of industry awoke before daylight to stoke boiler fires alongside opium addicts and smugglers. Bankers became bakers; missionaries became bricklayers; society ladies, secretaries, and prostitutes stirred cauldrons of porridge side by side in the kitchens.

Eric was asked to divide his time between teaching in the camp school and organizing athletic games. He was also elected to the Weihsien Christian Fellowship Committee, a group responsible for planning evangelical worship services and special meetings. In his usual way, he approached each assignment as a full-time job.

On April 18, just over two weeks after arriving, Eric sent a twenty-five-word Red Cross letter to Flo: "Simple hardy life under primitive conditions. Living with Josh and Bear in small room. Good fellowship, good games. Teaching in school, food sufficient, boundless love."

A subsequent message several weeks later carried the same reassuring tone while trying to give a realistic picture of camp: "Simple, hardy, open air, community life. All internal work done by ourselves, everyone a worker. We, busy, teaching in school. Tricia, Maureen, birthday remembrances. Love."

Eric shared a nine-by-twelve-foot room with two of his younger missionary colleagues, Edwin Davies and Joseph McChesney-Clark. With each bed placed over two steamer trunks along a wall, they had just enough space to come and go without tripping over each other. Josh Clark was a practical man and a bit of a loner who greatly missed his fiancée in England. "Bear" Davies, the theologian of the group, had the advantage of having his fiancée, Nelma Stranks, in camp. As different as the three roommates were, they enjoyed each other's company.

But not every living arrangement was as congenial as theirs. In some of the larger dorm rooms, single men had only eighteen inches separating them from the beds on either side. Sleep was interrupted by people snoring, tossing and turning, or using a chamber pot during the night. A. P. Cullen coped with the noise and lack of space by closing his eyes and mentally driving his favorite roads in England until sleep overtook him.

In other rooms, middle-aged single women, used to privacy and comfort, suddenly had neither. A month after going into camp, twenty-three-year-old Langdon Gilkey, who had been teaching in Peking, was summoned to a ladies dorm to quell a disturbance. As a young and reluctant member of the camp Housing Committee, Gilkey found the room divided between a group of young British secretaries and a contingent of older female missionaries. The secretaries resented hearing personal prayers said aloud at night and hymns sung early in the morning, while the missionaries deplored the secretaries' continual talk of their lurid sexual escapades. The conflict had culminated in a fistfight between a stocky missionary and a trim secretary. Both had suffered cuts and bruises in the fray. Gilkey looked around the room for someone who might help make peace and, finding no one, muttered that the committee would study the situation, then left before they turned on him.

In the men's quarters, the cold shoulder usually prevailed over the clenched fist. When two long-time antagonists were placed in the same room, they simply determined not to speak to each other for the duration of their internment. And that is exactly what they did.

But while conflicts were inevitable, the majority of internees entered into camp life with a willingness to work for the good of the community. Without this attitude they could not hope to survive. With a surprising array of talent available, a choral group sang Stainer's "Crucifixion" for Easter and began preparing the challenging oratorio "Elijah." A piano duo performed a Tschaikowsky concerto to packed houses on two successive nights. For the younger crowd with different tastes, a black American jazz band, whose members had played regularly at clubs in Tientsin and Peking, provided music for dancing on scheduled Saturday nights.

Humor often renewed the internees' spirits by allowing them to step back and laugh at themselves. At one variety show, the song "Weihsien Blues" premiered to thunderous applause:

> We used to be executives, and labored with our brains,
> With secretaries neat and quick to spare us any pains
> But if the ticker tape ran out we didn't touch the thing
> The office staff could see to that, we did the ordering.
>
> *CHORUS*
> Now we're in Weihsien, nothing's too dirty to do,
> Slops, spots or garbage, or stirring a vegetable stew.
> To shine in this delightful camp, you join the labor corps
> Where if you do your work too well, they work you more and
> more.

For since we've come to Weihsien camp, they've worked us till
we're dead.

Though now we're called the labor corps, we'll be a corpse
instead.

The Education Committee made sure that no one lacked the opportunity to learn in camp. Along with holding school for the children, volunteers taught classes for anyone wanting to learn Chinese, Japanese, Russian, German, and French. Courses in astronomy, philosophy, and accounting were offered along with gramophone concerts and lectures on subjects ranging from the Greek classics to Admiral Byrd. On Sundays, the church was in use throughout the day as various groups and denominations met for worship.

As the weeks lengthened into months, people tried everything to cope with the monotony and boredom. They gave fanciful names to the paths and lanes criss-crossing the camp. Park Avenue, Sunset Boulevard, and Downing Street offered reminders of home and of better things to come. Even though the kitchens served repetitious meals of soups and stews, menu boards appeared boasting a different fare each day. Proclamations of veal cordon bleu and medallions of beef brought wistful smiles from people standing in long lines and holding nothing but a bowl or a tin container and a spoon.

A few wags entertained themselves by starting a new rumor each day just to see how quickly it traveled and how widely it would be believed. Whether people actually thought that Churchill and Roosevelt had been on their way to liberate Weihsien when Churchill's camel got stuck in the sand at the edge of the Yellow River, they repeated it.

In late spring, neighbors shared flower and vegetable seeds for planting. Knowledgeable botanists identified sixty-one varieties of trees, including flowering paulonia and crepe myrtle, growing in the camp. Early summer brought warm sunny days and the welcome release of outdoor recreation.

Eric had no trouble getting people to turn out for sports. During the summer of 1943, evening softball games drew hundreds of enthusiastic spectators as a succession of teams tried to defeat the daunting company of Catholic priests. When it became known in early August that the much beloved fathers and sisters were to be sent to monasteries and convents in Peking, sadness gripped everyone in Weihsien. Not only were they losing people who had become friends, but also a company of men and women who had done much to keep morale high.

Camp accommodations were unbearably cramped, and the food amounted to little more than a starvation diet, but many of the Catholic missionaries who had served in remote locations in China found themselves in better circumstances than they had known for years. One of the priests noted that, for his order, "bread and tea was the usual morning meal." And although these men and women who had taken vows of poverty were quite content with what was provided, they set about to help others in need.

Father Patrick Scanlan, an Australian-born Trappist monk, endeared himself to scores of people through his fearless efforts to smuggle much-needed food into camp. Families with young children depended on the eggs, honey, and fruit that came through Father Scanlan's black market operations. While a few internees risked punishment to obtain opium, cigarettes, and a Chinese wine called *Pai ka'erh*, Scanlan took his chances for the children.

For weeks, the gregarious, forty-six-year-old priest eluded detection with the help of lookouts who warned him of any approaching danger. Through a drainage tunnel under the wall and in packets thrown over the top, goods worth thousands of Chinese dollars changed hands almost every night. But one evening, as a preoccupied young sentinel gazed into the eyes of a girl with whom he was talking, a Japanese guard nabbed Scanlan with a ten-pound sack of sugar in one hand and fourteen tins of jam in the other. He was brought before the camp commandant, who promptly sentenced him to two weeks in solitary confinement. News of the punishment was greeted with laughter throughout the camp as people assumed the priest had always lived a life of silence and prayer.

The truth was that for the previous fifteen years, as a teacher and later as guest master of a monastery, Scanlan had enjoyed wide contact with people. But he had never forgotten the lessons of his novitiate when for ten years he led a life of prayer, penance, and almost absolute silence. Of those solitary days he said, "It was a crucifixion, above all to my social instincts, to be thus cut off from my fellowmen, but it taught me to look to God alone."

Scanlan's incarceration inspired a humorous ditty titled "Prisoner's Song," written by a fellow internee. Two of the verses read:

> Oh they trapped me a trappist last Wednesday
> Now few are the eggs to be fried.
> Alone in a dark cell I ponder
> If my clients are hollow inside.
>
> For there is a big bag on the outside
> Overflowing with honey and jam
> But how can it come unto our side
> Till the bootleggers know where I am?

Late at night in Weihsien, when sounds of off-key singing came from Scanlan's cell, word spread that the priest was reciting his office in Latin. In fact, he was reviewing some American songs he had heard. But the sound so annoyed the guards, trying to sleep, that he was released a few days early if he promised to stop singing. When he returned from the Japanese area to the main part of camp, Father Scanlan received a tumultuous welcome from all his friends and loyal customers.

But when 400 fathers and sisters left Weihsien on August 17, people lined the streets and wept. Those who sang "God Bless America" were answered by others with "There'll Always Be an England." And one man who had no particular use for any religion was heard to remark, "I wish the bloomin' Protestants had left instead."

Two weeks later, another exchange of humanity dramatically altered the make-up of the camp. The arrival of some 300 students and teachers of the China Inland Mission school at Chefoo was followed a few days later by the departure of almost the same number of internees, mostly Americans, for repatriation. For those left in camp, the loss of so many friends and colleagues was bittersweet. While it raised their own hopes of being sent home in the near future, it left them facing a bleak winter in China while their more fortunate colleagues headed for reunions with family and friends.

Before the Chefoo students arrived, most children in camp had been with their parents. Now, a sizable number of youngsters from eight to eighteen years of age were there without mothers and fathers. The youngest remained in the charge of their Chefoo teachers, but the teenagers had a great deal more responsibility and freedom. Previously interned together at Temple Hill, near Chefoo, they were now thrown into the incredible mix of humanity in Weihsien.

As children of missionaries, most had been raised in the sheltered environment of Christian homes and a very conservative school. Now they were face to face with people and behavior from which they had been protected. The sight of a woman wearing dark lipstick and smoking a cigarette in public was enough to make some of the younger children stop and stare. During their first few days in camp, many Chefoo students learned the meaning of words they had never heard before.

On a more positive note, they soon discovered that the balding man in knee-length khaki shorts handing out sports equipment and refereeing their field hockey games was Eric Liddell, the Olympic champion. At another time and place they might have laughed at his gaudy floral print shirts, which they discovered were made from his wife's curtains. But after months of being interned, clothing had become functional rather than fashionable for everyone.

Eric communicated a genuine interest in all of the camp's teenagers, whether they came from the Christian community or not. Without his family there, he was free to answer every request for help. Soon, in addition to his regular teaching load, he was tutoring several students in chemistry. With no textbooks available, Eric created from memory a 100-page chemistry book, including valence tables, atomic weights, and the electrochemical list. Since no laboratory facilities existed in camp, he drew diagrams of experiments and talked each student through the process of combining various chemicals and noting the results. Inside the front cover of the book, Eric wrote: "The bones of inorganic chemistry. 'Can these dry bones live?'"

The Americans remaining in camp celebrated Thanksgiving Day by sharing a few precious treasures with their friends — a bit of jam, a freshly baked small cake, or some canned meat especially saved for that day. Meanwhile, their repatriated counterparts, nearing New York on the MS *Gripsholm*, had dined on a dinner of cream of corn soup, chateaubriand, spinach, fried potatoes, mocca cake, and coffee.

Diplomats continued to work toward further prisoner exchanges, and the hope of leaving Weihsien sustained those who had been left behind. But with the onset of winter, people in camp turned their attention to heating their living quarters by means of small, coal-burning stoves in each room. The only fuel issued to them by the Japanese was coal dust, which had to be mixed with mud and dried before it could be burned. Men who had once spent their days discussing tobacco imports and the international price of cotton now debated the merits of their recipes for making coal balls. In spite of every effort to maintain some perspective, life kept closing in on them.

Their only news of the outside world and the progress of the war was what the Japanese wanted them to have. Newspapers coming into camp reported glorious victories in every battle with Americans, along with the repeated sinking of the entire U.S. fleet. However, astute observers reading between the lines noted that each "glorious victory" in the Pacific occurred closer to the Japanese homeland. "Why" they wondered, "would a victorious army keep retreating?"

Letters sent from camp had been reduced to one twenty-five-word Red Cross message each month, with the occasional privilege of sending a one-hundred-word letter through Free China. Mail often took six months to reach Canada and another six months for the reply to come back. Much of the delay occurred in the post office at Weihsien, where mail might languish for weeks before being sent to Peking to be censored, creating a further delay. The whole process became so frustrating that many people simply stopped writing. But not Eric. If there was a chance of anything getting through, he would keep sending letters.

In late November, he wrote Flo saying that they had celebrated her birthday with a little party. He was keeping fit, not losing weight, and staying busy from morning till night. He was unable to add that he spent at least one evening a week mending hockey sticks with strips of cloth that used to be their bed sheets. Working in the hallway, out of respect for his roommates, he used a foul-smelling fish glue to secure the repairs, hoping they would last for another game or two.

On November 26, the day after her birthday, Flo wrote to him: "Daddy died peacefully Nov 13th. Failing since pneumonia summer. Margaret, Finlay, Louise here. Overwhelmed kindness friends, relatives. Mother magnificent — continuing here — all well. Dearest Love."

But there was no room to tell him how two-year-old Maureen had been the light of her grandfather's life during the previous weeks. Every morning after her bath she toddled in to sit on "Bumpa's" bed and encourage him to eat his breakfast by consuming most of it herself. Hugh MacKenzie might swallow a few bites for little Maureen, but not even she could re-ignite his will to live. It had been a sad morning when Flo closed the door to her father's room for the last time and tried to explain to the distraught Maureen that she couldn't go in because Bumpa had gone to live with Jesus in heaven.

Their letters crossed somewhere in the Pacific and arrived months after being sent. Perhaps it was good that every joy and sorrow was not immediately known by those apart. Their Father in heaven knew, and each day they could appeal to Him to meet the needs of those who were so far away in distance and time. Eric's copy of *Prayers for Daily Use* contained his tiny handwriting in the margin beside the "Prayer for Absent Loved Ones." In order, down the page, the names read: Flo, Tricia, Heather, Maureen, and on through every member of his extended family in Canada and Scotland.

His final letter of 1943, written on Christmas Eve, said: "Enjoying Christmas festivities; usual mission party tomorrow; rooms decorated; Christmas spirit abroad. Remembering you specially. Love to mum, dad, sisters, brothers, Tricia, Heather, Maureen and Flo."

Three days later, Amy Longman wrote her daughter, Perle, in Chungking saying: "Party repatriating shortly includes majority Chefoo School, H. T. Cook's family only British missionaries." Apparently another list had been posted with the names of those selected for the next group to leave Weihsien. But the talks broke down, negotiations failed, and the MS *Gripsholm* never returned to exchange Japanese civilians from the U.S. for the Cooks or the Longmans or anyone else in Weihsien.

Slowly, but with great certainty, the realization crept in that they were going to stay right where they were until one side or the other won the war.

NINETEEN

Going the Distance

1944

Weihsien—The Test

> Whether a man's happiness depends on what he has, or what
> he is;
> On outer circumstances, or inner heart,
> On life's experiences — good and bad — or on what he makes
> out of the materials those experiences provide.
>
> —Hugh Hubbard

On a frigid winter day, Eric Liddell awoke in the early morning darkness and lit a small peanut oil lamp. Fifteen feet away, another match flickered as Joe Cotterill did the same. Moving quietly to a packing-crate table in the center of the room, they opened their Bibles to the daily passage noted in Eric's manual of Christian discipleship. After reading silently for half an hour, they talked in hushed whispers, sharing the thoughts God had impressed on them from His Word, discussing the day ahead, and praying together, surrendering themselves afresh to the Lord. Before sunrise, Joe was off to his job as a stoker. If there was to be hot porridge for breakfast, he and his crew had to get the kitchen fires going.

The previous autumn, when rooms were reassigned after the American repatriation, Joe had joined Eric, Josh, and Bear in a small dormitory room on the top floor of the camp hospital. Since Joe and Eric both rose early, they decided to share their morning quiet time. And since that time, Joe had been constantly surprised by what Eric said and did.

One night, just before lights out, Eric returned to their dorm room reporting what a grand time he and Cullen had enjoyed playing bridge with friends. Cotterill had been brought up in a Christian circle that believed card games of any kind were a tool of the devil and should be avoided. How then could Eric Liddell, one of the finest Christians he knew, play cards and enjoy it? When Joe voiced his concern, Eric laughed in sympathy, not ridicule, then said, "I can understand why you feel that playing card games could lead to gambling, but it doesn't have to."

Even the idea of following a set pattern of daily Bible reading was somewhat foreign to Joe. But he began to discover that the Holy Spirit was not hindered by the structure of a reading guide. Each day's passage seemed to hold encouragement and instruction related to his deepest needs. Eric never tried to change Joe's theology. He simply encouraged him to come before God with a willing heart and a listening ear.

Twenty-six-year-old Cotterill welcomed Eric's friendship and wise counsel because, of all things to befall a young missionary interned in China, Joe had fallen in love. The trouble was that he and Jeannie Hills belonged to different missionary groups, neither of which thought it wise for one of their own to marry someone of a different theological persuasion. And to consider being married while still in camp was out of the question. Or was it?

When Eric enthusiastically encouraged them, and agreed to be Joe's best man, it came as a delightful shock. Even before the final permission arrived from their respective boards, Eric organized an "unofficial unengagement party" to celebrate with a gathering of close friends.

Flo called Eric "an incurable romantic" and loved the hidden side of him that others rarely saw. On March 27, 1944, he wrote to her: "You seem very near today, it is the 10th anniversary of our wedding. Happy loving remembrances; we must celebrate it together next year. Am celebrating it in thoughts and reliving some of our happy times.

"This week start exams, next week Easter holidays. Having excellent international hockey matches, keen rivalry.

"Lester heard wife reached Vancouver. Thanks for wonderful delayed letter via *Gripsholm* with two photos of children. Thrilled to receive them. Hope Tricia, Heather enjoying school, Maureen developing rapidly.

"Love to all the family. Let mother know I fit, busy and no complaints. Love, Eric"

As Eric observed his wedding anniversary, others noted that one year had passed since entering Weihsien. For most people, life had settled into a monotonous routine of "queues and stews." Three times a day they lined up with cups and tin containers to receive what had become known as SOS — most politely defined as "same old stew." The Japanese had shut down most of the black market trading, and the camp canteen sold eggs rationed at two per person per week.

The spirit of many in camp had shifted markedly from a concern for the common good to selfishness and "me-first." Some shouted at the food servers, saying they had been given less than the person ahead of them. Theft became a serious problem as kitchen workers often slipped a vegetable or a piece of meat into their own pockets. Flour and sugar disappeared from the bakery. Stokers took lumps of coal for their own stoves. Each item to which a person felt entitled reduced the amount available to the rest.

Life seemed to be little more than standing in one line after another for everything they needed — a pot of hot water in the morning, a bucket of coal dust in winter, a visit to the latrine, a weekly shower, and the detested roll call each morning. At 7:30 A.M., no matter what the weather, all internees except the sick and those on the job were required to assemble outside, in designated areas of the camp, and be counted. This could take up to an hour. Time and uncertainty were taking their toll on everyone except the young.

Among the boys from the Chefoo School, Eric saw the same playful spirit he and Rob had enjoyed when they lived in "the old barn" at Blackheath. Everything could be turned into a game. The guards were quite impressed with the ability of the Chefoo children to number off in Japanese, "Ichi-Ni-San-Shi" and so on up to ten. Once at roll call in Temple Hill, the first four boys in line had shouted, "Itchy-knee-scratchy-flea," which sent everyone into fits of stifled laughter and left the guards quite bewildered.

Eric found great delight in teaching the children how to play basketball and rounders — a British game similar to baseball. Once when a concerned adult spotted a pack of boys heading into a grove of trees at dusk, he investigated, only to find Eric leading them on a trek through the camp. To the children from Chefoo, whose parents were far away, he quickly became their much beloved "Uncle Eric." And his popularity among the teenagers reached such proportions that his roommates hung a sign on the door of their room indicating whether Eric was OUT or IN.

Some of the teenage interest could be attributed to hero worship, but their respect for Eric grew primarily because he was concerned and available. When the non-religious teens in camp objected to his policy of not organizing sports on Sunday, he allowed them to use the athletic equipment for pick-up games. And after a hockey match turned into a fight because no adult was present, he took the field the next Sunday afternoon to referee.

While boredom led many adults down the path of apathy, it beckoned adolescents toward experimentation. When it became known that a number of young teens from Tientsin and Peking had been holding sex parties in an unused basement and in the room of a condoning adult, a group of irate parents descended on the camp Discipline Committee demanding that they do something about it. Eric, along with a number of other missionary teachers, volunteered to organize weeknight activities to give teens another choice. After that, several evenings a week he was in the game room, participating in a square dance, playing chess, or helping someone build a model boat from scrounged pieces of wood.

One Friday night Joe Cotterill failed to appear for his assigned shift in the game room. When Eric happened by and found the activities unsupervised, he located Cotterill and delivered a sound reprimand. Having never seen Eric angry, Joe was somewhat stunned as he listened to a forceful explanation of the responsibility they had assumed and why it was essential that they carry it through. Eric's concern was for the young people struggling to find some present meaning to life when it seemed that the future had been snatched from their hands.

By the spring of 1944, eighteen-year-old Margaret Vinden had not seen her missionary parents in nearly five years. Her best friend, Kari Torjeson, blonde, vivacious, and extremely proud of her Norwegian heritage, carried the sorrow of her father's death in 1939 when the Japanese bombed his church in Shensi province. Norman Cliff had been ready to sail for university studies in England when he was caught in the aftermath of Pearl Harbor. When an adult in camp quipped, "Oh, the first five years are the hardest," it made these young people wonder if they would ever be free.

But when Eric spoke in church or led a Bible study group with them, he rarely dealt with what might happen tomorrow. Instead, he focused on what could happen today. During one small group discussion, he read aloud the words of Jesus in Matthew 5:43: "Love your enemies, bless them that curse you, do good to them that hate you, and pray for them which despitefully use you, and persecute you." Then he asked if this was merely an ideal or something practical they could actually do. Could they love the guards in camp and the Japanese people as a whole? Most thought it was only a lofty goal.

"I thought so too," Eric said, "but then I noticed the next words, 'Pray for them that despitefully use you.' When we start to pray," he said, "we become God-centered. When we hate then we're self-centered. We spend a lot of time praying for people we like but we don't spend much time praying for people we don't like and people we hate. But Jesus told us to pray for our enemies. I've begun to pray for the guards and it's changed my whole attitude toward them. Maybe you'd like to try it too."

❦

On successive Tuesday evenings during Whitsuntide 1944, Eric spoke on four gifts or fruits of the Holy Spirit — love, truth, humility, and faith. Each week, he tied his thoughts to a verse from one of his favorite hymns, "Gracious Spirit, Dwell With Me." On May 23, they sang:

> Gracious Spirit, dwell with me, I myself would gracious be,
> And with words that help and heal, would Thy life in mine reveal,
> And with actions bold and meek, would for Christ my Saviour speak.

An illustration he often used came from the running track. Speaking softly, with his hands holding the sides of the lectern, Eric told them a story:

> "Several years ago I sat in the grandstand at a great sports meeting where the finest athletes of the U.S.A. and the British Empire met in competition. There was an obstacle race in which competitors had to run round the course many times, jumping hurdles as they went. After several rounds the competitors were fairly well separated, except for the first two who were running within ten yards of each other.
>
> "As the first man took one of the hurdles his foot struck the top of it and knocked it over. The blow was not hard enough to affect him much, a slight stagger and on he went. The fallen hurdle left a gap. It gave the second man the chance to run through the gap instead of taking a jump and thus gain a slight advantage.
>
> "Ten yards behind means less than two seconds.
>
> "In the fraction of a second at his disposal a decision was made, he swerved to the side, jumped the hurdle next to the fallen one and then moved back in to the edge of the track again.
>
> "I can remember the thrill that went through me, and the answering cheer that rose from the crowd. That was the finest thing done that day.
>
> "He did not win; I have forgotten who did, but I can never forget that action. He could not act otherwise, he was

led by the Spirit of Sportsmanship. It was ingrained in him, part of himself.

"Sport is wonderful. The most wonderful part of it is not the almost superhuman achievements but the spirit in which it is done. Take away that spirit and it is dead.

"The Holy Spirit is to the Christian life what sportsmanship is to sport and more. Without Him in our lives, even at the best, we are little better than Tennyson's Maud:

"'Perfectly beautiful: let it be granted her: where is the fault?
All that I saw (for her eyes were downcast, not to be seen)
Faultily faultless, icily regular, splendidly null
Dead perfection and no more.'

"Or in terms of sport: —
A marvellous player, beautiful strokes, magnificent timing, perfect style, but no sportsmanship about him, Dead perfection, no more.

'Breathe on me breath of God,
Fill me with life anew
That I may love what Thou dost love,
And do what Thou wouldst do.'"

Only about fifty people attended Eric's weekly talks in a curtained-off portion of the large church. But for many of those who came, these talks marked a turning point in their attitude toward life and God. The meeting closed with a final verse from Eric's much-loved hymn:

Mighty Spirit dwell with me, I myself would mighty be
Mighty so as to prevail, where unaided man must fail
Ever by a mighty hope, pressing on and bearing up.
— Thomas Toke Lynch

On the night of June 9, 1944, two men escaped from Weihsien. Laurence Tipton, an executive with the British-American Tobacco Company, and Arthur Hummel, an English teacher at a Catholic school in Peking, went over the wall in a precisely timed maneuver assisted by three other internees. The plan had been such a carefully guarded secret that the people in camp didn't learn of it until the next day when the furious guards discovered the men were missing. The Japanese reprisals were swift but non-violent. All single men, including Eric and his roommates, were moved from the top floor of the hospital to the former high school building in the center of camp, and all internees were required to assemble for a laboriously conducted roll call twice a day.

Many people felt that the two men selfishly had placed everyone in jeopardy by escaping. But actually they had put themselves at risk for the good of the camp.

For several months Father Raymond DeJaegher, a Belgian priest, had been communicating with the outside world through a coolie who helped empty the camp latrines. The coolie, with his eye on DeJaegher, would bend over to blow his nose or spit on an ash pile, thus depositing a message in a tightly wrapped wad of waterproof paper. The priest would casually retrieve the pellet and leave out-going messages in a prearranged place.

Through this communication system, word had come from General Wang, a Chinese guerrilla commander, offering to storm the camp and set the prisoners free. But since he could not guarantee their safety outside the camp, he said they would need to arrange for American planes to come and fly them all to Chungking. Obviously the man needed to be dissuaded from such an attempt, but he could become a helpful ally. Tipton and Hummel arranged to link up with Wang's men after their escape, and soon, messages began to be smuggled into camp from the two escapees, giving the Council of Nine accurate information about the progress of the war.

The prisoners in Weihsien were far from forgotten by their own countries, but there was little their governments could do to help. The Swiss Consul from Tsingtao, a man named Egger, made regular visits to the camp, often sending reports on conditions to the British and American authorities. Mr. Egger worked tirelessly to get medicines and food parcels to the internees. Small amounts of "comfort money" for canteen purchases were also distributed to those in camp. In July 1944, Egger delivered 200 food parcels sent by the American Red Cross. The U.S. citizens who received them shared the powdered milk, Spam, chocolate bars, cigarettes, and other treasures with friends. Briefly, morale edged upward.

But when Brian Thompson, a sixteen-year-old Chefoo boy, was electrocuted after touching a low-hanging wire during roll call, spirits again sagged. How senseless it all seemed, and how desperately everyone longed for something to change.

Only the young seemed able to muster some enthusiasm for two contests sponsored by the Japanese commandant. Norman Cliff and his team won the rat-killing contest with a total of sixty-eight, eagerly claiming their prize of a tin of sardines. Ten-year-old John Taylor, a great-grandson of pioneer missionary Hudson Taylor, became champion fly-killer, offering a bottle containing precisely 3,500 dead flies.

With autumn and winter looming ahead, camp authorities repeatedly asked the Japanese commandant to allow the purchase of food and clothing from local Chinese merchants.

"These things are luxuries," he said. "You have it better than my own people."

His refusal said a great deal more than he intended about the course of the war in the Pacific.

In Eric's letters to Flo, with the twenty-five word limit imposed by the International Red Cross, he continued his efforts to ease her mind about the situation in Weihsien.

"Aug 24, 1944

"Large airy room with eleven others. Healthy, enjoying some reading. Constantly remember and picture you all.

Dearest love to all, everything sufficient. Longing for you, love. Eric."

Unknown to him, his mother died in Edinburgh on September 22. Flo sent news of her passing, wondering if he might even be repatriated and on his way home before the news reached him.

Eric's letter of October 25 said:

"Glorious weather. Winter activities begin. Good start teaching. Winter games, children's evening clubs, religious services. Kept busy. Remembering you all. Special love for special occasions. Eric"

He didn't want her to worry, even though, for the first time, he was beginning to realize that deep within himself all was not well.

TWENTY

Breaking the Tape

1944–1945

Joe Cotterill first noticed the change in Eric one November evening in their dormitory room. As one of their roommates fried a piece of bread in peanut oil, Eric reacted in an uncharacteristic way.

"What's that you're cooking?" Eric asked in a strained voice from his bed.

"The usual," came the off-hand reply.

"Well it smells horrible," Eric said without opening his eyes.

The humorless comment and acidic tone of voice were not like Eric at all. On the other hand, everyone in camp was worn down by the hard work and inadequate nutrition. Joe dismissed it as fatigue.

A few days later, Eric apologized to Joe for his remarks.

"I've been getting these terrible headaches," Eric said. "When they come, I just want to lie down where it's dark and quiet."

As Joe watched him walk away, he noticed that the spring was gone from Eric's step. He seemed slow, almost lumbering, as he trudged down the lane.

As the days passed, Joe began to notice other changes. In conversation, Eric's words came more slowly, and the little quips that so characterized him had gradually disappeared. Also, he had become more wistful about Flo and the children, often looking at their photograph and lamenting the fact that he had never seen Maureen, now three years old.

Early in January, Eric came down with the same flu and sinusitis that was afflicting many in the camp. The doctors treated him, but his condition did not improve. His headaches became more severe, and he frequently spent hours lying in bed with a damp cloth over his eyes. Some days he insisted on trying to meet his responsibilities, but often he was simply not able to get up for roll call. For many of the teens who depended on his energy and cheerful spirit, the fact that Uncle Eric was ill only deepened the winter doldrums that gripped the camp. There seemed to be little hope of anything changing for them in the near future.

Then, on a snowy day in mid-January, the camp suddenly came alive when a man shouted, "Look what's coming through the main gate! Can you believe it?" Cart after cart loaded with boxes marked American Red Cross rumbled up the main road toward the church. From their experience the previous summer, all knew exactly what was in each box. Visions of jam and Spam began to dance in their heads. A crew of men quickly gathered and began carrying the coveted boxes into the church. Two hours later, a man with a tally sheet declared, "Fifteen hundred. More than enough to give a full box to every person in camp."

But the euphoria over the arrival of much-needed food turned to disbelief when an official notice from the commandant appeared saying that the distribution had been delayed because a small contingent of Americans claimed that the boxes were clearly designated for U.S. citizens and should be given only to them. By their reasoning, each American should get seven-and-a-half boxes and everyone else in camp should get nothing. A proposed compromise offering one-and-a-half boxes to each American and one box to all other internees was rejected by the handful holding out for the entire shipment.

After two weeks of controversy while the parcels remained under guard in the church, the commandant declared that every person in camp would receive one box and the excess would be sent to prisoners in other camps. On the last day of January the internees were finally able to open the cardboard boxes and gleefully examine the four compartments, each containing powdered milk, cigarettes, tinned butter, Spam, cheese, concentrated chocolate, sugar, coffee, jam, salmon, and raisins. Before nightfall, trading began, with one packet of sixteen cigarettes worth two bars of chocolate, and one tin of coffee bringing two of Spam. It surpassed the best Christmas anyone could remember.

But Eric was too ill to enjoy it. Annie Buchan, the nurse from Siaochang, insisted that he be hospitalized, where she could take a special interest in his care. Many days he exhibited symptoms of depression. "The future seems like a blank wall," he told Annie. "I just can't see anything ahead."

A preliminary diagnosis suggested that overwork and fatigue had caused a nervous breakdown. Pondering that assessment, Eric felt a sense of spiritual failure. "There is just one thing that troubles me," he told a friend. "I ought to have been able to cast it all on the Lord, and not to have broken down under it."

On Sunday, February 11, he suffered a small stroke that left him with a slight limp and a strange cast in one eye. But within a few days he was up and walking again in the hospital, telling everyone he was feeling better. A steady stream of friends came to visit as the doctors allowed. When one asked if his head was better, Eric replied, "To answer that question I should require to know what is going on inside my head."

Joe Cotterill, now working in the hospital pathology lab, overheard the doctors discussing Eric's situation. The stroke had alerted them to the possibility of a brain tumor, but without an X-ray machine there was no way to know. All they could do was provide a quiet place with rest and good nutrition, hoping that would bring improvement.

Seventeen-year-old Joyce Stranks, who worked in the hospital kitchen, often stopped by to talk. Eric had coached her in softball, tutored her in chemistry, and even participated with her in a Christmas play the year before. Joyce was following the reading guide in his book on discipleship for her daily quiet time. January had found them discussing the topic of "Surrender" about which Eric had written: "As we start this course of readings we should first surrender our lives to God and dedicate ourselves to doing His Will. God's Will is only revealed to us step by step. He reveals more as we obey what we know. Surrender means that we are prepared to follow God's guidance, wherever or however He guides, no matter what the cost."

In the hospital, their daily visits were brief, and Joyce sometimes felt she was bothering Eric. But he always greeted her with a smile and seemed happy to hear about what was happening in camp. And he told her how he greatly appreciated the music of the Salvation Army Band directed by her father.

Every Sunday afternoon, even in winter, the Salvation Army Band played hymns outside the hospital. On February 18, they received a request from Eric to play "Be Still, My Soul." As the strains of "Finlandia" filtered into his room, Eric pondered the familiar words he loved so well.

"Be still, my soul: the Lord is on thy side;
Bear patiently the cross of grief or pain;
Leave to thy God to order and provide;
In every change He faithful will remain.
Be still, my soul: thy best, thy heavenly Friend
Through thorny ways leads to a joyful end."

Three days later, on February 21, possibly with the help of a friend, he typed a short letter to Flo: "Was carrying too much responsibility. Slight nervous breakdown. Am much better after month's rest in hospital. Doctor suggests changing my work. Giving up teaching and athletics and taking on physical work like baking. A good change. So glad to get your letter of July. Mrs. Longman is much better. Bear and Nelma making preparations for marriage on April 18. Will send particulars later. Wish you could enter into the celebrations. Joyce Stranks has been a great help to me in hospital, keeping me in touch with the news. Enjoying comfort parcels. Special love to yourself and children."

That same day, while talking with Joyce about complete surrender to God, Eric suffered a seizure and lost consciousness. Frightened, the girl ran to get Annie Buchan, who, in her concern for Eric, chided Joyce for bothering him.

"You should'na been here anyway," Annie scolded, drawing the curtains around Eric's bed. Joyce stood there in a flood of tears until a man put his arm around her and led her away.

Eric lay in a coma until 9:20 that night when he died.

The next morning, news of Eric's death spread through the snow-covered camp, causing shock and disbelief. "How could he be gone?" … ."He was only forty-three. … I saw him walking outside the hospital a day or two ago. … My wife baked a special cake, and we shared it with him last week during tea. … I heard him say he was feeling better. … Why would God let Eric Liddell die?"

Men who normally kept their emotions well in check wept openly on the streets of Weihsien as they pondered the loss of a man who was universally loved and appreciated in camp.

Joyce Stranks recoiled from the thought of visiting the morgue to see Eric's body. She didn't want to believe that he was dead. But at the gentle urging of her parents, she agreed to go. Accompanied by her father and Annie Buchan, Joyce forced herself to look at the lifeless form of the man who had so epitomized the love of Christ for her and so many others. And when she saw him, a wonderful feeling swept over her. The expression on his face was calm and restful. And deep within she knew that he was not there. As surely as Eric had lived and laughed among them, he had gone to be with the Lord he loved so well, and whose love he had shown to everyone he met.

She walked outside without speaking, numbed by the pain, yet feeling a strange sense of peace. Uncle Eric was gone. But he was home. And he was free.

On one of the most difficult days of Joe Cotterill's life, he participated in the autopsy to determine the cause of Eric's death. The examination revealed an inoperable tumor deep in the left side of his brain. Eric had not suffered a nervous breakdown, nor had he failed spiritually. Even in the world's finest hospital, little could have been done to save him.

⚜

Dr. Arnold Bryson, a veteran LMS missionary, led a short funeral service on Saturday, February 24. In his remarks, he sounded a theme that would be echoed many times in remembering Eric Liddell.

"What was the secret of his consecrated life and far-reaching influence? Absolute surrender to God's Will as revealed in Jesus Christ. His was a God-controlled life and he followed his Master and Lord with a devotion that never flagged and with an intensity of purpose that made men see both the reality and power of true religion."

For many of the people gathered for the service, the vocabulary of faith was unfamiliar. But they clearly understood from Eric's life of humility and service what it looked like to be a follower of Jesus.

"If anyone was ready for his Master's call," Bryson concluded, "it was our friend, whose happy, radiant face we shall see no more on earth, but his influence will surely live on in the hearts and lives of all who knew him."

After Bear Davies had led in a closing prayer, the pallbearers carefully lifted the rough wooden casket and carried it gently to the camp cemetery. One of them, eighteen-year-old Stephen Metcalf, had assisted Eric in keeping track of the camp athletic equipment. A few weeks earlier, Eric had given his only pair of running shoes to Stephen, saying, "You'll need these for the winter." Metcalf glanced down at the shoes, bound by Eric with tape and string, as he walked carefully along the snow-covered path into the Japanese area of camp, out-of-bounds to all but the small burial party.

Huddled together against the bitterly cold wind, they repeated aloud the Beatitudes, then lowered the casket into the frozen ground. As they did, Metcalf wondered, "Is this all that happens to honor such a great man? Is this all?"

A memorial service for Eric was held a week later, on March 3. Eight hundred people from every nationality and walk of life packed the camp church while others stood outside. A. P. Cullen, who presided at the service, said to those gathered: "This afternoon we are not here to dwell on the apparent tragedy nor yet upon the sense of irreparable loss. We are here, first and foremost, in this Memorial Service, to give thanks to God for the life so finely lived, the fight so nobly fought, the race so cleanly run, and to find renewed inspiration for ourselves in the example that Eric Liddell left us."

After reading selections from the Sermon on the Mount and St. Paul's "hymn of love"— 1 Corinthians 13 — the congregation sang "Be Still, My Soul."

Ted McLaren, the highly respected chairman of the camp Discipline Committee, paid tribute to Eric as an athlete. Recalling their days as teammates on the Scottish International Rugby team, McLaren said: "Never once did he show the slightest sign of bad temper or bad sportsmanship on the field; both, it seemed to me, were utterly foreign to him. Many a time he was lain for by his opponents, whose tactics were at least doubtful, but never would he repay them in their own coin — his method was invariable — he merely played better rugby and made them look like second-raters."

After Carl Longman spoke of Eric's role on the staff of the Anglo-Chinese College and Annie Buchan recalled the days of country work in Siaochang, Cullen offered his own deeply personal tribute.

"I have known Eric for thirty-three years. I have been in frequent contact with him for the last twenty years. After his family left for Canada, he and I lived together, just the two of us, in my flat till January 1942. From then until he came here fourteen months later, almost every day I went for a long walk with him. And from my knowledge of him, gained in this close association over many years, I say that Eric is the most remarkable example in my experience of a man of average ability and talents developing those talents to an amazing degree, and even appearing to acquire new talents from time to time, through the power of the Holy Spirit. He was, literally, God-controlled, in his thought, judgments, actions, words, to an extent I have never seen surpassed, and rarely seen equaled.

"The most noteworthy feature in Eric's life was the regular and rapid progress of his spiritual development. It is as phenomenal as the speed with which, in a 100-yards race, after being yards behind at halfway, he would catch up and pass the winning-post an easy first, leaving the other competitors standing. In the athletic world, no one knows how he did it — it remains a mystery; but for his progress in the spiritual race there is a very clear and definite explanation.

"First of all, absolute surrender to the Will of God. Absolute surrender — those words were often on his lips, the conception was always in his mind; that God should have absolute control over every part of his life.

"It was toward the attainment of that ideal that he directed all his mental and spiritual energies. It was no more easy for him than it is for us; let no one think that he did not have his temptations, just as we have, temptations to indolence, slackness, compromise, and what not. But he won his way through, by persistent study, regular times of devotion, constant meditation, insistent prayer, getting up early in the morning and spending one hour — two hours — in a concentrated search for God's will as revealed in the teaching of Jesus and the Bible generally.

"In recent years he laid much emphasis on the teaching in the Sermon on the Mount, which, he was convinced, embodied a really practical way of living, indeed the only practical way of living for a Christian. To him the supreme thing about God was God's love, even as love is the supreme necessity for a truly Christian life. Another of his favourite passages was the 13th chapter of 1st Corinthians.

"No sketch of Eric's life, however inadequate, would be complete without some reference to his gift of happiness and *joie-de-vivre*. He loved the good things of life as much as any of us. But *all* his happiness — the happiness that shone so radiantly in his face — *all* his happiness had its basis in his serene faith in God, his love for God, and his appreciation of God's gifts."

The final tribute came from P. A. Bruce, headmaster of the Chefoo School. Until they heard it that day from "Pa" Bruce, very few people knew that during the previous summer Eric had planned to sell the gold watch and chain given to him by the city of Edinburgh in order to buy much-needed softball equipment for the camp.

"Mercifully, 'Comfort Money' came in," Bruce said, "this need was met otherwise, and this sacrifice was not completed; a sacrifice willingly thought out and prepared for, so that these ball games might continue to give pleasure to scores of people."

Long after the service ended, some of the finest tributes to Eric came in private conversations as people recalled the ordinary man who had lived so extraordinarily among them.

A prostitute from Tientsin told a neighbor how Eric had put up a shelf on the wall of the room where she lived alone. "He was the first man to do something for me without asking for a favor in return."

One of Eric's roommates, a British businessman, said simply, "He lived a far better life than his preaching."

And an unnamed internee wrote in a personal diary: "He was not particularly clever, and not conspicuously able, but he was good. He was naturally reserved and tended to live in a world of his own, but he gave of himself unstintedly. His reserve did not prevent him from mixing with everybody and being known by everybody, but he always shrank from revealing his deepest needs and distresses, so that whilst he bore the burdens of many, very few could help to bear his.

"His fame as an athlete helped him a good deal. He certainly didn't look like a great runner, but the fact that he had been one gave him a self-confidence that men of his type don't often have. He wasn't a great leader, or an inspired thinker, but he knew what he ought to do, and he did it. He was a true disciple of the Master and worthy of the highest of places amongst the saints gathered in the Church triumphant. We have lost of our best, but we have gained a fragrant memory."

⁂

As spring approached in Toronto, it seemed that a curtain had fallen and no one, not even mission headquarters, was receiving any news from China. Flo and the girls continued to look for letters from Eric, but none came. As their eleventh wedding anniversary approached, Flo dared to hope that the talk of impending victory in Europe was true and that by next year, surely by then, they would be together again. For the first time in four years, she allowed herself to think about their reunion and how proud Eric would be to see his "mature and responsible" wife instead of the impetuous young girl he had married.

In mid-March, Rob Liddell, working at a hospital in Scotland, received an inquiry from Cocker-Brown at the London headquarters of the LMS: "Where would Eric go if he was repatriated."

"If Eric is given a choice," Rob replied, "of course he will make for Canada."

Then, on May 1, Cocker-Brown received a letter from the British Under-Secretary of State dated the day before:

Sir,

I am directed by Mr. Winston Churchill to inform you with regret that the Swiss representative at Shanghai has reported by telegraph that the Reverend Eric Henry Liddell died at Weihsien on the 21st February, 1945. The cause of death is not stated.

I am,
Sir,
Your obedient Servant,
I. W. O. Davidson.

Stunned, he immediately cabled the news to Rev. A. E. Armstrong at the United Church of Canada office in Toronto. Then Cocker-Brown rang Rob, asking him to pass the news to Jenny and Ernest.

That same day, in headlines as tall as a man's hand, the evening edition of the *Toronto Star* proclaimed HITLER DEAD. Talk of impending victory over Germany eclipsed all other news. The city was already making plans for a great celebration to greet the official announcement that the war in Europe had ended. But on the smaller stage, a more heart-wrenching drama was taking place.

On May 2, Rev. Armstrong, along with Rev. George King who had been repatriated from Weihsien the previous year, knocked at the door of 21 Gloucester Street. Flo invited them in but immediately sensed that they had come with bad news. Her first reaction was that something had happened to one of her brothers, Finlay or Kenneth, both serving in the armed forces.

"Is something wrong? Is it one of the boys?" she asked.

"It's not the boys," Mr. King replied. "It's Eric."

Eric! But that was impossible. He was not fighting in the war, and he was so vigorous and strong. It had never crossed her mind that anything could happen to him.

She wanted to know what and when and how, but all they could tell her was the date — February 21. He had been gone for two months and she hadn't known!

At the sound of their mother's weeping, Maureen and Heather rushed into the room. How could she tell them what she herself could not believe?

"Daddy is with Bumpa in heaven," was all she could manage before wrapping the little girls in her arms.

When Tricia came bounding into the house after school, she found it filled with somber friends, most of whom had been crying. The news of her first-place finish in a track meet that day turned to ashes when she learned that her father had died in China. She refused to believe it, telling herself there had been a terrible mistake and that very soon Daddy would turn up at the door and put everything right. But somewhere deep inside, she knew.

Jenny received the news of her brother's death by phone in the drawing room of her Edinburgh home. She had never been one to cry easily, but with great wracking sobs she stumbled outside, feeling that her chest would burst. "Did they torture him?" she wondered. "What had they done to make him die?"

As the news spread by newspaper and radio that Eric Liddell had died in a Japanese internment camp, all of Scotland mourned.

On Friday, May 4, the *Toronto Star* published a photograph of Eric and a brief article titled: "Rev. Eric H. Liddell Dies In Jap

Camp." It noted that a memorial service was scheduled the next afternoon in Carlton Street United Church.

At that service, tributes were given by Rev. George King, who had been interned with Eric for six months, and by Rev. T. T. Faichney, former pastor of Union Church in Tientsin.

The heartfelt words of appreciation and the sympathy of friends sustained Flo, who was numbed by grief. At times she felt like jumping off a bridge just to be with Eric again. But she knew she had to continue for the sake of their girls. More than her responsibility, they were her calling, the living portion of Eric and the life they had shared together.

The euphoria that engulfed the city of Toronto on May 7 seemed to mock her sorrow. Even though the next day was officially proclaimed V-E Day, with schools and offices closed, people couldn't wait. They flocked downtown to City Hall, where tickertape tangled the skies as people embraced strangers and danced in the streets.

But for thousands, the joy of victory came mingled with a deep sense of loss, captured poignantly by a newspaper message from a local furniture store. In this touching tribute to the celebration, a picture showed a young wife and a little girl looking out a window for a man who wouldn't be coming home. The printed message said: "On this day of victory — for our part — our thoughts are with all those whose irreparable sacrifices have made this day a reality."

TWENTY-ONE

The Race Goes On

21 Gloucester Street, Toronto, Ont. Canada
May 11, 1945

Dear Mr. Cocker-Brown:

It is over a week since Dr. Armstrong and Mr. King came to break the news to me that you had sent by cable. I wanted to write before this to thank you for your sympathy and that of the L.M.S. Fellowship which you also extended to me in that cable.

It was a stunning blow and I still can hardly believe it, but I have been *very* conscious of the prayers and thoughts of countless friends over in England and Scotland and here too.

My first reaction was, "That is why he has been so near me lately." I have dreamt more about Eric in the last few weeks than I have all the rest of the time I have been home. Every time (in the dreams) he was here we were all terribly happy and everything was so vivid. My reaction was "That is just wishful thinking getting the better of you."

Then in making plans for the summer and autumn I seemed to come up against a stone wall. Plans that seemed excellent at first seemed to get blocked. I don't know when I have been so conscious of a restraining hand and I simply couldn't understand it. I felt sure there was going to be some change in plans but I couldn't see what.

The thought flashed into my mind, "Could it be that Eric is really coming home and we may have to go over to England to meet him? No that's wishful thinking again."

Never once did I have any premonition of this and even after I knew I was so vividly conscious of Eric being happy. I could just see his sunny smile and twinkling eyes.

It has been a strange and wonderful experience. At times I have been numbed and overwhelmed by a sense of unreality — of pain — of fear for the future and then there has come welling up from within that power of faith which has carried me through. My faith has been wonderfully strengthened. In looking back I have so much to be thankful for. God has provided so wonderfully — we have been so happy and I know that He is working out his purpose and that good can come out of even this.

I have been overwhelmed by the kindness and thoughtfulness of my own immediate family — relations, friends, China friends, and people I don't even know.

My heart aches for Jenny, Rob, and Ernest. I wish they could have been at the Memorial Service that we had last Saturday. Beautiful, sincere tributes were paid to Eric by Mr. King who was repatriated from Weihsien and by Mr. Faichney who was the Minister in Union Church, Tientsin, for five years and was a great friend of ours.

I have just been hearing today of tributes paid to Eric's memory in several of the churches here on Sunday.

Please forgive me for rambling on like this. I have never had the pleasure of meeting you but I always remember how highly Eric spoke of you and how he enjoyed his visit in your home in June '40 while on deputation in the South of England.

I just wanted you and the other friends to know that I have been very conscious of your prayers and sympathies but you must not grieve for us.

I feel that Eric and I had as much happiness in our few short years together as many couples have in a whole lifetime and I thank God for the privilege of being Eric's wife.

I only hope that the children (they have been perfectly sweet and such a comfort to me) will take after Eric and follow in their Master's Footsteps.

Yours sincerely,
Florence Liddell

P.S. I am writing you a separate letter about business matters.

On the same day that she wrote this letter, Flo set her mind and hand to the pressing matters that faced her as a thirty-three-year-old single mother of three children. In the promised second letter, she wrote:

21 Gloucester Street, Toronto, Ont. Canada
May 11, 1945

Dear Mr. Cocker-Brown:
My brain still feels rather fuzzy and numbed when it comes to thinking of business matters, but I realize there are several matters that must be discussed at once and I would like your advice and information.

1st: I am enclosing a statement from the Treasurer's Office of the United Church of Canada of the money paid out to me since coming to Canada...

I feel very badly about having two increases in allowance since coming home when you folk in England who are donating the money have sacrificed so much and done with so little in these war years.

With wartime prices here I found it absolutely impossible to live without the increases. As it was I had to draw on our very limited savings for dentist and doctors bills.

I would like to know exactly where I stand as regards over-drawing or underdrawing on my salary during these four years. How much has been going to the Swiss Government for Eric? Wasn't there some arrangement for them getting something in the camps through the Swiss?

There will also be deductions for the payments on our insurance.

I understand that the Mission continues to pay the

ordinary allowance for six months after the husband's death. In this case does that mean six months from Feb 21st or six months from May 3rd?

Another point that is worrying me is, do I qualify for a Pension? I know Eric didn't actually join the L.M.S. until his first furlough. I have forgotten the ruling on pensions. Do I qualify and if so how much would it amount to? Dr. Armstrong has very kindly said I could still draw it through them as long as the wartime restrictions make it impossible for you to send direct to me.

Now about the insurances. ... Eric had two sets of insurance, one with the Australian Mutual Society (policies with you) and one with the Manufacturers Life Head Office here.

I have the policies for this second set here with me. I have phoned down to them and everything is in order except for a few snags. They are communicating with their office in London at once.

1st: There must be some proof of Eric's death but they tell me their office will probably get it from the Foreign Office.

2nd: The policy is in Sterling.

3rd: The policy is made out to the estate and not in my name.

Just before leaving Tientsin I went with Eric to the Mission Safe to get all our various papers and certificates, etc. We thought everything was in order but when I open the envelope marked his will, we find it is one he made out before we were married and definitely states is null and void when he marries.

I know he made another will because I saw it and simply can't understand how this has happened. By some fluke we must have destroyed the second one and kept this one. It's most unlike Eric. At first it didn't worry me because outside of the insurance there is absolutely no property and belongings to worry about. But I know nothing about English law and when the policy is made out to the estate and I have no will to show what happens.

I am terribly sorry to trouble you with all this but I didn't know what else to do.

Mr. King has been most helpful and so have the insurance people here. There is also a lawyer connected with the Mission Offices here but we haven't approached him yet as we thought it best to write to you and see what the situation was at your end.

I know that Rob or Ernest will be only too glad to take any of this responsibility off your shoulders if you will just let them know what they can do.

I know this will all take time but I know it will turn out alright eventually.

This is a most unbusinesslike letter and I hope you will forgive me for putting you and Mr. Diamond to so much trouble.

I would be very grateful if I could have a statement as soon as possible of how I stand financially with the L.M.S. because all my plans are at a standstill until then.

It is quite obvious I will have to go back to nursing but I am very thankful to be young and strong and to have a profession behind me.

However with the three children to think of, I'll have to get moving on plans at once.

Yours most gratefully,
Florence J. Liddell

As Flo struggled through her first weeks of widowhood, the people of Scotland prepared to honor their own beloved champion. On Sunday evening, May 27, a thousand people packed Edinburgh's Morningside Congregational Church to remember Eric Liddell. The next evening, Dundas Street Congregational Church in Glasgow overflowed as Scotland further honored the man whom the *Glasgow Evening News* said, "did her proud every hour of his life." At both services, D. P. Thomson spoke of Eric's deep spiritual commitment, while Rob described Eric's service in China. Men from the world of sport, education, and the church expressed appreciation for Eric and the challenge he had given them. Jenny and Ernest, along with their families, attended both services, learning something new from each one about their brother who so seldom spoke of his own success. Until those services, it had never occurred to Rob's daughter, Peggy, now eighteen, that her Uncle Eric had been a famous man.

When the school year ended, Flo decided that she and the girls would spend the summer at Port Albert, a small town on Lake Huron, 125 miles west of Toronto. While continuing to sort through the tangle of insurance policies, missionary pension, and salary issues, she needed time away to think, to heal, and to look ahead.

She found a rustic cottage, vacant for several years, which an American couple rented to her for $25 a month. She scrubbed it clean, moved the girls in, and settled down for three months without telephone or newspaper. Patricia considered it "pure heaven." Every day they walked, talked, swam, and sang together as Flo pondered the sort of life she wanted to make for her girls.

The four of them were still enjoying the quiet pace of life on the lake when they heard that the United States had dropped a giant bomb on Japan. On August 15, U.S. President Harry Truman announced the end of the war in the Pacific and declared it V-J Day.

For the 1500 people in Weihsien, the war ended two days later when an American B-24 Liberator buzzed the camp, then opened its belly and dropped seven paratroopers into the nearby gaoliang fields. Cheering internees rushed past startled guards and out the front gate to find the men and lead them back into camp.

Major Stanley Staiger, along with Ensign Jimmy Moore, a former Chefoo student, led the members of the rescue team into "The Courtyard of the Happy Way," where they took command of the camp. Standing on a small rise, the Salvation Army band played "Happy Days Are Here Again" and a medley of national anthems they had been secretly practicing for months.

The next day, supplies of food and surplus military clothing began raining down from giant B-29 bombers to fortify the internees until their evacuation.

Within two months, most of those who had been in Weihsien were on their way home. But a number of missionaries volunteered to go directly back to their old stations. George Luxon and A. P. Cullen returned to Tientsin to see what remained of the Anglo-Chinese College and restate the London Missionary Society's claim to the property. Cullen found his flat ransacked and thirty years of diaries, along with his personal library, gone. Scouring the second-hand shops of the city, he was able to re-purchase a few of his most cherished books. He and Luxon set about getting the college buildings repaired, contacting former students, and making plans to reopen as the Anglo-Chinese College on January 1, 1946. Their hearts were clearly still in China. "If you were here," Luxon wrote to the LMS office in London, "you would see how impossible it is to leave the Chinese when they are relying on us to help them re-organise their Christian work."

With autumn approaching, Flo knew that she must find a place for herself and the girls before returning to work. A few weeks after learning of Eric's death, her mother, Agnes MacKenzie, had remarked, "Here we are, two old widows together." Flo readily acknowledged her widowhood, but was not ready to be old or to continue living at home. After a frustrating search for housing, she rented three rooms in a house at 184 Browning Avenue, two miles east of downtown Toronto. Along with Flo and the girls, the landlady and her two daughters plus two secretaries occupied the three-story dwelling, sharing the kitchen and the costs.

A few weeks after moving in, Flo and the girls joined thousands of others in downtown Toronto to cheer the soldiers and sailors returning from war. Crowds lined the street as the men marched in formation toward the Parliament Buildings and Queen's Park, where the parade broke up and they were reunited with their families. Eight-year-old Heather watched in fascination as a beautiful young woman wearing a hat and veil threw herself into her husband's arms.

The pangs of grief she felt were not for herself, but for her mother. "I hope mom isn't looking at them," she said to herself, "because she's going to feel so bad. It's not fair. It's just not fair."

In mid-October an envelope from the Canadian Red Cross arrived containing three letters from Eric that she had never received. Two had been sent in 1944, and the last was the typewritten message posted on the day he died. A fresh wave of grief swept over her as she realized more of what Eric had endured during the final months of his life. The later return of Eric's personal effects, including his Edinburgh University blazer, was bittersweet as well. Although she had determined not to be mired in the past, the reminders of what might have been were everywhere.

December brought a letter from Eugene Huebener, one of Eric's roommates in camp. Enclosed was a photo of Eric's grave with a small wooden cross bearing his name.

"His death was a terrible shock to us all," Huebener wrote, "and I felt a great hole in my life for a little while, and after praying it over a calm settled on me, as if Eric was comforting me and saying that he had gone to a better place. Today I am trying to live more like he lived, because he lived like Christ lived. Because Christ liveth, I know Eric liveth and I know he has come to you in spirit and comforts you too.

"Rather than send you sympathy for your great loss, I would send you congratulations for loving and helping a man to show so many how to live."

Two days after Christmas, Flo wrote to Mr. Northcott of the LMS describing her current situation.

> "Last summer you asked me to inform you from time to time as to how my financial affairs were progressing.
>
> "So far nothing has developed. We are *hoping* that there is a chance of a copy of Eric's Will being in the Shanghai office. Rob has written about it and as yet we have had no word. If nothing turns up there we will have to have legal proceedings before I can obtain the insurance money. Rob has a lawyer on the case.

"I have had quite a hectic time since the summer looking for an apartment, packing, moving and settling in, but we have things pretty well organized now and we are very happily situated. Our landlady is from Edinburgh and is a perfect dear! I was terribly fortunate to find a place. I found you might as well have the plague as three children when it comes to house hunting.

"The children are very happy in their new school and church and I am all set to start nursing on Jan 7. I am starting with six hours a day Monday to Thursday. That will give me Friday to get caught up with the housework and have the week-end with the children."

On New Year's Eve, 1945, Toronto prepared to celebrate without war for the first time in six years. Those who could afford it booked dinner and dancing at the plush Royal Oak or King Edward Hotel. Others headed for a less extravagant dancehall like the Palais Royale at Sunnyside, the Club Kingsway, or the ever-popular Casa Loma. But none of this appealed to Flo on the last night of such a momentous year.

After tucking the girls into bed, she went downstairs and took Eric's Edinburgh blazer from the closet. Once a bright royal blue, it was faded and worn from the endless months in Weihsien. She slipped it on and hugged it tight around her. Sitting alone, she reviewed all that she had decided last summer at Port Albert. Deep in her soul, she had resolved to live and raise her daughters the way she and Eric had planned.

She would talk freely with them about the father they had hardly known yet deeply loved. When anger and feelings of abandonment threatened, she would try to help them understand how much he had loved them.

She would budget to the penny and spend nothing that she didn't have, but she would never let them feel poor. Their house would be filled with friends and singing and laughter and prayer. They would visit the art galleries and the museums not because they were free, but because they were worthwhile.

She would find a way to pay for dancing lessons. And every month she would take each daughter for a special day with her. They would have dinner at a nice restaurant like the Blue Room, where the china and crystal were set on white tablecloths. She would not use the occasion to teach etiquette, but to give the gift of her undivided attention. They would talk and have fun.

At home they would eat nutritious food. She would create, not simply cook. If they wanted a bologna sandwich on white bread with mustard, they would have to trade their sprouts and carrots with a friend at school. And they must never tell her if they did.

Flo stood and walked to the window as a puff of wind blew the snow from the steeply gabled roof, swirling it into the night and turning Browning Avenue into a snow-globe. Inside, they were warm and safe. And in heaven, Eric was safe in the arms of God, who would keep them too.

The trees outside appeared lifeless but they were only waiting. Their sturdy trunks, anchored deep in the earth, branched upward, stretching finally into fragile twigs. In time, the sun would find them and warm them into life again. Leaves would appear. Spring would come. She knew it.

Eric's race was over, but hers had just begun. She vowed to run it willingly, eagerly, and, at the end, to throw back her head to finish in triumph and joy. Eric had gone on ahead, and one day she would be with him again.

She needed neither hymnal nor piano as she softly sang:

Be still, my soul: the hour is hastening on
When we shall be forever with the Lord,
When disappointment, grief, and fear are gone,
Sorrow forgot, love's purest joys restored.
Be still, my soul: when change and tears are past,
All safe and blessed we shall meet at last.

Epilogue

FLORENCE LIDDELL remained in Canada, where she married Murray Hall, a widower, in 1951. They had a daughter, Jeannie, born in 1955. After Murray's death in 1969, Flo made three trips to Scotland to visit Eric's side of the family. She enjoyed a special preview showing of *Chariots of Fire*, but illness kept her from attending the premiere.

Eric and Flo's three daughters, Patricia, Heather, and Maureen, have nine children among them and make their homes in Canada.

Eric Henry Liddell (January 16, 1902 – February 21, 1945)
Florence MacKenzie Liddell Hall (November 25, 1911– June 14, 1984)

ROB LIDDELL never returned to China. After a career as a much-loved surgeon in Scotland, Rob and his wife, Ria, emigrated to Australia in 1958 to join their son, James Ralph (Jim), in a pioneer medical outreach. Both of Rob and Ria's children became doctors. Peggy lives in Edinburgh and Jim lives in Australia.

Robert Victor Liddell (August 27, 1900 – May 30, 1973)
Ria Aitken Liddell (June 29, 1895 – April 30, 1982)

JENNY LIDDELL SOMERVILLE returned from China in 1929 and spent the rest of her life in Edinburgh. She loved the film *Chariots of Fire* but disliked its portrayal of her as a worried sister who allegedly reprimanded Eric for devoting more time to running than to Christian work. "I never would have spoken to him like that," she said.

Her two daughters, Rosemary and Joan, live in Scotland.

Dr. Charles Somerville (December 26, 1877 – July 27, 1966)
Jenny Liddell Somerville (October 3, 1903 – June 8, 1994)

ERNEST LIDDELL sustained a severe head injury in 1941 and suffered from its effects for the rest of his life. Often forgotten in the story of his brother's life, he held a great admiration for Eric. Ernest pursued a career in banking in Scotland.

His only child, Susan, lives in Edinburgh.

Ernest Blair Liddell (December 4, 1912 – February 11, 1975)
Alice Rae Anderson Liddell (April 18, 1911 – February 16, 1997)

MARY LIDDELL, Eric's mother, died in Edinburgh on September 22, 1944. It is almost certain that word of her passing never reached Eric in camp.

Rev. James D. Liddell (September 6, 1870–November 11, 1933)
Mary Reddin Liddell (October 2, 1870 – September 22, 1944)

AGNES MACKENZIE, Flo's mother, lived in Ontario until her death at the age of 94. Her brood of seven children pursued a variety of professions. Flo's two remaining siblings, Finlay and Louise, live in Toronto.

Hugh MacKenzie (February 3, 1880–November 13, 1943)
Agnes Anne Hall MacKenzie (March 13, 1884–August 12, 1978)

CHINA—THE TIENTSIN ANGLO-CHINESE COLLEGE reopened after the war under the auspices of the London Missionary Society. A. P. Cullen served at the college from 1947 until it was taken over by the Communist government in 1950. He returned to England and retired in 1951.

The college buildings were destroyed by an earthquake in 1976. The Seventeenth Middle School of Tianjin occupies the site today. In a second-floor room, a glass case contains Eric's medal for his 440-yard victory over Dr. Otto Peltzer at the Min Yuan on November 25, 1929. Also on display is *The Disciplines of the Christian Life* (Eric's book on Discipleship) translated into Chinese.

The Second Middle School of Weifang (**Weihsien**) now occupies the site of the Japanese internment camp. A room in the school is devoted to the history of the former Presbyterian Mission and the Civil Assembly Center at Weihsien.

In 1990 a memorial stone, given by the University of Edinburgh, was erected at the school, near the Eric H. Liddell Sports Ground. On one side an inscription in English and Chinese gives a brief summary of Eric's life. On the other are these words from Isaiah 40:31: "They shall mount up with wings as eagles. They shall run and not be weary."

At Beidaihe (**Peitaiho**), modern condominiums have replaced the mission bungalows near Rocky Point and Eastcliff. White-haired tourists return for a final look at the places they loved as missionary children. The sea is warm, the breeze is fresh, and couples still stroll the beach at dusk with their arms around each other's waists.

1 Corinthians 13:4–7

Love is very patient, very kind.
Love knows neither envy nor jealousy.
Love is not forward or self-assertive;
love is not boastful or conceited.
It gives itself no airs.
Love is never rude, never selfish, never irritated.
Love never broods over wrongs, love thinks no evil.
Love is never glad when others go wrong.
Love finds no pleasure in injustice,
but rejoices in the truth.
Love is always slow to expose, it knows how to be silent.
Love is always eager to believe the best about a person.
Love is full of hope, full of patient endurance;
love never fails.

—paraphrase by Eric Liddell

The Dash Between the Dates

Napoleon's tombstone is huge. Churchill's is simple. The eternal flame burns over the grave of President John Kennedy. Very different lives, very different markers.

As different as each was from the other, their lives share at least one common mark: The dash between the dates. On every tombstone, whether simple or ornate, there is only one dash, or hyphen, between the dates.

The character and quality of our lives vary greatly. Yet, when all is said and done, we become precisely equal. They put one dash between the birth date and the death date.

We get one dash through life. That's it! No seconds! No restarts! Everybody finishes!

Some dash through life with great flair and style. Others become a quiet blur. Some run with long strides, leaving only toe marks in the sand. Most leave an erratic trail of footprints with more than a few heel marks. Many show evidence of being lost. Yet having lost their direction, they run all the faster.

The content of our "dash" varies. But in the end, the workmen still chisel only a dash. It reminds us of the stark truth: "Just as man is destined to die once, and after that to face judgment, so Christ was sacrificed once to take away the sins of many people... ."

In the end, men reduce all living to the cold mark on the stone. Those of us who "live a life worthy of the Lord," following in the footsteps of Jesus, find the end of earth's dash to be the beginning of heaven's glory.

—Joseph B. Fuiten

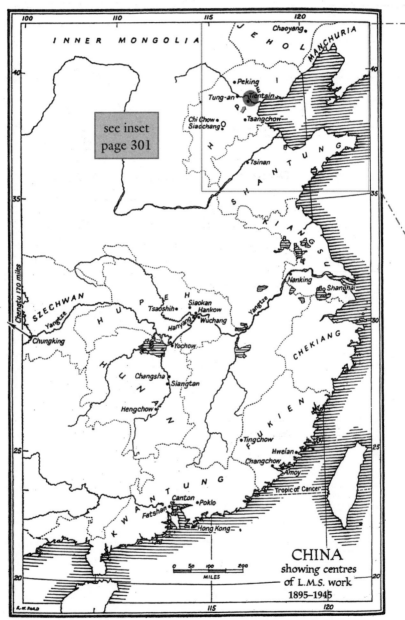

CHINA
showing centres
of L.M.S. work
1895–1945

From *A History of The London Missionary Society, 1895-1945* by Norman Goodall, Oxford University Press, 1954.

For modern spellings of locations in China, see pages 9–10.

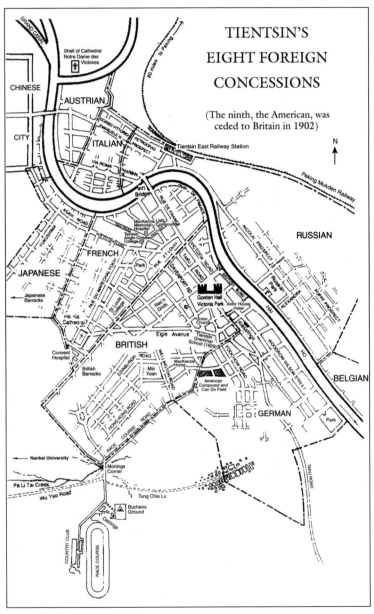

Adapted from *Little Foreign Devil* by Desmond Power, Vancouver, BC Pangli Imprint, 1996
Used by permission.

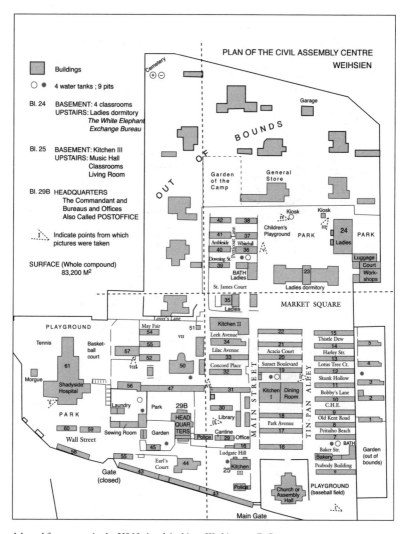

Adapted from a map in the US National Archives, Washington, D.C.

Eric Liddell's Races in Britain
1921–1925[*]

© Rev. J. W. Keddie, 2001, used by permission.

1921
May 28, Edinburgh Univ. Athletic Club Annual Sports, Craiglockhart, Edinburgh
100 yards — 1st 10.4   220 yards — 2nd
Invitation Relay Race — 1st, EUAC, 1:38.8

June 4, Queen's Park Football Club Annual Sports, Hampden Park, Glasgow
Inter-City Relay Race — 2nd, Edinburgh University

June 18, Scottish Inter-Varsity Sports, University Park, St. Andrews
100 yards — 1st 10.6   220 yards — 1st 22.4

June 25, Scottish Amateur Athletic Assoc. Championships, Celtic Park, Glasgow
100 yards — 1st 10.4   220 yards — 1st 22.6 (CBP)
Mile Relay — 1st, EUAC, 3:43.0 (CBP)

June 29, Edinburgh Pharmacy Athletic Club Sports, Powderhall Grounds
120 yards (Open) handicap — 1st 12.0 off scratch, with wind

July 2, Heart of Midlothian Football Club Annual Sports, Tynecastle Park, Edinburgh
100 yards (Open) handicap — 2nd (scr.)

July 9, Triangular International, Windsor Park, Belfast
100 yards — 1st 10.4   220 yards — 3rd

July 16, West Kilbride Athletic Club Annual Sports, Seamill Park, West Kilbride
100 yards handicap — 1st 10.0 (scr.)   220 yards handicap — 3rd (scr.)

July 23, Eglinton Harriers Sports, Victoria Park, Salcoats
100 yards handicap — 1st 10.0 (scr.)   220 yards handicap — 3rd (scr.)

July 30, Greenock Glenpark Harriers Meeting, Cappielow Park, Greenock
100 yards Invitational handicap — 3rd (scr.)

---

[*] Key to abbreviations is at the end of this section on page 310.

August 6, Rangers' Football Club Annual Sports, Ibrox Park, Glasgow
100 yards (Invitation) handicap — 1st 10.0 off 1 yard
300 yards (Open) handicap — 3rd (scr.)

August 13, Celtic Football Club Annual Sports, Celtic Park, Glasgow
100 yards handicap — 1st 10.2 off 1 yard
220 yards open handicap — 1st 23.6 (scr.)

1922
May 27, Edinburgh University Athletic Club Annual Sports, Craiglockhart
100 yards — 1st 10.2 (record)   220 yards — 1st 21.8 (record and Scottish
native record)   440 yards — 1st 52.6

June 3, Queen's Park Football Club Annual Sports, Hampden Park, Glasgow
100 yards (Invitation) handicap — 3rd (scr.)
100 yards (Open) handicap — 4th (scr.)
One Mile Inter-City Relay — 2nd Edinburgh 3:46.4

June 17, Scottish Inter-Varsity Sports, King's College, Aberdeen
100 yards — 1st 10.4   220 yards — 1st 22.8
One Mile Relay Race — 1st EUAC, 3:46.8

June 24, S.A.A.A. Championships, Powderhall Grounds, Edinburgh
100 yards — 1st 10.2   220 yards — 1st 22.6 (equals CBP)
One Mile Relay Race — 1st, EUAC, 3:40.0 (CBP and Scottish record)

July 8, Triangular International, Hampden Park, Glasgow.
100 yards — 2nd   220 yards — 2nd

July 15, Edinburgh and District Inter-Works Sports, Powderhall Grounds
150 yards (Open handicap) — 1st 15.0 (scr.), (equals Scottish native record)

July 26, North British Hotel Annual Athletic Meeting, Powderhall Grounds
100 yards (Open) handicap — 1st 10.1 (scr.)

July 29, Greenock Glenpark Harriers Meeting, Cappielow Park, Greenock
100 yards (Open) handicap — 2nd 10.0 (scr.), (equals Scottish native record)

August 5, Rangers Football Club Annual Sports, Ibrox Park, Glasgow
100 yards (Open) handicap, Heat — unplaced
220 yards (Invitation) handicap — 1st 22.0 (off 2 yards)

August 12, Celtic Football Club Annual Sports, Celtic Park, Glasgow
120 yards (Inv.) — 1st 12.2
220 yards (Inv.) handicap — 1st 22.4 (off 2 yards)

1923
May 26, Edinburgh University Athletic Club Sports, Craiglockhart, Edinburgh
100 yards — 1st 10.6   220 yards — 1st 22.4   440 yards — 1st 52.8

June 2, Queens Park Football Club Annual Sports, Hampden Park, Glasgow
100 yards (Invitation) handicap — 2nd (scr.)
Inter-City Relay Race — 2nd Edinburgh University 3:40.4

June 16, Scottish Inter-Varsity Sports, Craiglockhart, Edinburgh
100 yards — 1st 10.1 (record)   220 yards — 1st 21.6 (record and
440 yards — 1st 50.2 (record)   Scottish native record)
One Mile Relay — 1st EUAC, 3:40.8 (record)

June 23, SAAA Championships, Celtic Park, Glasgow
100 yards — 1st 10.4   220 yards — 1st 22.4 (CBP)
One Mile Relay Race — 1st, EUAC, 3:43.6

June 27, Edinburgh Pharmacy A.C. Annual Sports, Powderhall Grounds
120 yards (Open) handicap — 1st 11.9 (scr.)

June 30, Heart of Midlothian Football Club Annual Sports, Tynecastle Park
100 yards (Open) handicap, Heat — 1st   Semi-final — Unplaced

July 7, A.A.A. Championships, Stamford Bridge, London
100 yards — 1st 9.7 (CBP and British record)   220 yards — 1st 21.6

July 14, Triangular International, Stoke-on-Trent
100 yards — 1st 10.4   220 yards — 1st 22.6   440 yards — 1st 51.2

July 28, Greenock Glenpark Harriers Meeting, Cappielow Park, Greenock
100 yards (Open) handicap, Heat — 1st 10.6 (scr.)   Semi-final — Unplaced
100 yards (Invitation) handicap — Unplaced

August 4, Rangers Football Club Annual Sports, Ibrox Park, Glasgow
120 yards (open) handicap, Heat — 3rd (scr.)
300 yards (Special) handicap — 4th 31.8 (scr.)

August 6, British Games Meeting, Stamford Bridge, London
100 yards (Open) 1R, Heat 1 — 1st 10.2   2R, Heat 1 — 3rd 10.1
Final — 4th

August 8, Hibernian Football Club Annual Sports, Easter Road Park, Edinburgh
100 yards (Open) handicap, Heat 3 — 1st 10.8 (scr.)   Final — Unplaced
100 yards (Invitation) handicap — Unplaced

August 11, Celtic Football Club Annual Sports, Celtic Park, Glasgow
100 yards (open) handicap — 3rd (scr.)   220 yards (Open) — 3rd (scr.)

1924
April 25–26, University of Pennsylvania Relays, Philadelphia, Pa.
100 yards (Special Event) — 4th   220 yards (Special Event) — 2nd

May 19, Maryhill Harriers Meeting, Firhill Park, Glasgow
100 yards Invitation handicap — 2nd (scr.)
Invitation Relay Race — 2nd, EUAC 2:08.8

May 28, Edinburgh University Athletic Club Annual Sports, Craiglockhart
100 yards — 1st 10.2 (equals record)   220 yards — 1st 23.0
440 yards — 1st 51.5 (record)

May 31, Scottish Inter-Varsity Sports, Hampden Park, Glasgow
100 yards — 1st 10.2   220 yards — 1st 23.4   440 yards — 1st 51.2
One Mile Relay Race — 1st EUAC, 3:52.8

June 7, Hawick Common Riding Amateur Sports, Volunteer Park, Hawick.
100 yards (Open) handicap — 2nd (scr.) One Mile Relay — 1st, EUAC

June 14, SAAA Championships Hampden Park, Glasgow
100 yards — 1st 10.0 (equals CBP and Scottish native record)
220 yards — 1st 22.6   440 yards — 1st 51.2

June 20–21, AAA Championships, Stamford Bridge, London
220 yards, Heat 1 — 1st 22.3   2R Heat 1— 1st 21.8
440 yards, Heat 3 — 1st 51.0   2R Heat 1 — 1st 49.6
220 yards, Final — 2nd   440 yards Final — 1st 49.6

June 25, Edinburgh Pharmacy A.C. Annual Sports, Powderhall Grounds
150 yards (Open) handicap, Heat 3 — 1st 15.4 (scr.)   Final — 2nd

June 28, Heart of Midlothian Football Club Annual Sports, Tynecastle Park
300 yards Invitation handicap — 4th (scr.)

OLYMPIC GAMES
July 8, Colombes Stadium, Paris
200 metres, 1R Heat 3 — 1st 22.2   2R Heat 2 — 2nd

July 9, 200 metres, Semi-final 2 — 2nd 21.8   Final — 3rd 21.9 Bronze Medal
400 metres, 1R Heat 14 — 1st 50.2   2R Heat 4 — 2nd 49.3

July 11
400 metres, Semi-final 2 — 1st 48.2
Final — 1st 47.6 (Gold Medal, World and Olympic record)

July 19, British Empire v. USA (Relays), Stamford Bridge, London
One Mile Relay Race (4 x 440) — 1st, British Empire 3:18.2
One Mile Relay (440 x 220 x 220 x 880) — 1st, USA 3:29.8, 2nd, British Empire

July 26, Greenock Glenpark Harriers Meeting (Scotland v. Canada)
Cappielow Park, Greenock.   100 yards (International) — 3rd
440 yards (International) — 1st 51.2   One Mile Relay — 1st Scotland 3:57.0

August 2, Rangers Football Club Annual Sports, Ibrox Park, Glasgow
440 yards Open handicap — 1st 49.6 (scr.)

August 5, West of Scotland Harriers Meeting, Ibrox Park, Glasgow
220 yards Open handicap — 3rd (scr.)   300 yards (scr.) — 1st 32.0

August 16, Gala Harriers Sports, Netherdale Park, Galashiels.
100 yards Open handicap — 2nd (scr.)
440 yards Invitation handicap — 1st 54.0 (scr.)

1925
May 20, Edinburgh Univ. Athletic Club Annual Sports, Craiglockhart, Edinburgh
100 yards — 1st 10.4   220 yards — 1st 23.0
440 yards — 1st 51.4 (record)

May 31, Scottish Inter-Varsity Sports, University Park, St. Andrews
100 yards — 1st 10.2   220 yards — 1st 22.0   440 yards — 1st 55.8

June 6, Queen's Park Football Club Annual Sports, Hampden Park, Glasgow
440 yards (Open) handicap — 3rd 50.2 (scr.)
Inter-City Relay Race — 1st Edinburgh 3:39.8 (Scottish record)

June 13, Corstorphine AAC Sports, Union Park, Corstorphine.
440 yards — 1st 53.5 (East of Scotland Championship)

June 20, Edinburgh Southern Harriers Annual Sports, Powderhall Gds., Edinburgh
220 yards — 1st 23.4 (East of Scotland Championship)
220 yards (Open) handicap — 1st 22 1/4 (scr.)
300 yards Special invitation handicap — 1st 31.5 (scr.)

June 24, Edinburgh Pharmacy A.C. Annual Sports, Powderhall Gds., Edinburgh
120 yards (Open) handicap, heat 5 — 2nd (scr.)
One mile invitation relay — 1st, EUAC, 3:45.4

June 27, SAAA Championships, Hampden Park, Glasgow
100 yards — 1st 10.0 (equals CBP and Scottish native record)
220 yards — 1st 22.2 (CBP)   440 yards — 1st 49.2 (CBP)
One mile relay — 1st, EUAC, 3:40.2

CBP — **Championship Best Performance**
with wind — **A race in which the wind is at the runners' backs.**
Handicap — **A race in which some runners are given an advantage at the start.**
unpl. — **unplaced in race**
scr. = off scratch — **Starting at the original line in a handicap race.**

Acknowledgments

To all those whose names appear under Personal Interviews in the Bibliography, a special thanks for their time and effort.

Each person listed here provided an essential ingredient in the research and writing of this book. I am deeply grateful for their kind and generous assistance.

Canada

Mrs. Patricia Liddell Russell and Mrs. Heather Liddell Ingham for so warmly and openly sharing memories of their mother and father.

Mr. Finlay MacKenzie and Mrs. Louise MacKenzie McLean for answering my never-ending questions about their sister, Florence, and their remarkable family.

The late Dr. David Michell, OMF International, Toronto

Ani Orchanian-Cheff, Toronto Hospital Archives

Mr. Ken Wilson, United Church of Canada Archives, Toronto

People's Republic of China

Principal and staff, No. 17 Middle School, Tianjin;

Principal and staff, No. 20 Middle School, Tianjin

Principal and staff, No. 2 Middle School, Weifang

LeRoy and Jane Ramsey, Weifang—For the hospitality of their home and the walking tour of the former Weihsien Camp

Ken and Jan Wendling, Beijing—For gracious hospitality and help.

Mrs. Emma Wu, Tianjin—An excellent translator and intrepid guide.

United Kingdom

Dr. Norman Cliff — For his unflagging support, his expertise on China and his generosity in sharing his research materials.

Rev. Joe Cotterill — For patiently answering all my questions.

Mrs. Aline Faunce, MRA Archives, Cheshire

Mr. D. M. Green, Headmaster and Mr. David L. Jones, Archivist, Eltham College

Miss Ailsa Hamilton, Melrose, Scotland

Mrs. Carol Hemfrey, Drymen, Scotland

Phillip and Margaret Holder, Reading. For their warm hospitality and their open home.

Mr. and Mrs. Ceri R. and Beryl Jenkins, Morningside Congregational Church, Edinburgh.

Dr. Peggy Judge, Edinburgh. For unflagging cooperation and support.

Rev. John Keddie, Isle of Skye, Scotland. Sports historian extraordinaire.

Mrs. Joan Sommerville Nicol, Edinburgh. For so generously sharing her family photographs, and for a memorable visit to Carcant.

Mr. Bob Rendall, Director, The Eric Liddell Centre, Edinburgh, Scotland

Mrs. Rosemary Seton, Archivist, and the Special Collections staff at the School of Oriental and African Studies, London.

Rev. Adrian Varwell, St. Ninian's Conference Center, Crieff, Scotland

Fiona White, Librarian, Scottish Rugby Union, Edinburgh

Miss Isobel White, Walthamstow Hall, Sevenoaks, Kent

Mr. Jim Wigan, MRA Conference Centre, Tirley Garth

Ms. Vanessa Wood — For the invaluable resource of her great aunt's letters.

United States

Mr. Robert D. Foster — For 40 years of friendship and an unforgettable trip to China.

Sr. Andree Gaspard, Sisters of St. Francis, Milwaukee, WI

Mr. Larry Haise—For his wise and careful reading of the manuscript.

Mr. Fred Hollis, Day of Discovery television. For always saying "Yes" when I asked for more time to do research.

Mrs. Carol Holquist, Mr. Bob DeVries, Mr. Tim Gustafson at Discovery House Publishers for their patience and encouragement.

Mrs. Susan Fitch Liberta for freely sharing her father's Olympic diary.

Mrs. Judith Markham — For her superb editing skill.

Dr. Russell Ramsey — For early encouragement and help.

Dr. Chris Spink, Philadelphia — For sharing her Chefoo and Weihsien contacts.

Credits

Be Still My Soul, words by Katharina von Schlegel, 1752, translated by Jane Borthwick, 1855. Public domain. Composer: Jean Sibelius. Tune: *Finlandia.*

"The Dash Between the Dates," © Joseph B. Fuiten. Used with permission.

Bibliography

BOOKS AND PAMPHLETS

Bruce, Mary B. and Brown, Alison, *Drymen And Buchanan In Old Photographs,* Stirling, UK: Stirling District Libraries, 1988.

Bruce, Mary B., *Drymen and Buchanan: A Further Selection of Old Photographs,* Stirling, UK: Stirling District Libraries, 1993.

Buchanan, Ian, *British Olympians: A Hundred Years Of Gold Medalists,* Enfield, UK, Guinness Publishing Ltd, 1988.

Chang, Iris, *The Rape of Nanking: The Forgotten Holocaust of World War II,* New York: BasicBooks, 1997.

Cliff, Norman, *Courtyard of the Happy Way,* Evesham, UK: Arthur James Limited, 1967.

Cliff, Norman, *Prisoners of the Samurai,* Rainham, Essex, UK: Courtyard Publishers, 1998.

Cook, Thomas and Son, *Cook's Handbook for Tourists to Peking, Tientsin, Shan-hai-kwan, etc.,* Peking, 1924.

Cullen, A. P., *Making China's Men,* London: The Livingstone Press, 1937.

Cullen, A. P., *Lavington Hart of Tientsin,* London: The Livingstone Press, 1947.

De Jaegher, Raymond and Kuhn, Irene Corbally, *The Enemy Within,* Bombay: St. Paul Press, 1952.

Fairlie, F. G. L., *The Official Report of the VIIIth Olympiad, Paris 1924,* London: British Olympic Association, 1925.

Filey, Mike, *Toronto Sketches 4: The Way We Were,* Toronto: Dundurn Press, 1995.

Filey, *Toronto Sketches 5: The Way We Were,* Toronto: Dundurn Press, 1997.

Footman, Ray and Young, Bruce, *Edinburgh University: An Illustrated Memoir,* Edinburgh: The University of Edinburgh Information and Public Relations Services, 1983.

Frame, W. H., *Fire In His Bones: A Short Biography of D. P. Thomson, Church of Scotland Evangelist,* Privately printed, n/d.

Gale, Godfrey L. *Interned In China,* London: The Livingstone Press, 1946.

Gilkey, Langdon, *Shantung Compound,* San Francisco: Harper & Row, 1966.

Goodall, Norman, *A History Of The London Missionary Society 1895-1945,* London: Oxford University Press, 1954.

Hale, Hilda, *Indomitably Yours,* Victoria, B. C. Privately printed, 1999.

Helsby, Meredith and Christine, *He Goes Before Them . . . Even Into Prison,* Greenwood, IN: OMS International, 1993.

Henson, Herbert Hensley, *The Group Movement,* London, Oxford University Press, 1933.

Hoyt, Edwin P., *Japan's War: The Great Pacific Conflict 1935–1952,* New York: McGraw-Hill, 1986.

Keddie, John W., *Scottish Athletics 1883–1983,* Glasgow: Scottish Amateur Athletic Association, 1982.

Kluckner, Michael, *Toronto: The Way It Was,* Toronto: Whitecap Books, 1988.

Lean, Garth, *Frank Buchman: A Life,* London: Constable and Company Ltd., 1985.

Lean, Garth, *Good God, It Works!* London: Blandford Press, 1974.

Lennon, M. J., *Memories of Toronto Island,* Erin, Ontario: The Boston Mills Press, 1980.

Lester, Muriel, *It Occurred To Me,* New York and London: Harper & Bros., 1937.

Lester, Muriel, *It So Happened,* New York and London, Harper & Bros., 1947.

Liddell, Eric H., *The Disciplines of the Christian Life,* Nashville: Abingdon Press, 1985. (Edited version of Liddell's manuscript, *Discipleship.*)

Lin Yutang, *My Country and My People,* London: William Heinemann, Ltd. 1936. Revised edition, 1939.

Magnusson, Sally, *The Flying Scotsman,* London, Quartet Books, 1981.

Malcolm, Kari Torjesen. *We Signed Away Our Lives,* Downers Grove, IL: InterVarsity Press, 1990.

Martin, Gordon. *Chefoo School: 1881–1951,* Braunton, UK: Merlin Books, Ltd., 1990.

Massie, Allan, *A Portrait of Scottish Rugby,* Edinburgh: Polygon Books, 1984.

Masters, Pamela, *The Mushroom Years,* Placerville, CA: Henderson House Publishing, 1998.

McAll, Frances, *Hurdles Are For Jumping,* Oxford: New Cherwell Press, 1998.

McAll, Frances and Kenneth, *The Moon Looks Down,* London: Darley Anderson, 1987.

McPherson, Kathryn, *Bedside Matters: The Transformation of Canadian Nursing, 1900-1990,* Don Mills, Ontario: Oxford University Press, 1996.

Mervine, Marcus, *Japanese Concession in Tientsin and the Narcotics Trade* Nanking, Council of International Affairs, Information Bulletin, Vol. 3. No. 4, 1937.

Michell, David, *A Boy's War,* Singapore: Overseas Missionary Fellowship, 1988.

Moser, Don, *World War II: China-Burma-India,* Alexandria, VA: Time-Life Books, 1978.

O'Grady, Jean, Editor, *Famous People Who Have Met Me: The Life and Interviews of R. E. Knowles,* Toronto: Colombo & Company, 1999.

Pennell, W. V. *Tientsin, North China: The Port, Its History, and Rotary Club Activities,* The Rotary Club of Tientsin, 1934.

Phillips, Ellen, *The VIII Olympiad: Paris 1924, St. Moritz 1928* (Volume 8 in *The Olympic Century*) Los Angeles: World Sport Research & Publications Inc., 1996.

Power, Brian, *The Ford of Heaven,* London: Peter Owen Publishers, 1984.

Power, Desmond, *Little Foreign Devil,* Vancouver: Pangli Imprint, 1996.

Previte, Mary Taylor, *Hungry Ghosts,* Grand Rapids, MI: Zondervan, 1994.

Ramsey, Russell W., *God's Joyful Runner,* South Plainfield, NJ: Bridge Publishing, 1987.

Rasmussen, Otto Durham, *The Growth of Tientsin,* Tientsin: 1924

Reyburn, Wallace, *All About Rugby Football,* London and New York: W. H. Allen, 1976.

Riegler, Natalie, *Jean I. Gunn: Nursing Leader,* Markham, Ontario: Fitzhenry & Whiteside, 1997.

Rowlands, W. F., *The Plain and the People: Life Changing and Church Planting on the North China Plain,* London: The Livingstone Press, 1937.

Rowlands, W. F., *Christ Came To Bitter Market,* London: The Livingstone Press, 1951.

Scanlan, Patrick J. *Stars in the Sky,* Hong Kong: Trappist Publications, 1984.

Scovel, Myra, *The Chinese Ginger Jars,* New York: Harper and Row, 1962.

Servatia, Sister M. OSF, *A Cross In China: The Story of My Mission,* Fort Wayne, IN: Cuchullain Publications, 1989.

Swift, Catherine, *Eric Liddell,* Minneapolis: Bethany House Publishers, 1990.

Thomson, A. A., *Rugger My Pleasure,* London, Museum Press, 1955.

Thomson, D.P., *Men Christ Wants: Evangelistic Addresses,* (Abridged Edition) London: Marshall, Morgan & Scott, Ltd, 1952.

Thomson, D. P., *Personal Encounters,* Crieff, The Research Unit, 1967.

Thomson, D. P., *The Road To Dunfermline,* Dunfermline, UK: West Fife Publishing Co., 1952.

Thomson, D. P., *Eric Liddell: the Making of An Athlete and the Training of A Missionary,* Glasgow: The Eric Liddell Memorial Committee, 1945.

Thomson, D. P., *Scotland's Greatest Athlete: The Eric Liddell Story,* Crieff, The Research Unit, 1970.

Thomson, D. P., *Eric H. Liddell: Athlete and Missionary,* Crieff, The Research Unit, 1971.

Tipton, Laurance, *Chinese Escapade,* London, Macmillan & Co., Ltd., 1949.

Usher, C. M., Editor, *The Story of Edinburgh University Athletic Club,* Edinburgh, Athletic Club of the University of Edinburgh, 1966.

Vallance, Don, *The China Story: 1929-1949,* (The story of Dr. Geoffrey W. Milledge), privately printed, 1999.

Webster, F. A. M. Lt. Col., *Olympic Cavalcade,* London, Hutchinson & Co., 1948.

Wilkins, Joyce, *A Child's Eye View: 1904-1920,* Sussex, UK: The Book Guild, Ltd., 1992.

Wilson, Julian, *Complete Surrender,* Crowborough, UK: Monarch Publications, 1996.

Witting, Clifford, editor, *The Glory of the Sons: A History of Eltham College School for the Sons of Missionaries,* London: Board of Governors, Eltham College, 1952, Volume I in *Eltham College Past and Present,* 1992.

Woodhead, H. G. W., *Extraterritoriality in China: The Case Against Abolition,* Tientsin: Tientsin Press, 1929.

Zich, Arthur. *World War II: The Rising Sun.* Alexandria, VA: Time-Life Books, 1977.

PERIODICALS

The Chronicle (Magazine of the London Missionary Society)

Edinburgh Evening News

Eltham College Magazine

Glasgow Herald

The Honan Messenger/The Honan Quarterly (United Church of Canada)

National Geographic

North China Herald

Philadelphia Inquirer

School for Sons of Missionaries Magazine

The Scotsman

The Scottish Congregationalist

South Wales News

The Student – University of Edinburgh
Toronto Daily Star
The United Church Observer

UNPUBLISHED MANUSCRIPTS

Clark, Philippa Hart. *Four Women, Four Wars,* A biography of her father, Lavington Hart. Unpublished manuscript, 1996.

Hayward, G. W. *William Hopkyn Rees D.D. 1849–1924.* Unpublished manuscript, ©1999.

Liddell, Eric H. *The Sermon On The Mount: Notes For Sunday School Teachers,* Union Church Sunday School, Tientsin. Privately printed, 1937.

Liddell, Eric H. *Prayers For Daily Use,* Tientsin, China, Union Church, Privately printed, 1942.

Liddell, Eric H. *Discipleship,* privately printed, 1942.

PERSONAL LETTERS AND PAPERS

Cullen, A. P. Letters from China to his family, 1935–1942. © 1999 by Joanna Cullen Brown and Rowena Cullen Williams.

Longman, C. H. B. and Amy. Letters from China to their family. © 1999 by Perle Longman.

Peill, Roy F. Personal letters from China to his wife in England, September 1925–May 1926, ©1999, by Rosemary Harris.

Wood, Mary Myfanwy. Personal letters from China to her family, 1908–1935, ©1998 by Vanessa Wood.

PERSONAL MEMOIRS AND HISTORIES

Alderson, Sister M. Julian. *Franciscans In Shantung, China 1929–1948,* Milwaukee, Sisters of St. Francis of Assisi, 1980.

Bruce, J. W. G. (Jimmy) *Birds In The Fowler's Net: The Story of a Japanese Internment Camp,* privately printed, 1985.

Buchan, Annie Gray. *Adventure in Faith,* privately printed, 1973.

Buchan, Annie Gray. *A Scotswoman In China, 1925–1951,* William Speirs, editor. Privately printed, 1988.

Cliff, Norman. *Looking Back Fifty Years to Weihsien,* August 1995.

Fitch, Horatio M. *Olympic Diary,* June 12–August 6, 1924, © 1999, Susan F. Liberta.

A Ship's Log: 150th Anniversary School History of Walthamstow Hall, privately published by Walthamstow Hall, Sevenoaks, UK, 1989

Somerville, Jenny Liddell. *Memories of China Days,* privately printed.

Steel, Thomas A. *The Steel Story,* autobiography, privately printed, 1978. Chapter 23 — Eltham College.

TELEVISION

"The Flying Scotsman," BBC documentary, 1984.

ARCHIVES AND SPECIAL COLLECTIONS

The British Library, London

British Olympic Committee, London

D. P. Thomson Collection, The Church of Scotland, St. Ninian's, Crieff

Eltham College, Mottingham UK

Heriot-Watt University, Edinburgh

Library of Congress, Washington, DC

London Missionary Society (Council For World Mission), School of African and Oriental Studies, University of London, UK

MRA Archives (Moral Rearmament—formerly The Oxford Group) Tirley Garth, UK.

Morningside Congregational Church, Edinburgh

National Archives and Records Administration, Washington, DC

National Library of Scotland, Edinburgh

New Assisi Archives, Sisters of St. Francis of Assisi, Milwaukee, WI

New College, Edinburgh

Presbyterian Church (USA) Department of History and Records Management Services, Philadelphia, PA

Public Records Office, Kew, UK

Royal Geographic Society, London, UK
Scottish Rugby Union, Edinburgh
The United Church of Canada, Toronto
The Toronto Hospital Archives
Toronto Reference Library
The University of Edinburgh
Walthamstow Hall, Sevenoaks, Kent, UK
YMCA of the USA Archives, University of Minnesota, Minneapolis, MN

INTERNET

Website, Discover Tianjin — http://gao.fsn.net

PERSONAL INTERVIEWS — *indicates telephone interview

AUSTRALIA

Rev. J. Edwin and Nelma (Stranks) Davies*
Mr. Eric Liddell McKerchar*
Mrs. Dorothy (Rowlands) Wise [interviewed in Edinburgh]

CANADA

Mr. Douglas Finlay*
Mrs. Heather (Liddell) Ingham
Mr. Finlay MacKenzie
Mrs. Louise (MacKenzie) McLean
Rev. David Michell
Mr. Desmond Power*
Mrs. Patricia (Liddell) Russell
Dr. John Toop*

PEOPLE'S REPUBLIC OF CHINA

Mr. H. K. Cheng, Hong Kong
Dr. James Taylor, Hong Kong
Professor Yang Hsien-Yi, Beijing

UNITED KINGDOM

Mr. Peter Bazire

Mr. Ron Bridge

Mrs. Joanna (Cullen) Brown

Mrs. Susan (Liddell) Caton

Mr. Alan Chainey

Mrs. Philippa Hart Clark

The Rev. Dr. Norman Cliff

Mrs. Enid (Cullen) Coad

The Rev. Joe Cotterill

Mrs. Eileen Crossman

The Rev. Dr. Ian Doyle

Mrs. Jean (Bruce) Goodwin

Mr. Arthur Green

Miss Ailsa Hamilton

Mrs. Rosemary (Peill) Harris

Mrs. Ailie Hick

Mrs. Margaret (Vinden) Holder

Dr. Peggy (Liddell) Judge

The Rev. John Keddie

Miss Mary Lean

Miss Grace Liversidge

Mrs. Sylvia (Welch) Long

Perle Longman

Mr. Alec Luxon

Sally Magnusson

Drs. Ken and Frances McAll

Sir Arthur Marshall

Mr. Gordon Martin

Mr. George McKerchar

Mr. Stephen Metcalf

Dr. James S. Milledge

Mr. Robin Morris

Robert P.R. Murray, S.J.
Mrs. Joan (Sommerville) Nicol
Mr. David Parry
The Rev. Emmanuel Robertson
Mr. William Speirs*
Dr. Bill and Dorothy Toop
Mrs. Rowena (Cullen) Williams
Mrs. Rosemary (Sommerville) Wilson
Ms. Vanessa Wood

UNITED STATES

Dr. Marcy and Joyce (Stranks) Ditmanson
Dr. Langdon Gilkey
Mrs. Christine Helsby
Mrs. Evelyn Huebener*
Mrs. Susan Fitch Liberta*
Mrs. Kari (Torjeson) Malcolm
Mr. Jimmy Moore*
Dr. Russell Ramsey*
Mr. Thomas Steel

Index